1,000,000 Books

are available to read at

www.ForgottenBooks.com

Read online
Download PDF
Purchase in print

ISBN 978-1-331-87662-5
PIBN 10247867

This book is a reproduction of an important historical work. Forgotten Books uses state-of-the-art technology to digitally reconstruct the work, preserving the original format whilst repairing imperfections present in the aged copy. In rare cases, an imperfection in the original, such as a blemish or missing page, may be replicated in our edition. We do, however, repair the vast majority of imperfections successfully; any imperfections that remain are intentionally left to preserve the state of such historical works.

Forgotten Books is a registered trademark of FB &c Ltd.
Copyright © 2018 FB &c Ltd.
FB &c Ltd, Dalton House, 60 Windsor Avenue, London, SW19 2RR.
Company number 08720141. Registered in England and Wales.

For support please visit www.forgottenbooks.com

1 MONTH OF FREE READING

at
www.ForgottenBooks.com

By purchasing this book you are eligible for one month membership to ForgottenBooks.com, giving you unlimited access to our entire collection of over 1,000,000 titles via our web site and mobile apps.

To claim your free month visit:
www.forgottenbooks.com/free247867

* Offer is valid for 45 days from date of purchase. Terms and conditions apply.

English
Français
Deutsche
Italiano
Español
Português

www.forgottenbooks.com

Mythology Photography **Fiction** Fishing Christianity **Art** Cooking Essays Buddhism Freemasonry Medicine **Biology** Music **Ancient Egypt** Evolution Carpentry Physics Dance Geology **Mathematics** Fitness Shakespeare **Folklore** Yoga Marketing **Confidence** Immortality Biographies Poetry **Psychology** Witchcraft Electronics Chemistry History **Law** Accounting **Philosophy** Anthropology Alchemy Drama Quantum Mechanics Atheism Sexual Health **Ancient History Entrepreneurship** Languages Sport Paleontology Needlework Islam **Metaphysics** Investment Archaeology Parenting Statistics Criminology **Motivational**

NARRATIVE

OF THE

VOYAGE OF H.M.S. HERALD.

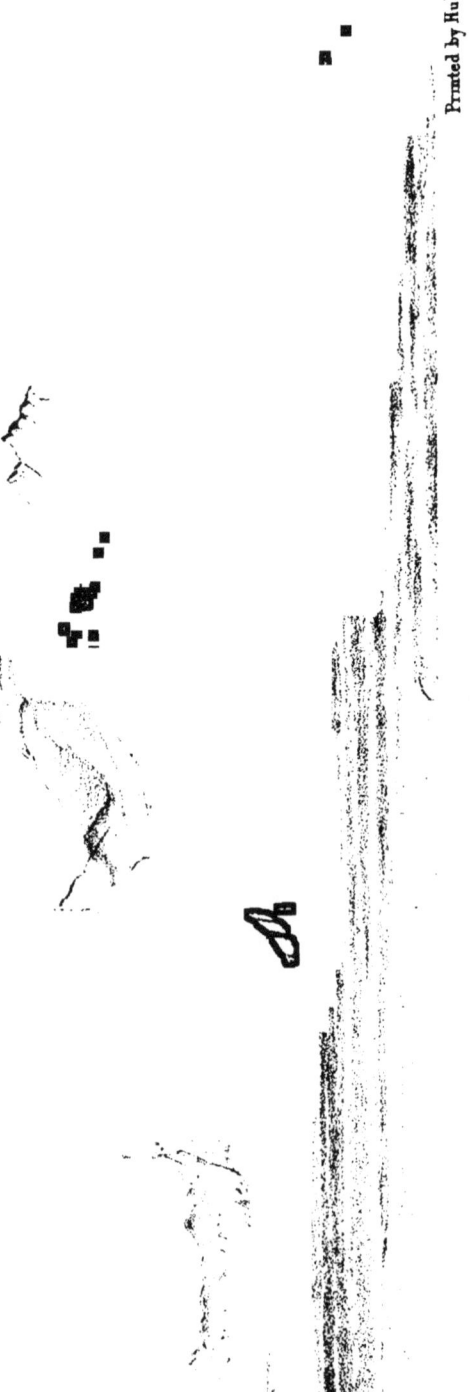

THE PORT OF PETROPAULOWSKI, KAMTSHATKA.

Printed by Hullmandel &

NARRATIVE

OF THE

VOYAGE OF H.M.S. HERALD

DURING THE YEARS 1845-51,

UNDER THE COMMAND OF

CAPTAIN HENRY KELLETT, R.N., C.B.;

BEING

A Circumnavigation of the Globe,

AND THREE CRUIZES TO THE ARCTIC REGIONS IN SEARCH
OF SIR JOHN FRANKLIN.

BY

BERTHOLD SEEMANN, F.L.S.,

MEMBER OF THE IMPERIAL L.C. ACADEMY NATURÆ CURIOSORUM,
NATURALIST OF THE EXPEDITION, ETC.

IN TWO VOLUMES.
VOL. II.

LONDON:
REEVE AND CO., HENRIETTA STREET, COVENT GARDEN.

1853.

JOHN EDWARD TAYLOR, LITTLE QUEEN STREET,
LINCOLN'S INN FIELDS.

CONTENTS.

CHAPTER I.

The Herald ordered to search for Franklin's Expedition—Historical Notice of the field of operation—First Voyage to the Arctic Regions—Departure from Panama—Sandwich Islands—Petropaulowski—Fort of St. Michael—Kotzebue Sound . . 1

CHAPTER II.

Behring's Strait—Western Eskimo-land—Its Geography, Climate, Plants, and Animals 11

CHAPTER III.

The Ice-cliffs of Eschscholtz Bay—Their Formation and Fossil Remains—Sir John Richardson's views on them . . . 33

CHAPTER IV.

The Eskimos—Their Dress—Arms—Food—Baidars—Habitations—Customs and Manners—Language 49

CHAPTER V.

Departure from Kotzebue Sound—Petropaulowski—Mazatlan—San Blas—Panama—Veraguas—Sandwich Islands . . 70

CHAPTER VI.

Second voyage to Behring's Strait—Departure from Honolulu—Kamtchatka—Kotzebue Sound—H.M.B. Plover—Search for Sir John Franklin—Cape Lisburne—Icy Cape—Wainwright Inlet 91

CHAPTER VII.

Separation of the two vessels—The Herald discovers a shoal and new islands—Cape Lisburne—Point Hope—Kotzebue Sound—Buckland River—Elephant Point—Departure for Mexico . 112

CHAPTER VIII.

The Plover's wintering in Kotzebue Sound—Mr. Pim's Journey to Michaelowski 130

CHAPTER IX.

Mazatlan—Surveying operations—San Jose—Guaymas—Islands and Ports of the Gulf of California 149

CHAPTER X.

Journey into the interior of North-western Mexico—Old Mazatlan—San Sebastian—The Sierra Madre—Copala—Santa Lucia—Durango—Santa Teresa—Return to the Port of Mazatlan . 159

CHAPTER XI.

Departure from Mazatlan—Third voyage to the Arctic Regions—Honolulu—Aleutian Islands—Kotzebue Sound—Cape Lisburne—Arrival of H.M.S. Investigator—Norton Sound—Grantley Harbour—H.M.S. Enterprise—The Herald returns to the Sandwich Islands 175

CHAPTER XII.

Historical Summary of the five years' search after Sir John Franklin, from the 1st of January, 1848, to the 1st of January, 1853, enumerated according to the dates on which the Expeditions left the British shores 189

CHAPTER XIII.

Continuation of the voyage of the Herald—Honolulu—King Kamehameha's Levee — Commencement of our homeward voyage—Arrival in Hongkong—Visit to Canton . . . 217

CHAPTER XIV.

The Island of Hongkong—Its geographical position—Geological formation—Climate and meteorology—Botany—Zoology . 234

CHAPTER XV.

Departure from Hongkong—Pulo Aor—Singapore—Straits of Sunda—Sumatra—Death of Mr. Woodward—Keeling Islands —Arrival at the Cape of Good Hope 246

CHAPTER XVI.

Stay at the Cape of Good Hope—Departure—St. Helena—Ascension—Flores and Corvo—Arrival in England—Conclusion . 264

APPENDIX.

Nautical remarks, by Henry Trollope, Com. R.N.—Heights ascertained with the Barometer and by Trigonometrical Measurement, by Captain H. Kellett, R.N., C.B. 283

INDEX 297

NARRATIVE OF THE VOYAGE

OF

H.M.S. HERALD.

CHAPTER I.

The Herald ordered to search for Franklin's Expedition—Historical Notice of the field of operation—First Voyage to the Arctic Regions—Departure from Panama—Sandwich Islands—Petropaulowski—Fort of St. Michael—Kotzebue Sound.

On our return to Panama, towards the end of April, we learnt to our surprise that the Herald, which up to that time had been a surveying vessel, was to enter upon a new career: the fate of Sir John Franklin beginning to excite apprehension, Captain Kellett was directed to proceed through Behring's Strait, in order to co-operate with H.M. Brig Plover in searching the north-western extremity of America, and the Arctic Sea, for traces of the missing voyagers. The Herald was made as comfortable as the limited means of the station and the urgency of despatch would admit, and officers as well as men, though debilitated by a prolonged stay in an unhealthy climate, heard with enthusiasm that their services were required in a cause so congenial to their feelings.

The region to which our operations were chiefly to be directed was discovered in comparatively recent times. The endless moorlands of the Arctic Circle, especially those of the New World, offered no temptation to the earlier adventurers, and, while navigation remained in its infancy, the icy masses rendered the exploration of the Polar Seas both irksome and dangerous; when however improvements in ship-building and increased knowledge had rendered seamen more confident, several expeditions were undertaken in this direction, and various attempts made to shorten the route to India by discovering a north-west passage. Thus, by degrees, Europeans became familiar with the north-eastern coast of America, but they remained in total ignorance of the north-western, where impediments of a more serious nature had to be overcome. The Pacific Ocean was in the hands of the Spaniards, a people who regarded all others, if venturing beyond the line of demarcation, as intruders; the distance of the Arctic regions from any civilized place was far greater than on the eastern side, and obtaining supplies consequently more difficult. Under such circumstances, it is not surprising that, after the discovery of the South Sea, a period of one hundred and thirty-five years should have elapsed before any attempt was made to penetrate into the higher northern latitudes; and, had not this been done by the accidental extension of the Russian dominions, a much longer time would probably have passed ere it would have been accomplished.

The first Russian expedition intended for the exploration of the Arctic regions was equipped in the year 1648, at the mouth of the Kolyma. It was commanded by a Cossack, and consisted of seven vessels, four of which were soon lost, and, although three succeeded in navigating through Behring's Strait, and thence to the Gulf of Anadir, the journals of these voyagers were so imperfect that little increase of geographical knowledge resulted from their labours. No further attempts by sea were made until the year 1728, when Vitus Behring, a Dane, was chosen to execute a plan which had originated with Peter the Great. Behring, having passed the strait now known by his name, sailed as far north as 67° 18'; he saw nothing of the coast of America, but was fully satisfied that he had proved the disconnection of the two continents. Another attempt which he made ended in shipwreck, and ultimate death, upon the island since denominated after him.

It was reserved for the immortal Cook to obtain the first view of the north-west coast, and fill up the blanks which had so long been left in the charts. Cook, in the hope of effecting the north-east passage, on the 9th of August, 1778, discovered Cape Prince of Wales, and accurately determined the breadth of the strait; elated by success, he pushed northward, and in lat. 70° 44' fell in with the packed ice, which extended as far as the eye could reach. After traversing the Arctic Sea from Icy Cape on the American, to Cape North on the Asiatic shore, the advance of the season and the injuries his ships had suffered compelled him to retrace his course to the Sandwich Islands, where he met his death. In the following year Captain Clerke, who succeeded to the command, also made an attempt, but his progress was stopped a few miles south of the position attained by his illustrious predecessor.

In 1816 Otho von Kotzebue, a German, sailed in a Russian ship, the Rurick, for Behring's Strait; he was accompanied by Adalbert von Chamisso, the poet and naturalist, whose writings have rendered this voyage so popular. Kotzebue discovered the sound called after him, but although an open sea presented itself to the northward, he sailed to the Asiatic shores, and thus lost a favourable opportunity of extending our knowledge of the north-west coast. In the following year he again repaired to the north, but did not meet with much success.

The discovery of the North-west Passage, always a favourite project with the British nation, lay dormant some time subsequent to the French Revolution, but when, in 1815, peace had been established and the agitation had abated, the solution of the great problem was resumed. In order to explore the Arctic Regions the Government despatched several expeditions, both by sea and land. In 1826 Captain Beechey, in H.M.S. Blossom, entered Behring's Strait, the principal object of his mission being to co-operate with Sir John Franklin, who was then exploring the shores of the Arctic Sea; Beechey failed to accomplish his design, but he made an accurate survey of the coast from Point Barrow to Grantley Harbour. During both summers in which he visited the Polar Sea, the extension of the ice was traced, the first year in lat. 71° 10′, the second in lat. 70° 50′.

Although the numerous attempts to effect the North-west Passage had proved abortive, yet the Government still entertained hopes of ultimate success. In May, 1845, the Terror and Erebus, under the command of Sir John Franklin, left England, accompanied by a storeship, from which they separated on the 26th of July. As since that date no intelligence respecting their fate has been received, the Admiralty, after allowing a reasonable period to elapse, deemed it necessary to take steps for their relief. In 1848 the Enterprise and Investigator, under the command of Sir James Clark Ross, were despatched to the eastern, the Herald, Captain Henry Kellett, and Plover, Commander T. E. L. Moore, to the western side, while Sir John Richardson penetrated overland to the shores of the Polar Sea.

Towed by H.M. Steamer Sampson, the Herald, accompanied by the Pandora, left the Bay of Panama on the 9th of May, 1848, and on the 11th she parted company with her tender, which was to communicate at Oahu with H.M. Brig Plover, and thence proceed to the Straits of Juan de Fuca, to complete the survey. On the 14th, in lat. 7° 19' north, and long. 89° 20' west, the Sampson, having towed us 660 miles, cast us off, and, giving us three hearty cheers, was soon out of sight. It had been supposed that by being towed several hundred miles to the westward we should soon fall in with the trade-wind, and thus escape the variables and calms. But we had not been taken far enough. We made hardly any progress, and it was not until we had reached lat. 9° 20' north, long. 116° 10' west, that we perceived the first signs of the trade-wind. On the 11th of July we sighted Bird Island, a rock belonging to the Hawaiian group, and on the 7th of August, after a tedious passage of ninety-two days, we entered Awatcha Bay, Kamtchatka, and anchored in the port of Petropaulowski.

The weather was delightful, and great was our surprise to find in Awatcha Bay, instead of naked hills and sterile plains, as we had anticipated, a luxuriant herbage, and, up to the line of perpetual snow of the volcanoes, a covering of brilliant green. It being August, the height of summer, nearly all the plants were in flower; the roadsides were covered with blue geraniums, Kamtchatka roses, and lilies, intermixed with *Pedicularis* and the white blossoms of *Spiræas*. Only two kinds of trees (*Pinus Cembra* and *Alnus incana*) were found; for the willows are only shrubby, and the *Pyrus rosæfolia*, called by Chamisso a tree, is never higher than ten feet. The poplar, reported to have been seen wild, was not met with by us in that state; in the governor's garden however we observed an avenue of these trees. *Alnus* is the most common. The town of Petropaulowski is built of its wood, which also furnishes the principal fuel. Of its bark the Kamtchadales make vessels for holding fluids, which they, like all the Siberians, call *tujes;* the same term when applied to a person answers to our word *simpleton*. The practice of mixing the bark of this tree with dough is not now in use at Petropaulowski, but is still prevalent among the natives in the interior.

If Nature has been scanty in her supply of larger woody plants, she has made up for it in the distribution of perennials; annuals are scarce on account of the short duration of the summer, and the suddenness with which the cold season sets in, which prevents many seeds from arriving at maturity. Among the officinal plants of Kamtchatka, the following are deserving of notice. The *Schelamanik*, or Intoxicator (*Spiræa Kamtschatica*, Pallas), is a fine perennial, six or eight feet high, and producing a corymb of conspicuous white flowers. A strong liquor is prepared from its root, although prohibited by the laws of the country. In the spring the young shoots, which have strong astringent properties, constitute, when mixed with fish or seal oil, a favourite dish of the inhabitants. The young leaves of the Marschownik (*Ligusticum Scoticum*, Linn.) are boiled and eaten, as those of *Urtica dioica* and *Ægopodium Podagraria* in Germany. The Guba (*Polyporus igniarius*, Fr., var.) is made into tinder, and, when burnt, its ashes are mixed with snuff.

The soil in the bay consists of rich mould; but notwithstanding this advantage agriculture is yet in its infancy. No grain of any kind is grown in the southern parts of the peninsula; it is said however that at Cape Kamtchatka, in lat. 56° north, rye and barley are raised. The inhabitants live chiefly on wild berries and fish, especially herring and salmon. It is only around their houses that little patches, cultivated with potatoes, cabbage, radish, lettuce, and turnips, are met with. The cabbages and turnips are excellent, but the potatoes very watery.

The Russian authorities behaved with great kindness, and did everything in their power to promote our object; but as, contrary to expectation, no tidings of the Plover had been received, and time was pressing, our stay was limited to a few days. On the 14th of August we departed steering for Norton Sound, North-west America, in order to obtain, at the Russian trading post of Michaelowski, baidars (skin-boats), and an interpreter for the Eskimo language. We reached the place on the 2nd of September, but in consequence of the heavy weather and the excessively exposed position of the settlement for a ship of the draught of the Herald, we were unable to communicate for two days.

The Fort of St. Michael, or Michaelofskoi, belongs to the Russian-American Fur Company, and supplies two other trading posts, situated some distance in the interior. It stands on a little tongue of land, on the south shore of Norton Sound, in lat. 63° 28′, long. 161° 51′ west, and is built in the form of a square, composed of trunks of trees, which are laid horizontally over each other, in the manner of the American block-houses. At each angle is a watch-tower, with loopholes; within the walls are the various store and dwelling houses; close by, a chapel, consecrated to the rites of the Greek church; and at a short distance a windmill for grinding corn. Grain is imported by way of Sitka, St. Michael's itself not producing it, nor indeed any cultivated vegetables, except a few turnips. About four hundred yards from the fort is an Eskimo village, the inhabitants of which are a much finer-looking race than the more northern tribes. The country adjacent is, like the greater part of the Arctic regions, a vast moorland.

The commandant of the fort could not supply us with baidars, but he furnished us with an interpreter, Paavil Oglayuk, afterwards known among us by the nickname of Bosky, which, for the sake of brevity, I shall adopt. He was a half-caste, and had been brought from Bodegas, in Upper California. Although ignorant of English, he had a slight knowledge of the Spanish language, by means of which our intercourse was carried on.

Having resumed our voyage, we had an exciting passage through Behring's Strait, and anchored on the 14th of September off Chamisso Island, in Kotzebue Sound, where we were extremely disappointed in not meeting with the Plover. Although on our part every exertion had been made to hasten the arrival on the field of operations, yet it was mortifying to find that the winter was fast approaching; the Eskimos had already left the coast, and several severe nights' frosts had destroyed the softer vegetation. In order to obtain an interview with the natives, Captain Kellett took the ship to Cape Krusenstern, but none were seen there. Having returned to Chamisso Island, a party from Spafarief Inlet was met with, and it was ascertained that some white men were travelling in the interior, a piece of information which opened a field for various but fruitless conjectures.

As may be imagined, the long passage to Behring's Strait had been extremely dull, and monotony, followed by its usual train, soon began to exercise its baneful influence. As a remedy, recourse was had to various kinds of diversion. After leaving Awatcha Bay, it was unanimously agreed to have a series of theatricals. Mr. Chimmo and Mr. Woodward painted the scenes, and Mr. Pim showed great skill in making ladies' dresses, including caps and bonnets. The first piece was performed in Kotzebue Sound, when Mr. J. G. Whiffin, the manager, produced, with a most powerful cast, a highly amusing play, and issued the following programme:—

"THEATRE ROYAL, KOTZEBUE.

"Grand Opening Night.—Off Chamisso Island, on Saturday, September 15, 1848, will be presented, by the Officers of H.M.S. Herald,

'THE MOCK DOCTOR; OR, THE DUMB LADY CURED.'

A comedy freely translated from the French of Molière, by Fielding.

Dramatis Personæ.

Sir Jasper, a knight	Mr. B. Pim.
Charlotte, his daughter	Mr. J. Anderson.
Leander, her lover, a military officer	Mr. B. Seemann.
Gregory, the Mock Doctor	Mr. T. Woodward.
Dorcas, his wife	Mr. J. Whiffin.
Davy, a poor man	Mr. T. Hull.
Dr. Hellebore, a mad doctor	Mr. W. Billings.
James, a groom	Mr. W. Parsons.
Harry, a footman	Mr. T. Bourchier.
Maid to Charlotte	Mr. W. Chimmo.
Squire Robert	Mr. H. Trollope.

"Doors open at half-past six. Performance commences at seven."

The play went off exceedingly well; the performers were repeatedly called before the curtain, and afterwards the midshipmen's mess gave a supper, to which Captain Kellett and the gun-room officers were invited.

Up to the 26th of September we had most delightful weather; but on the 27th the rapid approach of winter became evident. As the Plover did not make her appearance, a mark bearing the names of the Blossom and the Herald was erected upon the highest point of Chamisso Island, and on the 29th we beat out of the Sound.

Before we attempt to accompany the vessel on her voyage, it may be as well to give a sketch of Western Eskimo-land, its physical features, plants, animals, and inhabitants,—a brief summary of all we learnt during our three visits to the Arctic regions.

CHAPTER II.

Behring's Strait—Western Eskimo-land—Its Geography, Climate, Plants, and Animals.

THE coast of Western Eskimo-land, after describing Norton Sound, projects into a peninsula, which, in conjunction with the eastern shores of Asia, forms Behring's Strait. The distance between the continents in these parts is so small that, in passing through the strait, both Asia and America are visible at the same time,—a grand and imposing spectacle. From the peninsula the coast makes a deep curve, forming Kotzebue Sound, and then stretching towards the north-west, it again projects at Cape Lisburne, in lat. 68° 52′ 6″ north. Cape Lisburne is composed of two promontories, the north-eastern of which rises to the height of about 900 feet. Imaginative minds have suggested that at one time Asia and America were connected. Without indulging in similar speculations, it is impossible to look at a map without being struck with the parallel direction of their shores in these parts; and, if pushed together, how nicely East Cape would fit into Kotzebue Sound, and Cape Tchaplin join to Cape Prince of Wales. From Cape Lisburne to Point Barrow the land is almost a continued flat, and the coast, falling back to the north-east, forms Icy Cape, Wainwright Inlet, and ultimately Point Barrow, the northern extremity of Western America.

A few islands may be said to belong to this region. In Norton Sound there are Egg, Sledge, and Besborough Islands; a short distance below Behring's Strait, St. Lawrence; off Port Clarence, King's Island; and between Cape Prince of Wales and the eastern promontory of Asia, the Diomedes, three islands most appropriately named, for the albatross, after venturing from the northern confine of the tropic of Cancer, stops short at the Diomedes, making the very group bearing its name the northern limit to which its migrations extend. In Kotzebue Sound lies Chamisso Island, an everlasting monument to the memory of an illustrious poet and naturalist, towards Point Barrow the Sea-horse Isles, and almost midway between Asia and America, about lat. 71° north, Herald and Plover Islands, portion of a group as yet imperfectly explored.

The country has many rivers, but none of any great size, and, owing to the flatness of the region, all are sluggish. The Koeakpack, one of the largest, takes its rise in the north, and, running in a southerly direction, empties itself into Norton Sound; the Tokshuk, Kowala, and Buckland are smaller streams encumbered with shallows, and running north into Kotzebue Sound; the Noatak and Wainwright run in a southerly direction, and are, like the latter, unnavigable any distance even for large boats.

The climate is considerably milder than that of the eastern shores of America. The proofs we need not deduce from artificial tables, Nature herself has written them on the face of the country. The abundance of animal life, the occurrence of many southern plants, and above all the limit of the woods, if compared with the opposite shores, furnish indisputable evidence. On the eastern side of America no forests are found above the mouth of the river Egg, above the 60th degree of latitude; on the western, they extend as far as lat. 66° 44' north, or nearly seven degrees further towards the Pole. There are but two seasons, which follow each other in quick succession. Towards the middle of October the winter approaches. All life seems extinct; the sky is cloudless, the air calm, and most of the animals, the visitors of the mossy steppes during the few weeks of uninterrupted daylight, have left for milder regions, in order to obtain those supplies which the Polar world begins to deny them. For nearly nine months the waters are covered with ice, the land with snow; and the temperature is sometimes so low, falling as it does to 47° Fahr. below zero, that rum and quicksilver become solid the instant they are exposed. The air is so clear that voices may be heard at a distance of two miles, and even a whisper falls distinctly upon the ear. As the winter proceeds the days become shorter; in November they last but a few hours, in December the sun is hardly above the horizon, and in some latitudes never seen. Occasionally the darkness is dispelled by the appearance of the *aurora borealis;* from east to west an arch is formed, extending its brilliant coruscations up to the very zenith, and spreading a magic light over the wintry scene; sometimes the rays flash up in straight lines, at others they move irregularly like a flame when affected by a breeze*. It is in the depth of winter that the grandeur of the Arctic region is displayed. The stars, the moon, and a bleak expanse of snow and ice are the only objects visible. A death-like silence reigns far and wide: in vain does the wanderer listen,—no chiming of bells, no barking of dogs, no crowing of cocks, indicate the vicinity of civilization; his own breath, the solitary beating of his own heart, is all the ear perceives. It is in such moments, in the dreary steppes of the Polar region, that man feels he is not made to be alone, that there is something in his nature which longs for association and prompts him to seek circles where his exertion may be beneficial to his neighbours, and his wants be supplied by the aid of his fellow-creatures.

At last the sun returns; the days increase and the temperature rises. At the end of June the land is free from snow, and the ice breaking up. The summer sets in most rapidly. The landscape is quickly overspread with a lively green, flocks of geese and ducks arrive from the south, the plover, the snipe, and many other birds enliven the air with their notes, while the murmuring of rivulets and the hum of insects give evidence that winter has passed and summer fairly set it. The sun is now always above the horizon, and for some weeks there

* I observed on several occasions that whenever the arch was above an angle of thirty degrees the coruscations were undisturbed by the lower atmospheric waves; whenever it assumed a higher altitude the rays were visibly affected by the action of the wind, moving in a uniform direction with it.

is no distinction between day and night, except that at midnight the light is less bright than at noon, the former differing from the latter about as much as a November and a June day in England. The rays falling continually upon the surface of the earth prevent the temperature from cooling down much, and thus, notwithstanding the low altitude of the sun, a degree of warmth is produced which, under other circumstances, would not be possible; the thermometer rises as high as 61° Fahr. With a sun shining throughout the twenty-four hours the growth of plants is rapid in the extreme: the snow has hardly disappeared before a mass of herbage has sprung up, and the spots which a few days before presented nothing save a white sheet, are teeming with an active vegetation, producing leaves, flowers, and fruit, in rapid succession.

But it must not be supposed that during this time the sleep of plants is suspended. That function, though short, is as regular as in the tropics: with a midnight sun several degrees above the horizon, the leaves droop when evening approaches, partaking of that rest which seems to be necessary to the existence of both animal and vegetable life. If man should ever reach the Pole, and be undecided which way to turn,—when his compass has become sluggish, his timepiece out of order,—the plants which he may happen to meet will show him the way; their sleeping leaves tell him that midnight is at hand, and that at that time the sun is standing in the north. Human skill has long tried to construct instruments to aid those venturing to the Pole to find their way back. How curious if an all-wise Providence should have extended the range of a few leguminous plants to the very axis of our planet, and made some humble herbs the means of furthering the solution of the greatest of geographical problems!

The soil is always frozen, and merely thaws during the summer a few feet below the surface. But the thawing is by no means uniform: in peat it extends not deeper than two feet, while in other formations, especially in sand or gravel, the ground is free from frost to the depth of nearly a fathom, showing that sand is a better conductor of heat than peat or clay, and corroborating the observation of the accurate J. D. Hooker, who, after a series of experiments in India, arrived at the same conclusion. The roots of the plants, even those of the shrubs and trees, do not penetrate into the frozen subsoil; on reaching it they recoil as if they touched upon a rock through which no passage could be forced. It may be surprising to behold a vegetation flourishing under such circumstances, existing independent, it would seem, of terrestrial heat. But surprise is changed into amazement on visiting Kotzebue Sound, where, on the tops of icebergs, herbs and shrubs are found thriving with a luxuriance only equalled in more favoured climes. From Elephant to Eschscholtz Point there is a series of cliffs from seventy to ninety feet high, which present some striking illustrations of the manner in which Arctic plants grow, showing that terrestrial heat exercises but a limited and indirect influence upon vegetable life, and that to the solar rays we are mainly indebted to the existence of those forms which clothe with verdure the surface of our planet.

The whole country from Norton Sound to Point Barrow is a vast moorland, whose level is only interrupted by a few promontories and isolated mountains. The rain and snow-water, prevented by a frozen soil from descending, forms numerous lagoons, or, where the formation of the ground opposes this, bogs, the general aspect and vegetation of which do not materially differ from those of Northern Europe, being covered with a dense mass of lichens, mosses, and other uliginous forms. Places less crowded with plants are sometimes difficult to pass. The ground is soft, and covered with isolated tufts of *Eriophorum capitatum*; in walking over them some of the tufts give way, or the foot slides and sinks into the mud, from which it is often difficult to extricate it. Wherever drainage exists, either on the shores of the sea, the banks of rivers, or the slopes of hills, the ground is free from peat; such localities are generally clad with a luxuriant herbage, and produce the rarest, as well as the most beautiful plants.

The aspect of some spots is very gay. Many of the flowers are large, their colours bright, and, though white and yellow predominate, plants displaying other tints are not uncommon. Cape Lisburne, one of the most productive localities, looks like a garden. The *Geum glaciale*, with its fine yellow blossoms, is intermingled with the purple *Claytonia sarmentosa* and a host of anemones and white and yellow saxifrages, or the blue *Myosotis alpina*. But such spots are rare, they are like oases in deserts. The flora cannot be said to possess an imposing aspect. There is nothing to relieve the monotony of the steppes: a few stunted Coniferous trees and willows afford little variety, and even these, on passing the boundary of the frigid zone, are either transformed into dwarf bushes, or disappear altogether. About Norton Sound groves of white spruce-trees and *Salix speciosa* are frequent; northwards they become less abundant, till in lat. 66° 44′ 0″ north, on the banks of the Noatak, *Pinus alba* disappears. *Alnus viridis* extends as far as Kotzebue Sound, where, in company with *Salix villosa, S. Richardsoni*, and *S. speciosa*, it forms low brushwood. With the commencement of the Arctic Circle *Alnus viridis* ceases to exist; *Salix speciosa, S. Richardsoni*, and *S. villosa* extend their range further, but are only for a short distance able to keep their ground; at Cape Lisburne, in lat. 68° 52′ 6″ north, they are in the most favourable localities never higher than two feet, while their crooked growth and numerous abortive leaf-buds indicate their struggle for existence. All attempts to spread their dominion towards the north prove unsuccessful; two degrees higher, and they are seen no more. At Wainwright Inlet a boundless plain presents itself. No tree interrupts the uniform line of the horizon, no shrub shows itself above the level of the turfy vegetation; all woody plants are prostrated to the ground, and only maintain life by seeking shelter among the mosses and lichens. The polar wind, which never affects the graceful palm, and is incapable of injuring the hardy oak, yet at last succeeds in laying low the offspring of Flora in these regions. Here they are doomed to slumber two-thirds of the year without sun, without warmth, in an icy bed, till the return of the great light restores the brightness of day and enables them to resume, for a few weeks, the busy operations of organized beings.

The region is as yet unchanged by human efforts. The Eskimos, by their migratory habits, by spreading from Greenland to the Aleutian Islands, and by their annual journeys, as well as by their intercourse with the Tchukchis of Asia, may have helped to extend the range of certain species; but since cultivation of the soil is unknown, they can have exercised but a limited influence on the aspect of the flora. Villages exist, yet all that our minds associate with them is wanting. On approaching we expect to meet with roads and bridges and smiling fields, to behold peaceful dwellings peeping through green boughs, and the steeple of the church towering heavenwards: in an Eskimo village these pleasing features are looked for in vain. At the commencement of summer the habitations are deserted, the natives having left for the coast, in order to lay in a stock of whale and seal blubber. The underground dwellings look cheerless and are filled with water, the surrounding ground is strewed with bones and fragments of skin, broken sledges, and other remnants, the paths are overgrown with herbage,—the whole presenting a picture of misery and desolation. The Eskimos have not yet learned that migratory habits and progress in civilization are opposed to each other; nor have they learned to make the soil supply more than it is willing spontaneously to yield: the whole region is in a state of nature, and up to the year 1850 the only plants cultivated were a few turnips, which the commandant of a Russian trading-post had sown near the fort of St. Michael. The natives care little for vegetable food, though they cannot entirely dispense with it. In the spring the leaves of the sorrel (*Rumex domesticus*, Hartm.) are eagerly sought, in order to arrest the ravages of scurvy; and again, towards autumn, the roots of the Mashu (*Polygonum Bistorta*, Linn.). As a stock for the winter, raspberries, whortleberries, and cranberries are collected, placed in boxes, and preserved by being frozen into a mass so hard that in order to divide it recourse must be had to the axe, or some other sharp instrument. Nor do the Eskimos make more use of vegetable substances for other purposes. Fuel they scarcely need, except for cooking. In their summer tents they require no fire, and their subterranean dwellings, on being heated, become uncomfortable, and begin to thaw and leak; the flames of a few lamps, the wicks of which are made of a moss (*Sphagnum fimbriatum*, Wils. et Hook.), supply the necessary heat. Birches and willows furnish material for bows, spruce-trees for arrows, while drift-wood affords means for constructing the skeleton of the *baidars*, or the walls of the hut. Man cannot be charged with having defaced the primeval aspect of this region; he has left everything as it was in the beginning. The mineral wealth rests undisturbed in the bowels of the earth; the vegetable kingdom still exercises an absolute sovereignty; and the animal creation swarms over the boundless steppes, rarely disturbed by the sight of the hunter, and uncontrolled by the voice of the herdsman.

It is not often that a botanist is able to investigate a flora so strictly original. Out of 243 Phanerogams, 2 are trees, 23 shrubs, 195 perennials, 7 biennials, and

12 annuals. Nature does not seem to have trusted to the region many plants whose propagation depends solely upon the ripening of their seeds,—an uncertain harvest in a district where the quick approach of winter puts a sudden stop to the operations of vegetation. Nor are the physical circumstances favourable to the formation of wood; most of the ligneous plants are mere *fruticuli*, very dwarfish, and more under the ground than above it. Only a few willows, a rose, the red currant, a birch, and a *Spiræa* are deserving of the name of shrub. Trees are still more scarce, no more than two kinds (*Pinus alba* and *Salix speciosa*) having as yet been discovered. The white spruce occasionally attains a height of forty or fifty feet, and a circumference of from four to five feet. The largest willow (*S. speciosa*) seen was twenty feet high and nearly five inches in diameter; it had such a juvenile appearance that, judging from the growth of trees in milder climates, it would have been pronounced to be five or six years old, yet on closer examination its age proved more than eighty years, while that of some white spruce-trees was proved to exceed a century and a half.

The greater number of the plants are common to the Alps, the Rocky Mountains, and the northern portions of Europe and Asia; some even are inhabitants of the Antarctic countries. Few are peculiar to Arctic America, and only four (*Artemisia androsacea, Eritrichium aretioides, Oxytropis polaris*, Seem., and *Polytrichum cavifolium*) have been found exclusively in Western Eskimo-land. Formerly a considerable number were thought to belong to the Polar regions of the north; in proportion however as knowledge increased, the endemic species have either been reduced to mere forms or varieties, or have proved to be plants common also to other countries. Now only a few remain, and there is reason to suppose that even these few will be found to extend their range over a much wider extent of surface than is at present assigned to them. The corroboration of this supposition would be productive of important results; it would throw additional light upon the geographical distribution of vegetable forms, and prove that the diffusion of plants had taken place, not from north to south, but from south to north,—a direction which, even in the absence of these data, may be supported by plausible arguments.

A peculiar feature of the vegetation is its harmless character. Poisonous plants are few in number, and their qualities are by no means virulent. The traveller need not fear to get blinded or giddy by entering a thicket; no members of those families to which the manzanillo, the upas-tree, or the nightshade belong, inhabit the extreme north. He need not be afraid of being hit by an arrow dipped in the sap of the deadly wourali—no *Loganiacea* extends its range to these latitudes; nor need he be much on his guard against spines and thorns: save the *Geum glaciale*, and a rose—which forms no exception to the rule incorporated in a popular adage,—there are no plants bearing arms, belonging to that group which has been termed the " milites." The Fauna presents an analogy. Reptiles do not venture into the Subarctic and Arctic regions: physical circumstances seem to have exercised upon that tribe the same check as, according to tradition, the presence of St. Patrick has done in one of the British islands. Some of the quadrupeds are ferocious, but not to the same degree as in the tropics. How the bear may be trained we have frequently an opportunity of seeing, and how easily the rein-deer may be domesticated is well known. Even the wolf,—the dismal howling of which seems to be a fit concert in the wilderness of the north,—becomes under the care of man a useful animal: the Eskimo dog is to all appearance the result of such treatment; from being the enemy, the wolf becomes the friend of man, and draws the sledge of the very master whom hordes of his wild relatives are ready to attack and devour.

From the Flora we turn to the Fauna. The polar bear (*Ursus maritimus*) sometimes attains the height of nine feet, and inhabits the icebergs of the Arctic Sea, preying upon the seal, which, with one blow of its powerful paw, it secures and destroys. This bear rarely, if ever, approaches human habitations, and the icebergs adjoining the coast of Asia appear to be its favourite resort. The Eskimos however find the skin too useful to suffer the animal to remain in quiet, and have invented an ingenious artifice to secure it. A thick and strong piece of whalebone, about four inches broad and two feet long, is bent double; while in this state, some pieces of blubber are wrapped around it, and the contrivance placed in the open air, where a low temperature renders it hard and compact: it is now ready for use. The natives, being armed with bows and arrows, and taking the frozen mass with them, depart in quest of their prey, and as soon as the animal is seen, one of them deliberately discharges an arrow at it; the bear, feeling the insult, pursues the party, now in full retreat, but meeting with the frozen blubber, dropped expressly for it, swallows the lump. The chase, the exercise of running, and the natural heat of the inside, soon cause the dissolution of the blubber; the whalebone, thus freed from incumbrance, springs back to its old position, and makes such havoc with the intestines, that the beast discontinues the chase, and soon dies.

The other bears are comparatively diminutive. The most common is the brown bear (*Ursus Arcticus*), which inhabits the woods, and is not seen much to the northward of them. The natives kill considerable numbers about Kotzebue Sound. It commits great depredations upon the Russian fishing-stations in Norton Sound, and is so daring and voracious that nothing save a well-directed shot puts an end to the mischief.

Not unlike the bear is the wolverine (*Ursus luscus*, Linn.), which is also limited to the woods, and rarely, if ever, seen to the northward of them. Although small, it has been known to drag an entire deer to its den. The natives never openly face it, but always resort to stratagem. It preys upon any animal that may fall in its way, indiscriminately making a meal from the rein-deer or the mouse. Its skin is highly prized, and holds the first rank in Eskimo currency.

The marten of Eskimo-land appears to be a somewhat intermediate species between the sable of the Old and the marten of the New World; it partakes of the dark colour of the former, and the thick soft fur of the latter, while the fur on the under part of the foot is a character common to both species. It does not extend its peregrinations beyond the limit of the woods; on the contrary, it appears to increase in size and number as it recedes from that boundary. The peninsula to the south of Kotzebue Sound abounds in it; and still further south, inland from Norton Sound, nearly all the natives have outer coats of its fur, which however are not considered so valuable as those of deer-skin. Of several hundred skins that I have seen, the colour was never entirely black. The ermine (*Mustela Erminea*) is common, and inhabits the banks of rivers. During the winter it possesses, like the Arctic hare, a white skin with a black-tipped tail. It is occasionally trapped, though, from the number required for a single dress, it is not often molested, and its skin, as an article of exchange among the natives, is considered of trifling value. The otter (*Lutra Canadensis*) is highly prized and much sought after; its skin is used as trimmings for dress, and bartered at a high price with the Russian traders. The fox (*Canis vulgaris*) is of a bright red colour, and is principally found about the coast, where it obtains plenty of food throughout the year by preying on the ptarmigan and hares. The Russians give a good price for the skin. The white fox (*Canis lagopus*), so common on the Asiatic shores, is rarely met with.

Wolves are seldom seen alone, generally running down their prey in packs. They do not hesitate, if pressed by hunger, to attack a single individual, although, if two or three people are together, they are easily scared. Scarcely a winter passes without some of the natives being destroyed; this, their own assertions, "and my personal knowledge," says Mr. B. Pim, "sufficiently testify. It is always necessary to be on the alert: I remember that it once fell to my lot to cook for the party to which I was attached; and having prepared some venison steaks for my companions, I fell asleep. Some wolves however had been in the vicinity all day, and kept better watch than myself. Upon awaking, I found to my surprise that the frying-pan was empty, and no remnants of the repast were to be seen. Pursuit was hopeless, and my companions returning, they had to go supperless to sleep." The wolf-skin is much prized by the Eskimos, and the animal itself is often caught for the purpose of crossing their dogs, and thus adding to their size and strength.

The lynx (*Felis rufa*) is scarce, but destructive to the deer. It takes its place among the branches of trees, and pounces upon its prey beneath. The skin, though the fur is very soft and thick, is not valuable, because it is remarkably thin. The flesh is made by the natives into broth for the sick and aged, as chickens are with us.

The different species of seal in the Arctic Sea are numerous, and form one of the necessities of life to the Eskimos. Their flesh is an esteemed article of food, and their skins are used for various domestic purposes. Of still greater importance is the morse or walrus (*Trichechus rosmarus*), without which the condition of the natives would be wretched indeed. Its skin forms the outer covering of their baidars and kayaks; from its tusks are made weapons, sledge-runners, and a variety of useful articles; and its flesh and blubber afford both food and light. Even to a European the walrus-meat is not disagreeable: Captain Cook calls it marine beef; and on board the relief ships, soup made from it frequently appeared at table.

Rats and mice are numerous, and, as the aborigines put everything to some use, the former are trapped for their skins, the latter as food. Marmots (*Axtomys Parri*) abound all along the coast; they are of a yellowish-grey colour, inclining to russet. The skin is esteemed, forming, as it does, a warm covering. The marmots burrow in holes, and remain in a state of lethargy during the winter.

Beavers (*Castor Fiber*) are caught or trapped in numbers, and, like the marten and others, are found in greater abundance towards the south. The natives obtain a good price for the skins, which the Russians appear to consider the most lucrative branch of their fur-trade, and import vast numbers into China, in exchange for tea.

The hare (*Lepus glacialis*) roams over the vast moorland, and several killed on Choris Peninsula averaged fourteen pounds in weight. During the winter they are entirely white, with the exception of the tips of the ears, which are black; but in the summer the colour changes, until in September it can hardly be distinguished from that of the hares of Europe. The skin serves as the inner coat of the Eskimo, and surpasses all others in softness and warmth.

Of the whole fauna perhaps no animal is better adapted to the country, or more useful to the inhabitants, than the rein-deer (*Cervus Tarandus*). From its skin, clothing and tents are made; from its bones, arrow-heads, etc.; and from its sinews, bow-strings, thread, etc.; while its flesh forms a most nutritious food. The teeth are used as ornaments by the women, and the horns converted into handles and the heads of darts. The rein-deer is migratory, proceeding to the northward when the snow melts, and returning southward when the frosts of winter render the Arctic steppes uninhabitable. The migrations southward extend little beyond Norton Sound. The rein-deer are very tenacious of life, and, unless hit in a vital part, they are not even stopped in their career by a musket-ball. The hunter sometimes exhausts his whole quiver of arrows before he secures his prey. There is however a quicker method of attaining the end. The natives make a semicircular pound, of staves driven into the ground, and affix to it nooses of walrus-hide; the animals are at first gently driven towards them, and then, frightened by loud outcries, they rush headlong to destruction.

Porpoises are seldom seen, but they seem to be replaced by white whales, which are a little larger. In June and the beginning of July they are taken in considerable numbers; during the rest of the summer they are hardly approachable. There are, besides, the Greenland whale, the spittle-back, and the finner. Many whale-ships have been attracted in consequence. Each vessel is capable of containing about 3500 barrels of oil; and as whales generally yield from forty to fifty barrels each, it is necessary to capture at least eighty-five to obtain a full cargo. The effect of this slaughter is already apparent, and the ships have to enter the icy masses in order to drag their prey from its last refuge; but even there success does not always attend their efforts.

The black crow and the ptarmigan are the only birds that remain in the Arctic regions throughout both the summer and winter seasons. The crow is supposed by the natives to have been the maker of the universe; but this belief does not induce any veneration, on the contrary, the bird was frequently pointed out as a fit mark to fire at. The ptarmigans change their plumage every month, and approach nearest to white in December; but after that time the tail, wings, and head gradually become black, until in June the feathers assume a brownish-red. In April the ptarmigans begin to pair, and during that time they have a peculiar cry, sounding almost like the words "go back, go back." As the month of May advances, and diffuses warmth around, flocks of geese, gulls, divers, puffins, shags, and swans, quickly followed by ducks, teal, and wigeon, spread themselves over the country. The smaller birds, such as owls, snipes, plovers, curlews, and sparrows, appear to spring from the ground, and their nests are soon to be found in every direction. The number of birds is very great, as they are seldom frightened, or, with the exception of the ptarmigan, snared by the natives.

Many varieties of fish abound. Salmon, so frequent in Norton Sound, are not found to the northward of the river Buckland; they appear however to be superseded by the mullet, which attains a considerable size. Herrings and whiting are caught in Hotham Inlet in great quantities, and some of the smaller streams produce a few trout.

An immense number of shells, star-fish, crabs, shrimps, and Radiata, occur in the Arctic Sea; the beach also, in some places, is strewn with mussels; of land-shells only a single species seems to prevail.

Insects are few in proportion to the rest of the fauna. A species of butterfly, a bee, two beetles, a jumping spider, and the mosquito, may be considered as comprising the whole; the latter however makes up for the paucity of other insects. In the tropics mosquitoes are often troublesome, but in the worst mangrove-swamps they are never so numerous as in the northern regions: indeed, they tormented us so much that the blood was often streaming from every unprotected part of our bodies. The tropical mosquitoes are small and swift, and although it generally proves a vain attempt to kill them, yet they may be driven away. Far different are these northern ones. They are much larger, sluggish in their movements, and, after having once taken up their position, they are with difficulty frightened. Fifty to a hundred may be destroyed by a single dash of the hand; yet all is of no avail: their places are instantly occupied by fresh recruits, and at last a person becomes so fatigued, after so many unsuccessful attempts to free himself from his tormentors, that he is obliged to give up killing them in despair, and submit patiently to their irritating operations.

The only domestic animal of the natives is the Eskimo dog, which, according to some naturalists, is to be considered as a tame wolf. The resemblance between the two is indeed striking. Both have the same low melancholy howl, and, although the head and ears of the dog are shorter, its eyes smaller and more sunk, its tail handsomely curled over the back, its paws smaller and less spread, and its colour of every hue, yet these distinctions are not sufficiently characteristic to raise it to the rank of a separate species. The natives are very proud of their dogs, and some of the principal men have teams corresponding in colour and size, as a wealthy European would have his horses. The dogs are employed for no other purpose than that of drawing the sledges and baidars. While yet puppies they are placed in harness, and thus early accustomed to the labour they are to perform. When tied to a sledge they evince their joy by the wildest antics, and set off at a quick pace, which however soon changes to a steady trot. The females are seldom used for draught, and only a few kept for breeding. The dogs, upon scenting, will start in full pursuit, but unless driven by hunger never attack the deer. The natives treat them with kindness and attention, and never use harsh measures; a word is generally sufficient to quicken their pace or bring them to a halt. The women even go so far as to chew the food for the pups, and give them a share of the furs. This treatment indeed differs essentially from that inflicted by the Tchukchis, on the north-eastern shores of Asia, who beat their dogs most unmercifully.

When considering the country in a commercial point of view, we find, as far as our present knowledge enables us to see, no vegetable productions which would play a prominent part in the traffic of civilized nations. Of wood there is only a limited quantity, and that is too far inland; the leaves of the *Rumex domesticus* and the different scurvy-grasses, as well as the roots of some *Polygonums*, may, in the absence of better vegetables, serve for culinary purposes, and they may even, under cultivation, become more palatable; the various kinds of berries may be highly useful to the Eskimos, destitute as they are of any other fruit, and they may be most welcome antiscorbutics to those voyagers whose daring leads them to the Polar Seas; the Iceland moss and other lichens may be useful tonics and dyes; but all these productions are of little or no commercial importance. Should the country be ever inhabited by a civilized people, they will have to look to the animal creation for those means which procure the commodities of more favoured climes, and they will have to exchange walrus-tusks, eider-down, furs, and train-oil, for the spices of India, the manufactures of Europe, and the medicinal drugs of tropical America.

CHAPTER III.

The Ice-cliffs of Eschscholtz Bay—Their Formation and Fossil Remains—Sir John Richardson's views on them.

THE ice-cliffs* of Eschscholtz Bay, in Kotzebue Sound, well deserve attention. They extend along the southern side of the bay, east and west, from Elephant Point to Eschscholtz Point; they are from forty to ninety feet high, and consist of three distinct layers. The lower layer is ice, the central clay, containing fossils, and the uppermost peat. Partly from the action of the waves, partly from the thawing of the ice, that side of the cliffs facing the sea is cut perpendicularly, and presents a clear view of the internal structure of the formation.

The ice, or lower layer, as far as it can be seen above the ground, is from twenty to fifty feet thick, but is every year decreasing. In the months of July, August, and September a considerable quantity melts, which causes the downfall of the two upper layers, and gives

---

* For a view of these cliffs see Plate I. of the 'Botany of the Voyage of H.M.S. Herald.'

the whole a very confused aspect, by mixing together peat, clay, plants, bones, and ice in a most disorderly manner. The ice was thought by some of the earlier visitors to be only a superficial coating; but this supposition was disproved in 1849, when enormous portions were found to have separated from the main body, testifying beyond a doubt that it forms part of a solid iceberg. Others, who comprehended the real nature of this lower layer, endeavoured to explain its presence by assuming that the water of the surface penetrated through the peat and clay, gradually accumulated, changed into a mass of ice, and thus caused the rising of the cliffs. This hypothesis at first sight appears plausible, but if examined it falls to the ground. In temperate climates we often find moorlands rising, like a sponge, in consequence of the mass of water which has accumulated in them; in Kotzebue Sound however, where the soil is always frozen at a depth of two or three feet from the surface, no water can possibly sink to the depth of several fathoms, and consequently no rising can take place.

The second or central layer varies in thickness from two to twenty feet, and consists of alluvial clay intermingled with gravel, sand, and fossil bones, the whole emitting the peculiar smell common in burial-places. In one spot was found some long black hair, together with a quantity of light brown dust, evidently decomposed animal matter. The fossils are sometimes of great size. In 1848 we collected eight tusks of the antediluvian elephant, the largest of which, though broken at the point, was eleven feet six inches long, one foot nine inches in circumference at the base, and weighed 243 lbs. Molar teeth, thigh-bones, ribs, and other fragments of this gigantic animal, and a great number of horse and deer bones, were disinterred. The species found in these cliffs are the mammoth (*Elephas primigenius*), the fossil horse (*Equus fossilis*), the moose-deer (*Cervus Alces*), the rein-deer (*Cervus Tarandus*), fossil musk-ox (*Ovibos moschatus*), *Ovibos maximus*, fossil bison (*Bison priscus?*) the heavy-horned fossil bison (*Bison crassicornis*), and the big-horn (*Ovis montana*).

The uppermost layer, or surface, is from two to five feet thick, consisting of peat, entirely destitute of fossils. It bears the kind of vegetation to which it owes its existence—plants peculiar to moorlands. Among them many mosses, lichens, sedges, and several *Ericaceæ* and willows may be recognized, the occurrence of which demonstrates the possibility of the growth of plants in a soil frozen beneath, a fact formerly much disputed.

As the ice could not have been formed by water percolating through the clay and afterwards becoming frozen, it is natural to conclude that it was in its present site previous to the arrival of the clay. This conclusion is strengthened by the evidence afforded by the clay itself, for the fossils are solely confined to that layer. If these were indiscriminately distributed, we might be led to suppose that the whole had undergone the same revolution; such not being the case, we are forced to believe that the clay with its fossils arrived after the ice had been firmly established, and, as these fossils belong to the antediluvian period, the ice must be very old.

Sir John Richardson, with that accuracy for which he

is so distinguished, has, in the 'Zoology of the Voyage of H.M.S. Herald,' described the bones collected by us, and prefaced his description by the following philosophical observations:—

"The science of chemistry, as at present taught, justifies our belief that animal substances, when solidly frozen and kept steadily in a temperature below the freezing-point, do not undergo putrefaction, and may be preserved without change for any conceivable length of time. The depth to which, in northern countries, the summer thaw penetrates, varies with the nature of the soil, but, except in purely sandy and very porous beds, it nowhere exceeds two feet in American or Siberian lands lying within the Arctic Circle. The influence of the sun's rays is not perceptible at this depth until towards the close of summer, which occurs at a varying period of from five to ten weeks from the time that the surface of the earth was denuded of snow by the spring thaw. During the rest of the year, even in the forest lands, though not so long there as in the open barren grounds, or *tundras*, the soil is firmly and continuously bound up in frost. The thickness of the permanently frozen substratum is more or less influenced by its mineral structure, but is primarily dependent on the mean annual temperature of the air acting antagonistically to the interior heat of the earth. Unless the mean heat of the year in any given locality falls short of the freezing-point, there exists no perennial frozen substratum at that place. It is not necessary that we should here endeavour to trace the isothermal line of 32° Fahr., as the reader may obtain a correct idea of its general course by consulting Baer's charts. It will suffice to say, that on the continent of America it passes some degrees to the southward of the sixtieth parallel of north latitude, and that while it undulates with the varying elevation of the interior, it has a general rise northwards in its course westerly.

"Where the permanently frozen subsoil exists, it is a perfect ice-cellar, and preserves from destruction the bodies of animals completely enclosed in it. By its intervention entire carcases of the extinct mammoth and tichorhine rhinoceros have been handed down in arctic Siberia from the drift period to our times, and, being exposed by landslips, have revealed most interesting glimpses of the fauna of that remote epoch. Conjecture fails in assigning a chronological date to the time when the drift and boulders were spread extensively over the northern hemisphere: the calculations that have been made of the ages occupied in the formation of subsequent alluvial deposits are founded on imperfect data; and we merely judge from the absence of works of art and of human bones, that the drift era must have been antecedent to the appearance of man upon earth, or at least to his multiplication within the geographical limits of the drift. Whatever may be our speculations concerning the mode in which the carcases in question were enclosed in frozen gravel or mud, their preservation to present times in a fresh condition indicates that the climate was a rigorous one at the epoch of their entombment and has continued so ever since. Moreover, as large carcases could not, without decomposition, be conveyed from a distance by water, it is fair to conclude that the animals lived in the districts in which they are now found, or in their immediate neighbourhood, and not, as some have supposed, in warmer and more distant regions.

"It seems also to us to be impossible that ice could have been the vehicle by which whole bodies or complete skeletons could have been brought from warmer parallels and deposited in the vast cemeteries of polar Siberia or in Eschscholtz Bay, for the simple reason that ice is not the product of these warm countries. Nor does the difficulty seem less of explaining how such a group of pachyderms and ruminants could have been brought down by travelling glaciers from warmer southern valleys of mountain ranges no longer in existence, without admitting such extensive changes in the surface-level of the district, as would confound all our ideas of the distribution of the drift as we at present find it.

"It is easier to imagine that the animals whose osseous remains now engage our attention ranged while living to the shores of an icy sea, and that by some sudden deluge or vast wave or succession of waves they were swept from their pasture-grounds. It is not necessary that we should here discuss the extent of this deluge, or inquire whether it covered simultaneously the north of Europe, Asia, and America, or operated by a succession of great waves or more local inundations. What more immediately concerns our subject is, to know that in the drift containing marine shells of existing species, and boulders borne far from their parent cliffs, we have evidence of diluvial action extending from the *ultima Thule* of the American polar sea to far southwards in the valley of the Mississippi.

"The identification of the fossil mammoth and rhinoceros of England and Europe with those of Siberia by the first of living comparative anatomists, might lead us to conclude that the same fauna inhabited the northern parts of the new and old world; but I think that we shall find evidence in the bones of bovine animals brought from Eschscholtz Bay, that an American type of ruminants was perceptible even in that early age.

"At the present time the moose-deer and mountain sheep inhabit districts of America suited to their habits up to the most northern limits of the continent; while the musk-ox and rein-deer go beyond its shores to distant islands; and the arctic hare is a perennial resident of the most northern of these islands that have been visited, or up to the seventy-sixth parallel. Supposing the climate of North America, at a time just antecedent to the drift period, to have been similar or nearly so to that which now exists, the habits and ranges of the ferine animals at the two dates, though the species differ, may have had a close analogy. The mammoth and other beasts that browsed on the twigs of willows or larger trees may have ranged as far north, at least in the summer, as the moose-deer does now, or up to the seventieth parallel; and lichenivorous or herbivorous ruminants may have extended their spring migrations still further north;—these journeys in quest of seclusion and more agreeable food being quite compatible with the co-existence of vast wandering herds of the same species in more southern lands, reaching even beyond the limits over which the drift has been traced, and where the final extinction of the entire races may be owing to causes operating in comparatively recent periods.

"The St. Petersburg Transactions, and other works, contain accounts of the circumstances attending the discovery of the entire carcases of a rhinoceros and of two mammoths in arctic Siberia; and one cannot avoid regretting that they were beyond the reach of competent naturalists, who might, by examining the contents of the stomach, the feet, external coverings, and other important parts, have revealed to us much of the habits of these ancient animals and of the nature of the country in which they lived. The inexhaustible deposits of organic remains in the Kotelnoi or New Siberian Archipelago, lying off the Sviatoi Noss, may yet disclose some equally perfect carcases; and their exploration by a scientific expedition is a project that promises a rich return for the labour and expense of such an undertaking.

"In arctic America such remains have been discovered in its north-western corner alone, and as yet, bones, horns, and hair only have been obtained, without any fresh muscular fibre; but all the collectors describe the soil from which they were dug as exhaling a strong and disagreeable odour of decomposing animal matter, resembling that of a well-filled cemetery. In August, 1816, Kotzebue, Chamisso, and Eschscholtz discovered, in the bay which now bears the name of the last-mentioned naturalist, some remarkable cliffs, situated a short way southwards of the Arctic Circle, and abounding in the bones of mammoths, horses, oxen, and deer. The cliffs were described by their discoverers as pure icebergs one hundred feet high, and covered with soil, on which the ordinary arctic vegetation flourished. These novel circumstances excited strongly the attention of the scientific world; and when Captain Beechey and his accomplished surgeon Collie, ten years later, visited the same place, their best efforts were made to ascertain the true nature of the phenomenon. Dr. Buckland drew up an account of the fossil remains then procured, with illustrative plates, and Captain Beechey published a plan of the locality.

"This plan comprises a nearly square section of country, having a width and length of about fourteen miles. The Buckland river, where it bends to the northward to fall into Eschscholtz Bay, flanks the district on its inland or eastern border. From the mouth of this river the coast-line trends nearly due west to Eschscholtz Bluff, and forms the south side of that bay; the shore for one-half of the way, or about seven miles, between the Bluff and Elephant Point, being composed of the high icy cliffs, and for the remainder of the distance, or from Elephant Point to the river, the coast is low and slightly incurved. The west face of the land fronts Kotzebue Sound and is formed of slaty gneiss rocks, which terminate on the north at Eschscholtz Bluff, and ten or twelve miles to the southward the rocky eminences, taking an inland direction, are flanked by low, marshy ground. A ridge of hills runs nearly parallel to the western shore at the distance of a mile and a quarter, and at their southern angle, where they bend inland, there stands still nearer the coast-line one of the loftiest bluffs, ascertained to be 640 feet high. From this corner the course of the range is south-easterly, the swampy country above-mentioned running along its base. The banks of the Buckland are also represented as being high, if not hilly, and they enclose, in conjunction with the range, a sloping valley or basin, drained by numerous rivulets, and opening to the north on the low coast eastward of Elephant Point. At the western entrance of the Buckland there is a minor display of frozen mud-cliffs; similar deposits exist also on its eastern bank as well as on the north shore of Eschscholtz Bay, likewise on various points of the coast between Behring's Strait and Point Barrow; but fossils have been detected only in Eschscholtz Bay, and on the banks of a few rivers that join Behring's Sea between it and Mount St. Elias.

"The following extracts from the Narrative of Captain Beechey's Voyage contain a description of the cliffs by a skilful observer.

"'We sailed up Eschscholtz Bay, 28th July, 1826, which was extremely shallow, and landed at a deserted village on a low sandy point where Kotzebue bivouacked when he visited the place, and to which I gave the name of Elephant Point from the bones of that animal being found near it. The cliffs are from twenty to eighty feet in height, and rise inland to a rounded range of hills between four and five hundred feet high above the sea. In some places they present a perpendicular front to the northward, in others a slightly inclined surface, and are occasionally intersected by valleys and watercourses, generally overgrown with low bushes. Opposite each of these valleys there is a projecting flat piece of ground, consisting of the materials which have been washed down the ravine, where only good landing for boats is afforded. The soil of the cliffs is a bluish-coloured mud, for the most part covered with moss and long grass, full of deep furrows, generally filled with water or frozen snow. Mud in a frozen state forms the surface of the cliff in some parts; in others the rock appears with the mud above it, or sometimes with a bank half-way up it, as if the superstratum had slid down and accumulated against the cliff. By large rents near the edges of the mud-cliffs they appear to be breaking away, and contributing daily to diminish the depth of water in the bay.' (p. 257.)

"'Such is the general conformation of this line of coast. That particular formation, which, when it was first discovered by Captain Kotzebue, excited so much curiosity, and bore so near a resemblance to an iceberg as to deceive himself and his officers, remains to be described. As we rowed along the shore the shining surface of small portions of the cliffs attracted our attention, and directed us where to search for this curious phenomenon, which we should otherwise have had difficulty in finding, notwithstanding its locality had been particularly described; for so large a portion of the ice-cliff has thawed since it was visited by Captain Kotzebue and his naturalists, that only a few insignificant patches of the frozen surface now remain. The largest of these, situated about a mile to the westward of Elephant Point, was particularly examined by Mr. Collie, who on cutting through the ice in a horizontal direction found that it formed only a casing of the cliff, which was composed of mud and gravel in a frozen state. On removing the earth above, it was also evident, by a decided line of separation between the ice and the cliff, that the Russians had been deceived by appearances. By cutting into the surface of the cliff, three feet from the edge, frozen earth similar to that which formed the face of the cliff, was found at eleven inches' depth, and four yards further back the same substance occurred at twenty inches' depth*.

" 'This glacial facing we afterwards noticed in several parts of the Sound, and it appears to be occasioned either by the snow being banked up against the cliff or collected in its hollows in the winter and converted into ice in the summer by partial thawings and freezings, or by the constant flow of water during the summer over the edges of the cliffs, on which the sun's rays operate less forcibly than on other parts in consequence of their aspect. The streams thus became converted into ice, either in trickling down the still frozen surface of the cliffs, or after they reach the earth at their base, in which case the ice rises like a stalagmite and in time reaches the surface. But before this is accomplished, the upper soil, loosened by the thaw, is itself projected over the cliff, and falls in a heap below, whence it is ultimately carried away by the tide.

" '[September, 1826, p. 323.] The cliffs in which the fossils [collected by Mr. Collie] appear to have been imbedded, are part of the range in which the ice for-

* "Had the pits been sunk at a distance from the edge of the cliff to the depth of three or four yards, information of a more decided character would have been obtained; for the experiments do not of themselves prove satisfactorily that the frozen mud which was reached so early in the summer as the end of July, at the depth of twenty-two inches, was not merely an unthawed layer of the superficial soil, reposing on pure ice at some distance below.

mation was seen in July. During our absence of five weeks, we found that the edge of the cliff in one place had broken away four feet, and in another two feet and a half, and a further portion of it was on the eve of being precipitated on the beach. In some places where the icy shields had adhered, nothing now remained but frozen earth from the front of the cliff. By cutting those parts of the ice which were still attached, the mud in a frozen state presented itself as before, and confirmed our previous opinion of the nature of the cliff.'

" The above description of these remarkable cliffs has been quoted at length, as it is not only perfectly clear but also concise. The opinions of Captain Beechey and his officers respecting the origin of the ice-cliffs are discussed at considerable length in Dr. Buckland's paper, printed as an appendix to the Narrative of the Voyage. Mr. Collie describes the fossiliferous cliff as facing the north and extending two miles and a half in a right line with few interruptions, and as having a general height of about ninety feet. It is composed of clay, he says, and very fine quartzy and micaceous sand, assuming a greyish colour when dry. The land rises gradually behind the cliff to an additional height of one hundred feet, and is clothed with a black boggy soil, that nourishes brown and grey lichens, mosses, several *Ericeæ, Gramineæ*, and various herbaceous plants, and is intersected by valleys pervaded by streams, and having their more protected declivities adorned with shrubs of willow and dwarf birches. 'The specimens taken out of the *débris* at the foot of the cliff (none were dug out of the cliff itself) were in a better state of preservation than those which had been alternately covered and left exposed by the flux and influx of the tide, or imbedded in the mud and clay of the shoal. A very strong odour, like that of heated bones, was exhaled wherever the fossils abounded.' (p. 509.)

"After an interval of twenty-four years, the recent voyage of the 'Herald' to this interesting spot has given a third opportunity of collecting fossil bones and examining the structure of these now far-famed cliffs. Captain Kellett, Berthold Seemann, Esq., and John Goodridge, Esq., with the works of Kotzebue and Beechey in their hands, and an earnest desire to ascertain which of the conflicting opinions enunciated by these officers was most consistent with the facts, came to the conclusion, after a rigid investigation of the cliffs, that Kotzebue was correct in considering them to be icebergs. I have been favoured with papers on the subject from each of the Herald's officers named above, and shall quote as fully from them as my limits allow, after premising a few general observations on the frozen cliffs of other parts of the arctic coast that have come under my personal observation.

"At Cape Maitland, in Liverpool Bay, which forms the estuary of the Beghula River, and lies near the seventieth parallel, there are precipitous cliffs from eighty to one hundred feet high, composed of layers of black clay or loam enclosing many small water-worn pebbles and a few large boulders. With the exception of about eighteen inches of soil on the summit, which thaw as the summer advances, these cliffs present to the sea a constantly frozen wall, that crumbles annually under the action of the rays of a summer sun, but the fragments being carried away by the waves and prevented from accumulating, the perpendicular form of the cliff is preserved. Elsewhere on the coast cliffs equally vertical, but having a different exposure, were seen masked by a *talus* of snow, over which a coating of soil had been thrown by land-floods of melting snow pouring down from the inland slopes. The duration of these glacier-like snow-banks varies with circumstances. When the cliffs rise out of deep water, the ice on which the *talus* rests is broken up almost every summer, and the superincumbent mass, previously consolidated by the percolation and freezing of water, floats away in form of an iceberg. In other situations the snow-cliffs remain for a series of years, with occasional augmentations marked by corresponding dirt-bands, and disappear only towards the close of a cycle of warm summers. In valleys having a northern exposure and sheltered by high hills from the sun's rays, the age of the snow may be very considerable; but it is proper to say that though aged glaciers of this description do exist on the shores of Spitzbergen and Greenland, they are of very rare occurrence indeed on the continental coast of America. The ice-cliffs of Eschscholtz Bay may have had an origin similar to that of the Greenland icebergs, and have been coated with soil by a single or by successive operations. I find it difficult, however, to account for the introduction of the fossil remains in such quantity, and can offer to the reader no conjecture on that point that is satisfactory even to myself. The excellent state of preservation of many of the bones, the recent decay of animal matter shown by the existing odour, quantities of hair found in contact with a mammoth's skull, the occurrence of the outer sheaths of bison horns, and the finding of vertebræ of bovine animals lying in their proper order of sequence, render it probable that entire carcases were there deposited, and that congelation followed close upon their entombment. A gradual improvement of climate in modern times would appear to be necessary to account for the decay of the cliffs now in progress and the exposure of the bones. The shallowness of the water in Eschscholtz Bay, its narrowness, and its shelter from seaward pressure by Choris Peninsula and Chamisso Island, preclude the notion of icebergs coming with their cargoes from a distance having been forced up on the beach at that place. Neither is it more likely that the bones and diluvial matters were deposited in the estuary of Buckland's River and subsequently elevated by one of the earth-waves by which geologists solve many of their difficulties, for ice could not subsist long as a flooring to warmer water. In short, further observations are still needed to form the foundations of a plausible theory."

The Eskimos—Their Dress—Arms—Food—Baidars—Habitations—
   Customs and Manners—Language.

THE inhabitants call themselves "Innuit," a term signifying, in their language, *Man;* the more usual term, Eskimos, or Esquimaux, is said to be a corruption of *Eskimantik, i.e.* raw-fish-eaters, a nickname given them by their former neighbours, the Mohicans. They are one of the most widely-spread races existing, ranging through 140 degrees of longitude, or an extent of 3500 miles. But this enormous surface is thinly inhabited. The very nature of the country and climate seems opposed to a rapid increase of the population, or any large aggregation of communities; indeed, a rough estimate of merely the coast of Western Eskimo-land—for of the interior we are ignorant—would give no more than three souls for every two square miles, or a total number of 2500.

By comparing the accounts transmitted by different writers, we find that the various tribes, however widely separated geographically, differ but slightly from each other in appearance, manners, customs, or language. They are however by no means as uniform in size as might have been expected: those inhabiting the vicinity of Norton and Kotzebue Sounds are by far the finest and tallest, while those living between Cape Lisburne and Point Barrow are, like the tribes of the eastern portions of America, much shorter in stature, and bespeak the inferiority of the districts in which they live.

Both sexes are well proportioned, stout, muscular, and active. The hands and feet are small and beautifully formed, which is ascribed by some writers to their sedentary habits, but this cannot be the case, as probably no people take more exercise or are more constantly employed. Their height varies: in the southern parts some of the men are six feet; in the more northern there is a perceptible diminution, though by no means to the extent generally imagined.

Their faces are flat, their cheek-bones projecting, and their eyes small, deeply set, and, like the eyebrows, black. Their noses are broad; their ears are large, and generally lengthened by the appendage of weighty ornaments; their mouths are well formed, their lips are thin, and, in the men, distorted by large beads or circular ivory labrets, protruding from diagonal cuts under them. These labrets correspond in shape and size with those formerly in use among the ancient Mexican warriors. This fact might be considered merely as one of those curious coincidences so frequently met with among nations widely separated from each other, if there were not another consideration more important. During the winter—by far the greater portion of the year—the

Eskimos are frequently obliged, on account of the excessive cold, to take them out. From this it would appear that the custom could not have originated in the frigid zone, although it may have been retained after having been once adopted. We know that the Aztecs came from the north, and are able to trace them with tolerable accuracy to about the latitude of the Straits of Juan de Fuca; we may therefore well ask, May not the Eskimos have come from the same quarter, or at least have adopted the custom when living in milder regions? In Mexico the labrets were worn only by the soldiery, among the Eskimos they are in use with the men indiscriminately; but in the society of the former the warriors constituted a separate class, among the latter every one exercises that office. Their very name, '*Innuit*' (man), shows the estimation in which they hold themselves. The fact also that the labrets are only worn in Western Eskimo-land is deserving of consideration.

The teeth of the Eskimos are regular, but, from the nature of their food, and from their practice of preparing hides by chewing, are worn down almost to the gums at an early age. Their hair is straight, black, and coarse; the men have it closely cut on the crown, like that of a Capuchin friar, leaving a band about two inches broad, which gradually increases in length towards the back of the neck; the women merely part their hair in the middle, and, if wealthy, ornament it with strings of beads. The possession of a beard is very rare, but a slight moustache is not infrequent. Their complexion, if divested of its usual covering of dirt, can hardly be called dark; on the contrary, it displays a healthy, rosy tint, and, were it not for the custom of tattooing the chin, some of the girls might be called pretty, even in the European acceptation of the term. A few individuals however differ in their countenances from the normal cast. A man belonging to the Hotham Inlet tribe bore so strong a resemblance to a negro, that, in order to settle the question satisfactorily, he was subjected on board the Plover to much scrutiny, an investigation which so frightened the poor fellow, that it was some time before he could be induced to renew his visits to the ship. Another man, from Spafarief Inlet, possessed to a remarkable degree the hooked nose and large black eyes peculiar to the Hebrew race.

The dress of the Eskimos is admirably adapted for the country they inhabit, and it is hardly possible to conceive the degree of comfort it affords in an Arctic winter. The garments consist of a double suit, both corresponding in size and shape, and only differing in the way they are worn: the inner has the hair next to the body, the outer *vice versá*. The boots, trowsers, and outer coat are made of deer-skin; the inner garments are made of fawn or the skin of some fur-bearing animal. The men wear a coat which reaches to a little above the knee, and is confined closely to the body by a belt, having behind the tail of some animal; a hood, tastefully trimmed with wolf-skin, is attached to this garment, and renders any other covering for the head unnecessary. The trowsers reach a little below the knee, and are overlapped by the boots, to which they are secured by a string. In the soles of the boots straw is placed, which is frequently changed, and appears to afford considerable warmth. Their gloves are generally made of the skin of young deer, but as these would not sufficiently exclude the cold, large thick mittens are worn over them. During the summer, when on whaling or sealing excursions, a coat of the gut of the whale, and boots of seal or walrus hide, are used as waterproof coverings. The *walguti*, a pouch containing pipes, tobacco, flint, and steel, or, in the absence of the latter, two sticks for procuring fire, is worn at the belt, and completes the costume. The clothing of the women differs but slightly: the coat reaches lower down, has a scollop before and behind, and a hood sufficiently large to carry an infant; the trowsers and boots consist of one piece only, and the tail behind is wanting; in other respects they can hardly be distinguished from the men.

The arms of the natives are adapted rather for the chase than for warfare. Their spears are made of driftwood, principally that of the white spruce, and pointed with ivory obtained from the tusks of the walrus. Their lances, darts, and arrows consist of the same material, and are variously pointed with flint, bone, slate, or ivory. Their bow, made of beech if procurable, is most ingeniously strengthened by thongs of deer-sinew, which are neatly plaited; the string consists of fine deer-sinew threads, laid together like the hairs of a fiddle-bow. The old ivory knives and flint axes are now superseded, the Russians having introduced the common European sheath-knife and the hatchet. The board for throwing darts is in use, and is similar to that of the Polynesians.

Animal food is abundant, and forms the chief portion of their diet, which consists principally of venison, seal, and whale and walrus blubber. The blubber is never cooked, and, being considered a delicacy, is given as such to children: that of the walrus is not disagreeable, indeed I have tasted some which greatly resembled cheese; that of the whale is rancid. It appears to be a matter of indifference whether the food be raw or boiled, fresh or tainted. The venison, even when it has undergone the process of cooking, is always accompanied by a plentiful sauce of train-oil. The oil is sometimes mixed with berries, and then forms a dish which ranks high in the native fare. Fish is eaten raw, and generally forms a stock for journeys; it is preserved either by being dried in the sun, or buried directly after being caught in the frozen soil. Vegetable food must necessarily form the smaller portion of the subsistence of a people who neither cultivate the soil nor inhabit a region where such productions are valuable. The acid leaves of the sorrel (*Rumex domesticus*, Hartm.), immediately they appear above the ground, and indeed throughout the summer, are eaten by handfuls as an antiscorbutic. The root of the Ma-shu (*Polygonum Bistorta*, Linn.) is another article of food: after being roasted in the ashes, it is not unlike the potato, though not so soft and nutritious. The principal winter stock is obtained from berries, of which nature has provided prodigious quantities, of eight different kinds—*Empetrum nigrum, Rubus acaulis, R. Chamæmorus, Vaccinium uliginosum, V. Vitis-Idæa, V. Oxycoccus, Cornus Suecica,* and *Arbutus alpina*. They are gathered in the autumn, and preserved by being frozen in wooden boxes, out of which they have to be cut by an axe or some other sharp instrument. Many other vegetable substances might be used with advantage; for instance, wild garlic (*Allium Schœnoprasum*, Linn.), various lichens, and scurvy-grass (*Cochlearia* sp. pl.). Their beverage is water; in very cold weather however they drink train-oil, and assert that it produces a higher degree of bodily heat. Intoxicating liquors are fortunately unknown among the northern tribes, but in Norton Sound, from constant intercourse with Russian traders, a predilection for them appears to have been acquired.

The *baidar*, or *omiak*, can hardly, as on the eastern side of the continent, be called a woman's boat, because it is used indiscriminately for many purposes. Its length is about thirty feet, extreme breadth six feet, and depth three feet. It tapers uniformly towards the bow and stern, and somewhat resembles the Madras Massulah boat. The frame is made of drift-wood, chiefly pine, and dovetailed and lashed together with thongs of walrus-hide and whalebone. The floor is flat, and there are generally six thwarts, or seats. The whole frame is covered with walrus-hides, which, while yet wet, are tightly and neatly stitched. A *baidar* is capable of holding from fifteen to twenty men, without drawing more than one foot of water; when more heavily laden, inflated seal-skins are lashed on the outside, which prevent the boat from capsizing. Although propelled by twelve or fourteen paddles, their speed is not great, and against a strong wind and on a rough sea they hardly hold their way. The paddles are about fifteen feet in length, and have a handle at the top. A long piece of wood, secured to the gunwale of of the bow, is used as an oar—a bad imitation of our method of propelling boats. The office of steersman is generally taken by an old man, who is provided with a paddle rather longer than the rest. A sail made of walrus-gut or deer-skin is also employed, but as the peculiar construction of the boats renders them incapable of beating to windward, it is only set in a fair wind. The *kayaks* are only sixteen feet long and two feet broad, and so light, that on a sailing or whaling excursion they are placed in the *baidar*, and not taken out until the prey is in sight. They taper and turn upwards at each end, and have at the centre a circular hole large enough to admit the body of the owner. The river and sea kayaks differ in their construction; the latter are rather smaller, more slightly made, and not so high out of the water. On pressing occasions two men may be seen in the same kayak, though it was a matter of surprise that even one should be able to maintain his erect position. A double-bladed paddle is used to propel them, and this operation is performed with great rapidity and speed. The paddle is, in the hands of the Eskimo, what the balancing pole is to a tight-rope dancer, and people who seat themselves for the first time in these kayaks, without being aware of this peculiarity, are sure to turn completely over.

Their sledges are formed of wood, and differ in construction from those of all other nations. They average twelve feet in length, two feet six inches in height, two feet broad, and have the fore part turned up in a gentle curve. The runners are narrow, and shod with the bone taken from the jaws of the whale, which is affixed to them by wooden pegs. The floor resembles a grating without cross-bars, and is almost a foot from the level of the snow. Thongs of deer-sinew, walrus-hide, and whalebone are used to secure the different parts, which are sufficiently strong to bear a weight of from 500 to 700 lbs.

Their houses, or *yourts*, unlike those of the Eastern Eskimos, are never constructed of snow, but built more substantially of drift-wood. They are more than half underground, and generally situated on low, and, if possible, sandy ground. An excavation, about twenty feet square and eight feet deep, is lined with trunks of small trees, and caulked in the interstices with moss; the rich inhabitants plank this part with boards which have previously been smoothed with an axe. The roof shelves from the centre of a large square aperture, exactly resembling the combings of a hatchway, through which light is admitted and the smoke escapes; every other part of the roof is covered with turf. The entrance leads underground through a passage thirty or forty feet long, and level with the floor, and has an easterly direction from the house. At each extremity is a small chamber, the one communicating upwards by a hole with the house, the other with the open air; the latter serves for shaking off the loose snow from the clothes before going into the warm hut. Both extremities are carefully closed with deer-skins, to keep out the cold air. The floor is marked out with sleeping-places on each side, except that of the entrance; the bedsteads are merely boards raised eighteen inches from the ground by being placed on trunks of trees,— in some huts they are strewed with branches of willow, over which at night the furs are placed. A few stones form the fire-place, which, like the rest of the centre, is covered with a few loose planks, moveable at pleasure when it is required to light a fire. The square aperture is covered with a piece of whale-gut, which admits the light and is sufficiently strong to resist a heavy fall of snow. In each corner is a stone, hollowed out to contain oil, in which a little moss (*Sphagnum fimbriatum*, Hook. et Wils.) is placed as a wick, thus forming a lamp, over which a sort of net-work is spread for the reception of wet or damp clothes. The fire in the centre is never lit merely for the sake of warmth, as the lamps are sufficient for that purpose, and great heat would cause the thawing of the roof, and consequent wetting of the whole apartment.

The interior of some of the huts is kept clean and tidy. The degree of comfort within is surprising. The lamps diffuse warmth and light; and when the traveller has put off his wet clothes, and reclines on the soft deer-skins regardless of the boisterous and snowy weather without, the pity he felt for the condition of the poor Eskimos rapidly evaporates, and he finds that, remote as they are from civilization, their condition is by no means so deplorable as is generally considered. The reception met with also strengthens this idea: the contents of the larder are placed before him, a dance, with its accompanying songs, follows, and every one exerts himself to the utmost for the gratification of the strangers; after the performance each brings a small present, and although he is certain of a return, it would be unfair to deny an evident hospitality and wish to please.

During the winter, when thickly covered with snow, the huts are not easily distinguished, and they would often be passed unobserved were it not for a tall stage near them, intended to elevate the kayak, harness, etc., above the reach of injury from the dogs. Each hut has its underground storehouses dug out of the frozen soil, and lined with straw mats; they are distinct from the *yourts*, and contain fish, berries, blubber, venison, etc. A sort of pigeon-house raised on poles, used for the reception of skins, garments, furs, or any article not in use, is placed near the stage, and assists in pointing out the locality of the huts.

It is rare to find a village without its accompanying dance-house,—a building erected by the united efforts of the whole community, and constructed on the same plan as the common dwellings, but larger, and, the floor being raised some three feet from the ground, more free from wet. The walls are decorated with tambourines and sometimes with wooden masks; lamps, to which each man contributes his share of blubber, are kept burning all round.

When the warmth of summer dissolves the snow, the floors of the winter-huts are covered with water several inches deep, and it then becomes necessary to take refuge in tents. The tents are made of untanned deer-skins, are of a conical form, and without any aperture at the top, as fires are never kindled within; they are pitched in a few minutes, and as quickly repacked. A small fire just outside the entrance, tended with care, keeps off the mosquitoes.

The government,—if the loose tie which connects an Eskimo tribe is deserving of that name,—is a combination of the monarchical and republican forms. Slavery, even in its mildest aspect, is totally unknown; every one is on a perfect level with the rest of his countrymen; yet all acknowledge an hereditary chief, whose authority however is very limited: he receives no tribute from his subjects, nor can he dispose of their labour or property: making treaties, or granting permission for hunting on the grounds belonging to his own tribe, appears to be the whole extent of his power.

The distance to which the Eskimos travel, for the purpose of exchanging their furs, is surprising. Some of the natives of Hotham Inlet were well acquainted with Cape Lisburne, and had even been close to Point Barrow. It is on the snowy waste that they appear in their proper element: followed by their sledges, they will walk about twenty-five miles a-day; at night unload, spread out their deer-skin, and, however inclement the weather, sleep as soundly as in their own huts. Their greatest hardship is the want of water. Upon coming to fresh ice, they dig a hole through it, the water bubbles to the surface, and the requisite supply is procured. As this good fortune however does not occur very often, and they require an incredible quantity to quench their thirst, recourse is had to another expedient—a halt is called about every hour, and tobacco, chopped with wood, smoked; "I fancied," says Mr. Pim, " that it afforded relief, and it is probable that the natives experience it in a greater degree, as they inhale the smoke in their lungs, and allow it to escape afterwards from their nostrils."

When the snow is soft, snow-shoes are worn. They are from two to three feet long, a foot broad, and slightly turned up in front; the foot is supported in the centre by a net-work of walrus-hide, and further secured by a thong leading across the toes and round the heel. From constant practice the Eskimos use them with surprising speed; in Norton Sound, one of them indeed succeeded in overtaking a deer: after having in the excitement of the chase lost all his weapons, even to the knife, he had the greatest difficulty in killing his prey, and received severe injury in the combat.

Hunting and fishing form almost the sole occupation of the men, who, with their small means, exhibit great ingenuity, as is shown by their method of overcoming the polar bear. Their bravery is quite as much put to the test, and well exemplified, in their capture of the whale, an animal many times larger than the baidars, and quite capable of swallowing the diminutive kayaks. As soon as the whale is seen rolling on the surface of the water, the kayak is paddled within a few feet of it, and the harpoon darted into the blubber. At the least lateral pressure the ivory top of the weapon disengages itself from the staff, which latter floats on the surface of the water and is picked up again, while the top, with the line and the seal-bladder attached, remains fixed to the animal. Many darts of the same kind are inserted, till at last the prey, with its many bladders impeding its progress, yields to the lances of the pursuers, and is towed in triumph to the shore. The capture of the seal and walrus is effected in the same manner. Salmon and other fish are caught in nets; the line and hook are used only towards the breaking up of the season, in order to obtain a supply of whiting.

In summer the Eskimos are in a most disgusting state

of filth; in winter they look quite the reverse, although their antipathy to water is then quite as strong. Occasionally they wash their bodies with a certain animal fluid, but even this process is seldom gone through.

Their method of eating is primitive. A wooden platter, full of meat, and another vessel containing train-oil, are placed in the centre of the party, who squat down on their hams. Every one selects the piece of meat he prefers; if it proves too large to be at once introduced into the mouth, a slice is cut off: one end of the meat is held with the teeth, the other with the left hand, while the right goes through the process of severing it asunder; the knife passes thus in dangerous proximity to the nose. Sometimes the meal is finished by a dish of berries mixed with seal-oil,—which, by the bye, is not to be despised. A smoke then follows, and the breakfast, dinner, supper, or whatever it may be called, for they have no stated hours for their meals, is concluded. Our food and method of eating, being so different from theirs, caused at first great surprise, but left a sufficiently favourable impression to induce them in various instances to adopt our plan. Spoons and forks rose in value; and it soon became unnecessary to take them with us on excursions in the vicinity of Kotzebue Sound. The women take their meals by themselves, and are not permitted to join the men, which reminds one of the Ecuadorian highlands, where the same bad taste prevails.

Their songs, like those of all the aboriginal Americans, are in flat keys and without rhythm. The key in which they are pitched always renders them melancholy, while the total want of rhythm makes them difficult to retain in the memory; their effect upon the ear of a European is unsatisfactory, and their end appears abrupt and unnatural. These characteristics are not easily accounted for. It has indeed been said that a people who have long groaned under oppression, as for instance several of the Sclavonic tribes, have their tunes in flat keys. This remark however can hardly be applied to the New World, for although in the southern portions of that continent the most complete despotism prevailed, yet many of the northern communities always enjoyed a considerable degree of freedom. Nor is it less surprising that the aboriginal Americans should have made so little progress in music as to be ignorant even of rhythm, which seems to us so natural that we adopt it unconsciously in thrashing and many other domestic operations. The tunes in use among the Eskimos appear not to exceed four in number; they are never used except for accompanying their dances. Music indeed seems to have little effect,—at least our fiddles and flutes made no impression whatever. The accordion was an object of curiosity, rather on account of the manner in which the sounds were produced than for the sounds themselves. The women, instead of quieting the children with nursery ditties, put a slip of blubber in their mouths, which appears to have an equally tranquillizing effect.

Their dance is of the rudest kind, and consists merely in violent motion of the arms and legs. It is generally performed by one man, but any number of individuals may join. The performer before commencing generally changes his dress, putting on a white coat and gloves, and placing a band around his head, the beak of a bird or the snout of some animal in the centre of his forehead, and a feather over each ear. He begins by stamping violently with the right foot, and throwing out his arms in wild gesticulations, besides leering horribly on the surrounding spectators, and shaking his head. He then uses the left foot, and changes again when inclined. The exertions are too violent to be long sustained, the performer is therefore often relieved by another. Sometimes several men take part in the dance, and occasionally the women join, but the latter merely move the body and wave their arms, without changing the position of their feet. The men sometimes shout, but the women never utter a sound.

In their power of imitation the Eskimos are almost equal to the Chinese. Whenever they saw any of our articles which they could adopt with advantage, they invariably tried to imitate it, and generally succeeded in making it similar in appearance, although perhaps not so perfect in construction. Knives, forks, spoons, were thus copied, and even a fiddle was once attempted, of course quite incapable of producing harmonious sounds. This turn of their mind will become of importance; and when they are more civilized, and have received proper tuition, they may, during their long winter, manufacture a variety of curious and elaborate articles.

It has been the fault of many writers to hold up the savage as a model of excellence, his character as inartificial, and his actions as honourable. How such a conclusion could have been drawn, with scenes of blood enacting under the very eyes of the observers, appears an anomaly. The American Indians, for example, were educated in deceit, and exercised their cunning and bloodthirstiness upon every occasion. The Polynesians, that numerous class of islanders, had the same characteristics; intoxicating drink and every vice common in civilized countries existed amongst them. The West Indians also were well acquainted with the useless habit of smoking, and even had, as some contend, a well-known contagious disease, which they communicated to their discoverers. On the whole therefore the belief that intercourse with civilized nations can teach savages any new vices is without foundation. The character of the Eskimos is a mixture of good and bad qualities, but considering it is without moral guidance it makes a favourable impression. Hospitality is never refused by them. At their meals the stranger joins as a matter of course, and the best the household affords is set before him. If the party is large the men assist in any work that may be going on, while the women cluster together, and aid each other in making coats and boots. A scene familiar in most households at home ensues: one, perhaps, a good boot-maker, imparts her mode of cutting out; another, skilled in tailoring, relates her peculiar method for the benefit of the hostess. Amongst themselves honesty is strictly observed; towards us this principle was not always acted upon: several things were pilfered from us, but as these were of inestimable value to them, every allowance ought to be made. Their attachment to children is great, but their treatment varies according to the sex: a boy is petted, while a girl becomes a drudge at an early age. Mothers as well as fathers entertain the same opinion on these points, and they both express their regret on the birth of a female infant. Still infanticide, a crime so common among savages, does not appear to exist, and was always indignantly denied. Bartering children is never resorted to. The women are treated, although not as equals, at least with more consideration than is customary among barbarous nations, for the Eskimo, not being a warrior, can find time to enjoy the comforts of domestic life; and, as in more refined communities, it not unfrequently happens that the woman is the chief authority of the house; the man never makes a bargain without consulting his wife, and if she does not approve, it is rejected. Old age is not reverenced,—it is, on the contrary, subjected to derision, and occasionally to maltreatment; the aged however never suffer from want of food, nor are they deserted on the bleak steppe to die a lingering death, as is said to be the practice of the Eskimos of the eastern side of America.

The mode of marriage is curious. When a man has fixed upon his choice, he proceeds to the girl's mother, and asks at once for the daughter's hand: if the mother is satisfied that he can support a wife by the produce of the chase, and besides has nothing objectionable, she gives her consent. The bridegroom then gets a complete suit of clothing, and tenders it for the girl's acceptance; the bride takes it to her mother, and, returning dressed in it, is considered his wife. In the same manner two men sometimes marry the same woman—a custom which seems to have its origin in the paucity of the softer sex. After the marriage ceremony has been performed infidelity is very rare.

When any person is sick, a perfect Babel ensues. For the cure of the patient the natives evince more gratitude than for any other benefit conferred. Their diseases are few: cutaneous eruptions are the most common, and these would probably be prevented by cleaner habits. Deformities are rare: only one hunchback and a man with goitre came under our observation. The dead are never interred; the corpses, with the clothes, trinkets, arms, and other implements of the deceased, are wrapped in a walrus-hide, and deposited on a stage raised about three feet from the ground; their position with regard to the points of the compass is not taken into consideration; they are covered with planks, and these again surrounded with trunks of trees, which are piled in a conical shape, and prove far too heavy for any wild animal to disturb.

The Eskimos of the country under consideration, with the exception of a few in Norton Sound who have become converts to the Greek church, appear to be without any religion whatever. Their idea of a future state is most vague: they believe that after death a certain amount of consciousness remains, but whether it continues for ever or terminates at a certain period they seem never to have considered. The crow, as has been mentioned, is deemed the maker of the world, and a high opinion entertained of its cunning, but it is nevertheless not venerated. It was always pointed out to us as a fit mark for our guns, probably with the belief that we could not kill it: how much this supposition was shaken when the bird fell like others, I am unable to state.

Respecting the origin of the white men their opinion

is equally vague. An old chief, on being asked where he thought we had come from, replied, "It is unknown, but I suppose you are trees grown in the same soil as the drift-wood, only living, while the wood left on our shores is dead." Whether the latter part of this answer was a mere metaphor, or whether the chieftain actually believed that we were a kind of tree, our slight knowledge of the language did not allow us to determine.

The Eskimo language is very guttural, but not inharmonious; it is rich in expressions, and is one of agglutination. Like the people that speak it, it is widely diffused, spreading over Greenland, Labrador, the whole of the northernmost portions of America, and the Aleutian Islands. From having occasionally been heard from the lips of the Tchukchis, a nation inhabiting the northeastern shores of Asia, it has been supposed to be related to theirs. This opinion is however erroneous; the Tchukchis have acquired it during their intercourse with their eastern neighbours, and only use it when communicating with them, or other strangers; just as the Chinese inhabiting the seaports would, in addressing a foreigner, employ the Canton "jargon"—that odd mixture of English, Portuguese, Chinese, and Dutch. The Eskimo language, as might be expected from its want of a literature, and its extensive range, is divided into many dialects, which often vary so much that those who speak one are unable to understand the others. The natives of Kotzebue Sound, for instance, have to use an interpreter in conversing with their countrymen in Norton Sound; towards Point Barrow another dialect prevails, which however is not sufficiently distinct to be unintelligible to the Kotzebue Sound people. By the indefatigable labours of the Moravian missionaries, the Labrador dialect has been reduced to writing, and the Bible already translated. Let us hope that the germ of truth which has been sown in the east may quickly spread its benign influence to the west, and tend to rescue from barbarism a remote portion of the human family.

CHAPTER V.

Departure from Kotzebue Sound—Petropaulowski—Mazatlan—San Blas—Panama—Veraguas—Sandwich Islands.

WEIGHING on the morning of the 29th of September, we beat out of Kotzebue Sound, and passed Behring's Strait on the evening of the 2nd of October, in a heavy snow-storm. Once more we directed our course to the capital of Kamtchatka, our place of rendezvous, to inquire whether, during our absence, any information respecting H.M.B. Plover had been received; we arrived on the 16th, but, as before, nothing had been heard of that vessel. We landed Bosky, our interpreter, as we could not conveniently take him back to Norton Sound, where, on account of the lee shore, ships are exposed to some danger from the want of shelter against the violent winds during the autumn. The interpreter received for his services a remuneration of one dollar a-day, and Captain Kellett moreover ordered the paymaster and purser to supply him with some few articles of clothing necessary for the rigid climate in which he was to pass the winter.

As the inhabitants of Petropaulowski, and especially the Governor, had treated us with great kindness, both on our first and this second visit, we were desirous to show that we entertained the same feelings towards them. All our "actors" having been informed that they must exhibit their dramatic talents before the belles of the Kamtchatka capital, a spacious building on shore was hired. It was necessary to have the entertainment on *terra firma*, because, on a previous occasion, when Captain Kellett gave a dinner-party on board, several ladies had been affected by the motion of the vessel, and felt symptoms of sea-sickness. Great was the delight of the Russians on seeing our theatrical performance, and, though few of them were able to understand what we said, the applause we were favoured with was as hearty as we could have wished. After the play was over, the visitors were conducted to the supper-room, when another strange scene presented itself to our friends. It is customary at Petropaulowski, at the conclusion of a ball or party, for the ladies to go home quite unattended, and for the gentlemen to remain and take a good supper. The company was therefore not little surprised when—the number of guests being great, and the room too small—all the places at table were offered to the ladies, and the gentlemen had to follow our example and wait upon them. Meanwhile the stage was cleared away, and when supper was finished dancing commenced, and was kept up until morning. The next day the ladies expressed themselves highly pleased with the entertainment, but nothing seemed to be more appreciated than that we had broken through an absurd custom, and given them the precedence at supper, which they looked upon as a forerunner of a reform in that direction.

On the 21st of October we departed, and on the 14th of November found ourselves on the Californian coast in sight of Guadelupe, an island, the northern point of which is dotted with pine-trees. We intended to send a boat on shore, but were prevented by the high surf. We continued our voyage without delay, and on the 24th we anchored in the port of Mazatlan, Mexico. The Pandora had left that harbour a few days previously, on her voyage from the Straits of Juan de Fuca to Panama.

Our voyage from Taboga to Mazatlan occupied 199 days. During this time we lost one man, our fiddler, by death; with this exception, the health of the crew was good until within a few days of making this port, when symptoms of scurvy began to manifest themselves. Captain Kellett says, in his report to the Admiralty: " I cannot account for the appearance of this disease; there could not possibly have been better provisions than we used, in addition to which Sir George Seymour had sent an ample supply of preserved meats, which were served out twice instead of once a week. On our first visit to Petropaulowski there was no salt meat issued, the men having had for six days abundance of fish, without vegetables. To the north, in Kotzebue Sound, they had as many berries as they had time to pick. At Petropaulowski, the second time, they had four days excellent beef and vegetables, an abundance of fish, and an unlimited supply of lime-juice. During our voyage to Mazatlan we were ten days on fresh provisions, fish and beef, and had fifty days preserved meats and rice. My impression, until the scurvy made its appearance, was that we might have protracted our voyage for any length of time, with the same precautions and a similar issue of such provisions; the absence of vegetables is the only reason I can assign for the disease, unless the men may have been predisposed to it from the debilitating effects of their long service in the hot and moist climate of Choco. I have been thus lengthy in my description of the appearance of this disease, and of the precautions taken to avoid it, as preserved meats have now become an article of issue to the ships' companies; which, with rice, does not appear to be so conducive to their health as with the potato. The general health of the crew is good; and with the assistance of a double allowance of vegetables, and a run on shore, all traces of scurvy will be soon eradicated."

As the Herald was to remain a few days at Mazatlan, Mr. Robert Pakenham, a midshipman, and myself, made a journey to the town of San Sebastian, and thence, accompanied by an old Spaniard, Don Alejandro Bueso, we went to the Cerro de Pinal, which gave us a good idea of the mountain scenery of Mexico*. After our return to the port, the Herald lifted anchor on the 4th of December, reached San Blas two days after, stayed there a few hours, and then directed her course towards Panama, where she arrived on the 19th of January, 1849, having been absent from that place nearly nine months.

* This tour, however interesting, I shall not here describe, as I traversed the same district in the following year, and should have to go twice over the same ground. Those who may be interested in it will find an account of it in 'Hooker's Journal of Botany,' vol. i. p. 148.

Pleasing though it was to see again a place so familiar to us, the state of the country was little calculated to allow of any further intercourse than was absolutely necessary. The accounts of the discovery of gold in California, having reached the United States, had brought to the Isthmus a number of emigrants, who, finding that the usual conveyances, food, lodgings, etc., failed, and disregarding the rainy season, had endeavoured to overcome the obstacles by walking across, sleeping in the woods, and eating quantities of fruit. The consequence was that vast numbers fell sick, and, the cholera ravaging the country at the same time, a great many died. For this reason the Herald communicated with Panama merely through the consulate, and went to Taboga to take in her supplies.

On the 29th of January the Herald left the Bay of Panama, to prosecute the survey of the coast of Veraguas and Costa Rica, while I proceeded to explore the canton of Alanje. I disembarked at the island of Aguacate, and went in a canoe to the Puerto de Remedios; thence I hired horses and rode to the village of Remedios, a place I had visited the year before. On my road thither I found the *Cedron* (*Simaba Cedron*, Planch.), a tree which has attained great celebrity, and is well deserving of particular notice. The most ancient record of it which I can find is in the 'History of the Buccaneers,' an old work published in London, in the year 1699. Its use, as an antidote for snakes, and its place of growth, are there distinctly stated; but whether on the authority of the natives, or accidentally discovered by the pirates, does not appear. If the former was the case, they must have learned it while on some of their cruizes on the Magdalena, for in the Isthmus the very existence of the tree was unsuspected until about 1845, when Don Juan de Ansoategui ascertained that the *Cedron* of Panama and Darien was identical with that of Cartagena. The virtues of its seeds however were known, years ago, from the fruits imported from the Magdalena, where, according to Mr. William Purdie, the plant grows in profusion, about the village of San Pablo. In the Isthmus it is generally found on the outskirts of forests in almost every part of the country, but in greater abundance in Darien and Veraguas than in Panama. The natives hold it in high esteem, and always carry a piece of the seed about with them. When any one is bitten, a little, mixed with water, is applied to the wound, and about two grains, scraped into brandy, or, in the absence of that, into water, is administered internally. By pursuing this treatment the bites of venomous snakes, scorpions, centipedes, and other noxious animals, have been unattended by dangerous consequences. Doses of it have also proved beneficial in cases of intermittent fever. The *Cedron* is a tree, from twelve to sixteen feet high; its simple trunk is about six inches in diameter, and is clothed on the top with long pinnated leaves, which give it the appearance of a palm. Its flowers are greenish, and the fruit resembles an unripe peach. Each seed, or cotyledon I should rather say, is sold in the chemists' shops of Panama for two or three reals (about 1*s*. or 1*s*. 6*d*. English), and sometimes a much larger price is given for them.

Remedios lies on the high road which connects David,

Santiago, and Panama, the three chief places of the Isthmus. The road is perfectly safe: highway robberies are never committed, and attacks upon the life of travellers have never been known. All the people go unarmed,—a striking contrast indeed to Mexico, where one is never sure that the person approaching is not a bandit. There is however one part of the road, the beach of Chiru, which is rather dangerous; at least I have good reason to consider it so. I was once on my way to Panama, and having travelled all day, I arrived much fatigued, about eight o'clock in the evening, at the beach of Chiru, where I had to wait for the ebbing of the tide, for this beach can only be traversed when the sea has retired. Having on one side a wall of almost perpendicular rocks, on the other the ocean, it must be approached with caution by every traveller, for woe to him who is too late, and overtaken by the flow! Nothing can save him: he is either drowned by the returning waves or dashed to pieces against the cliffs.

About midnight my servant informed me that the ebb was just making, and the beasts were ready for starting. I hastily threw my poncho over my shoulders, put on my straw-hat and spurs, and a few minutes after had left the hospitable roof under which the first part of the night had been passed. In less than a quarter of an hour we stood on the beach of Chiru. The moon, just peeping behind dark clouds, dimly illumined the broad Pacific, which in solemn grandeur stretched before us. The ebbing had commenced, and the time for passing the beach arrived. The waters had retired, leaving all along the strand a road of hard sand, the whiteness of which, and its reflection of the sun's rays, are objections to traversing this beach during the daytime. We had continued our journey for about an hour without interruption, when one of the beasts, being a little lame, was unable to proceed, and it became necessary to distribute its load among the others. Quickly as this task was performed, it took nearly three-quarters of an hour. In every other locality such an accident would have been hardly noticed, but happening on the beach of Chiru it was highly dangerous. The guides were fully sensible of it: having completed the arrangements they used every means of quickening the pace of the animals; and whenever there was an occasion for regulating the burdens, it was done with an activity which signally contrasted with their former indolence, and fully revealed their apprehensions.

Yet all precaution was of no avail. We had scarcely travelled two hours more when the waters exhibited symptoms of approach. The moon had now entirely disappeared,—darkness reigned far and wide,—but at a distance fiery masses seemed to rise one above the other. They came nearer and nearer. "Ave Maria purissima! Madre de Dios!" exclaimed the guides, "the tide is setting in." We pushed on as fast as the exhausted state of the beasts would admit, but had a terrible persecutor. The ocean already washed the feet of the animals. Every moment the danger became more evident, and, aided by a strong breeze, the sea rose with more than usual rapidity. The beasts could hardly keep a footing, and to prevent them from being carried away, we took a rope, connected with it the different cargoes, and laid hold of it ourselves. Whenever fresh rollers reached us, we halted, and directly they retired proceeded a few steps.

Our progress was extremely slow, and in vain did we look ahead to discover the road to San Carlos; in vain did the people invoke the holy Virgin and call on all the saints to protect them: no miracle interposed. The ocean continued roaring, and the water reached to our saddles. Terrible moment! All hopes of deliverance seemed to vanish. Our only safety lay in pressing forward. I felt my heart beat heavily, and I had already mentally bidden farewell to my friends and relations, when suddenly the cry of "The road to San Carlos!" restored me to life. Between two rocks opened the long-expected road. We were now safe, and in a few minutes we all stood on solid ground.

The roaring of the elements seemed now to have reached its height; with fearful energy the phosphorescent waves were thrown against the stony masses,—the road behind us appeared like one great fire. I could hardly believe that that was the way we had come. My feelings overcame me; my strength began to fail: the sudden change from the anticipation of death to the consciousness of life was too great. I felt my eyes growing dim, my thoughts departing, and, exhausted by fatigue and anxiety, I fell senseless to the ground.

From Remedios my road led through an immense forest, the Montaña de Chorcha, and after passing the villages of San Felix and San Lorenzo, I reached on the 14th of February the town of David, where I was kindly received by James Agnew, Esq., an American gentleman, who many years ago settled in the country, and now possesses some very large plantations of coffee. After a short stay I proceeded to Boquete, a farm situated on the extinct volcano of Chiriqui. Although I had visited that place the previous year, yet it afforded me a great addition of new species, and will probably yield a rich harvest to any one who makes a prolonged stay.

On the 1st of March I rejoined the Herald at Boca Chica, and proceeded with her to the Paredez Island and Point Burica. The nautical survey having been finished, Captain Kellett sailed for the Sandwich Islands on the 19th of March, and falling in with the trade-wind on the 7th of April (lat. 8° 30' north, long. 87° 10'), arrived at Honolulu, Oahu, on the 9th of May.

Of the twelve islands which compose the Sandwich, or, as it is now generally termed, the Hawaiian group, Oahu is one of secondary magnitude, covering a superficial area of 533 square miles. It owes its origin to volcanic action and the accumulation of corals, and is traversed from north-west to south-east by a ridge of steep mountains, the summits of which are nearly always enveloped in clouds or deluged with rain. Numerous streams descend from these heights, sometimes as little springs, more frequently forming cascades, which, after irrigating the lower lands, and diffusing freshness and verdure, discharge their waters into the Pacific Ocean.

The valley of Nuuanu, in the vicinity of Honolulu, which was formerly a mere wilderness, is now intersected by substantial roads, and converted into plantations and gardens, between which the still primitive huts of the natives, and the country houses of the foreign inhabitants of Honolulu, shaded by numerous Koa, Hau, and Kukui-trees, display themselves; while at a distance the mountain-chain arises, presenting, from the constant moving of the clouds overhanging it, the luxuriance of its vegetation, and its deep nooks and groves, a variety of tints and a change of light and shade truly enchanting.

In advancing towards the north of the island the road gradually ascends until it reaches a broad chasm, where the mountain seems to have been torn asunder. A strong breeze rushes into your face, you stand on the edge of a yawning precipice, the celebrated *Pali*. You shudder at the thought that here the victorious Kamehameha drove over his vanquished enemies, and that here the unfortunate wretches, instead of finding refuge in the fastnesses of the mountains, were doomed to perish. Your cheeks flush, your pulse beats quicker, as imagination paints with vivid colours that historical scene, and you fancy you see the fugitives one after the other pushed over the edge,—their bodies falling, touching the bottom, and dashed to atoms.

Having recovered from the surprise, a view opens which quickly dispels the gloomy thoughts of bygone days, and the fear which the unexpected appearance of the precipice and the violence of the wind were calculated to produce. Beneath stretches the smiling district of Koolau, a grassy undulating country, dotted with groves of screw-pines and breadfruit-trees, the true physiognomy of a Polynesian landscape. Here and there are rivulets winding their courses through verdant plains, farms surrounded by plantations, and, at a distance, on a fine-looking bay, arises the village of Kaneoe, with its church, its court-house, and its extensive fish-ponds, the whole beautifully contrasting with the broad ocean, which, like a silvery belt, encircles all, and bounds the view on the distant horizon.

Oahu, although situated within the limits of the tropics, and deprived of the cooling influence of snow-capped mountains, has by no means a hot climate. During nine months of the year, from the beginning of March to the end of November, the sun's rays are moderated by the trade-winds, which sweep with more or less force over the islands, and occasion a considerable reduction of temperature. In the rainy season, the three months that the trade-wind does not blow, the sun has travelled too far to the south to cause an oppressive degree of heat; the thermometer never rising above 80° Fahr., nor falling below 50°. In summer the air is pure and refreshing, the sky of an azure blue, and the sun brilliant. No wonder that in such a climate little sickness prevails, that epidemics are almost unknown, and that contagious diseases, except those of a cutaneous nature, have not yet extended their influence to these shores.

The Flora is neither strictly tropical, nor does it exhibit the features common in the temperate zone, rather a mixture of both. This remark however only applies to the aspect; in analysing the vegetation more closely we find that the greater number of its components are derived from the eastern parts of Asia, and that Polynesia, the shores of Australia, and the continent of America, have contributed their share. To the philosopher who attempts to account for the geography of plants, the Hawaiian Flora presents a problem difficult to solve. That the greater part of the vegetation, like the branch of the human family which inhabits the group, should originally have come from a *direction contrary to that of the trade-wind*, must ever excite speculation, and suggest the idea that in the distribution of organized beings Nature probably employed other means than merely those afforded by the currents of the atmosphere, the waves of the ocean, or the caprice of man.

A considerable portion of the vegetation—nearly one-third—consists of Ferns, those graceful forms which engage the attention of every observer. Of palms only a single species, the Cocoa-nut, is found in Oahu, but two kinds of *Livistonia* in the other islands of this group. The rest of the Flora is principally composed of myrtles, grasses, sedges, *Mimoseæ*, and *Arums*. It is strange that there are so few plants peculiar to the group, and there is reason to suppose that when the surrounding countries have been thoroughly examined, the number will be still less.

But whatever may be the component parts of the Hawaiian flora, or from whatever quarters it may have been derived, it presents a great variety of useful plants. Some afford the choicest wood, equally adapted for ornamental furniture and the construction of coarser architectural works; others yield spontaneously abundant harvests of delicious fruit, only waiting for hands to gather them; while again a considerable number bear tubers and corms which contain a quantity of farinaceous substance, enabling the natives to prepare not only their own food, but also arrow-root for exportation.

Some of the islands, especially Maui and Hawai, produce several species of beautiful fancy wood. In 1850 King

Kamehameha III. presented to Her Britannic Majesty a circular table solely composed of these. In its centre were inlaid the royal arms, well developed with the different woods, but the greater part of the table consisted of the Koa (*Acacia heterophylla*, Willd.), the light yellow tint and feathery appearance of which render it an elegant material for every kind of ornamental furniture, while its toughness and durability equally qualify it for the construction of the native canoes*. The Ohiaai (*Jambosa Malaccensis*, DC.) and the Kou (*Cordia subcordata*, Lam.) also have a wood used by cabinet-makers and carpenters. That of the Ohiaai was considered sacred in the time of paganism, and served for carving idols. The Oahu Sandal-wood (*Santalum paniculatum*, Hook. et Arn.), the Iliahi, or Laau ala (fragrant wood) of the Hawaiians, is now to be found in only one place, called Kuaohe, where it grows on the slopes of hills, close to the sea. Of the splendid groves, with the produce of which formerly so many ships were laden, but a few isolated bushes, which do not exceed three feet in height and an inch in diameter, remain, and these would probably have disappeared had they not been protected by the law, and thus escaped being converted into fuel.

Numerous plants are used as articles of food. The root of the Ki (*Dracæna terminalis*, Linn.), which has a sweetish-bitter taste, is baked between heated stones, and eaten; formerly an intoxicating beverage was extracted from it. The stem of the plant, it may be added, is used for hedges, and the leaves for thatching and for

* The statement of a recent traveller, that the canoes of the Hawaiians are made of the trunk of the cocoa-nut palm, is erroneous.

wrapping up bundles of food, fish, charcoal, etc. The leaves serve also among the native women as a medium of communicating ideas, which appears to be somewhat similar to the Quipos of the ancient Peruvians; the leaves are reduced to narrow shreds, and by making in them certain folds and knots the object is effected. The unexpanded fronds of the Kikawaiko, a fern, are considered a delicacy by the Hawaiians; but it must be confessed that to a European they taste insipid, resembling in flavour more the white of a raw egg than any other substance. The fleshy trunks of the *Ape*, an *Aroidea*, with leaves measuring from eight to twelve feet in circumference, after having been roasted, and thus deprived of their acridity, are eaten. The fruit of the *Physalis pubescens*, Linn., is brought to Honolulu, where the white residents make it into tarts and pies, terming it native gooseberry. The fruit of the Lahala (*Pandanus odoratissimus*, Linn.), the Ohiaai (*Jambosa Malaccensis*, DC.), the Ulei (*Osteomeles anthyllidifolia*, Lindl.), the Noni (*Morinda citrifolia*, Linn.), the Kilica (*Morus Indica*, Linn.), and many others, are eaten. The berry of the Kilica when ripe is black, but inferior in flavour to any of the mulberries cultivated in Europe. This *Morus* has proved useful for silk plantations; its foliage is small, yet one taken from the fields at random, of eight months' growth, produced three pounds and a half of leaves, and within six weeks after being wholly stripped, it had so much recovered that it could not be distinguished from those which had not been so treated. The Sandwich Islands arrow-root is prepared from the *Pia* (*Tacca pinnatifida*, Linn.). The Pia grows spontaneously in dry sunny places, and is also cultivated to a considerable extent; it is about two feet high, and every part of it is extremely bitter. The fecula made from its tubers is equal to the best West Indian arrow-root, and is much used by the inhabitants for culinary preparations, starching linen, and various other purposes. It sells in Honolulu at about five cents a pound, and, according to official returns, 43,683 lbs. of it were exported in 1845; 10,000 lbs. in 1846; in the three following years the quantity sent to foreign countries was less; in 1850 it again increased. More important than the Pia is the Kalo* (*Colocasia esculenta*, Schott), the favourite vegetable of the Hawaiians. It is chiefly grown in artificial swamps, but also, as in Central America, on dry ground. As is the case with all vegetables long cultivated by man, a great number of varieties exist, distinguished from each other by the colour of the corms and foliage, as well as by the height of the entire plant and the shape of the leaves; those varieties however in which a bluish colour prevails are considered the best, and the tribute to the chief has always to be discharged with them. Besides the Kalo, there are at present under cultivation sugar-cane, sweet potatoes, water-melons, cucumbers, potatoes, bananas, pumpkins, and coffee. No pains are taken with the breadfruit, as the natives, unlike those of the Society Islands, do not eat it. Cocoa-nut palms are grown on the seaside, but do not thrive well; they have evidently attained their northern limit. Under the old despotism, their fruits were reserved for the men, women

---

* Spelt "Taro" by the early voyagers, though incorrectly, as there is neither *t* nor *r* in the Hawaiian alphabet.

not being allowed to partake of them; with the overthrow of the *tabu* system and the heathen superstitions, this custom, like many others, was discontinued, and cocoa-nuts are now eaten by both sexes.

Various vegetable substances are employed for miscellaneous purposes. The cloth (*kapa*) of which the natives make many of their dresses is obtained from the bark of two trees—the Wauke (*Broussonetia papyrifera*, Vent.) and the Mamaki (*Bœhmeria albida*, Hook. et Arn.). Formerly much cloth was made from the Kilica (*Morus Indica*, Linn.), but as its bark is of inferior quality, it is at present, when European manufactures may be had at a cheap rate, little used. Cordage is obtained from the Hau (*Paritium tiliaceum*, St. Hil.), and two sedges, Akaakai and Ahuawa. The two latter go through processes of preparation similar to those of flax. The vessel out of which the natives eat their *Poi*, *i.e.* fermented Kalo (*Colocasia esculenta*, Schott), is called *Ipu*, and consists of the shell of *Cucurbita maxima*; the network surrounding it is prepared from the bark of the Hau (*Paritium tiliaceum*, St. Hil.). The water-flasks, or *Huewai*, are sometimes handsomely ornamented, and are obtained from the bottle-gourd (*Lagenaria vulgaris*, Ser.). The kernels of the Kukui (*Aleurites triloba*, Forst.) are used for making oil, and are also employed instead of candles; a number of them strung upon a stick will burn for hours, throwing out a clear and steady light.

The Hawaiians display an intimate knowledge of the vegetable kingdom. They possess vernacular names for nearly every plant, and have almost invariably succeeded in discovering the uses to which the various herbs, shrubs, and trees may be applied. These they are always ready to communicate, with the exception of the medicinal properties. The knowledge of the latter is chiefly confined to the native physicians and the "wise women," who, deriving from it a lucrative return, observe a strict silence on these points, and, if questioned, give an evasive answer. Their sovereign remedy seems to be a decoction made from the root of the Awa (*Piper methysticum*, Forst.), a plant cultivated in different parts of the kingdom; but as formerly great quantities of intoxicating liquor were extracted from it, its cultivation is at present restricted by a law, according to which, in the whole Hawaiian dominions, only four fields, each not to exceed four acres in extent, are allowed to be planted with it.

There exist a number of beautiful land-shells in Oahu, some of which fell into our hands. For shell the Hawaiians have the rather more descriptive than elegant name of "ka iwi mawake o ka io,"—literally, the bones outside and the flesh within. Several species of the genus *Achatinella*, especially the *A. Stewartii*, Nuttall, have the peculiarity of making a sound not unlike that of crickets. The "singing," as it is called, commences about midnight, and ends towards dawn; the natives discern in it a regular rhythm, and possess the following verse, the sounds of which are made to correspond with those of the shells:

"Kahuli aku kahuli mai
Kahulileula lee akolea
Kalekolea e kii ka wai
I wai i wai i waiako
Lea kolekolea."

Thinking that a translation of these lines might throw

some light upon the food, habits, or history of the animal, I submitted them to several of the best scholars. Some considered them as mere sounds without sense, others declared that a meaning was attached to them, and that several expressions could be clearly made out, but that the peculiar construction of the Hawaiian poetry rendered the whole very obscure, and a translation, without the aid of some intelligent natives, difficult.

The vernacular tongue of the Sandwich Islands is the Hawaiian, a branch of the Polynesian language, which is spread over most inhabited spots of the Pacific Ocean, and extends as far as New Zealand. It shows in the construction a certain resemblance to the Hebrew, which, faint as it is, has furnished an argument to those who maintain that the Hawaiians are a part of the scattered tribes of Israel. All sounds purely Hawaiian may be represented with only twelve letters, *a, e, i, o, u, h, k, l, m, n, p, w*. The letters, in whatever position they may occur, are always pronounced alike, as is the case to a considerable extent in Russian, Spanish, Italian, and German. It is the principle of the language that every syllable should end with a vowel,—indeed it is with difficulty that an adult native can be brought to pronounce two consonants without a vowel between them; the word "Kristo" is the only exception that has been admitted in writing. In consequence of this peculiarity the number of vowels greatly predominates over the consonants, which makes the language sound to our ears more like the early babbling of children, than the conversation of grown-up people. Though specific names exist almost to any extent, yet throughout the language there is a great want of generic terms. This fact shows, more than any other proof which can be adduced from historical and other sources, that the Hawaiians have never been a thinking people, nor had among them men of philosophical acquirements; for no community has any use for generic terms until it begins to reason*.

Next to the Hawaiian the English language is the most widely diffused; it is however a mistake of many who have visited the seaports, to suppose that every native is more or less conversant with it. Although it is taught in the higher schools, yet few Hawaiians can speak it with any degree of fluency, and by far the greater number are ignorant of it. The peculiar construction of their own, disqualifies them in a great measure for acquiring foreign languages. English however is rapidly gaining ground, and after the extinction of the aboriginal race it will become the vernacular tongue. In Honolulu nearly all the boatmen, and those connected with shipping, understand it tolerably well, but speak it in a broken and disjointed manner. The chiefs have generally a good knowledge of English, and several converse in it fluently. Some writers have blamed the American missionaries for not introducing, together with the new doctrine and the arts of civilization, some European language, and others have insinuated that the

* Those who are anxious to obtain a more intimate acquaintance with the Hawaiian language, are referred to an interesting article in the 'Hawaiian Spectator,' vol. i. p. 392–420, and to the various publications of the great Hawaiian scholar, L. Andrews, especially the 'Hawaiian Grammar,' the 'Hoakakaolelo no na Hualolelo Beritania,' and 'A Vocabulary of words in the Hawaiian language,' all published at Lahainaluna.

reason why the Christian teachers adopted the native dialect was because they wanted to make it the medium of preserving their power, and exercising a censorship over the people, little inferior to that which the Jesuits maintained in Paraguay, or the Inquisition enforced in Europe. Opinions so absurd must be taken for what they are worth. Every one acquainted with the working of a vernacular tongue knows that nothing is more difficult than to suppress one language by substituting another. A foreign language may gradually creep in, but it cannot be at once introduced; this must be the work of ages.

CHAPTER VI.

Second voyage to Behring's Strait—Departure from Honolulu—Kamtchatka—Kotzebue Sound—H. M. B. Plover—Search for Sir John Franklin—Cape Lisburne—Icy Cape—Wainwright Inlet.

HAVING completed the preparations for our second northern voyage, we left the harbour of Honolulu on the 19th of May, and passing to the southward of Oneehow and Lisiansky Island, and close to the position of Byer's and Morrell's Islands, without meeting with either of the two latter, we sighted Kamtchatka on the 22nd of June; there we picked up a fresh gale off the land, which ran us within a mile of Cape Gavarea, and left us in a dead calm. Our position would have been critical had we not found at this distance bottom in thirty fathoms. At daylight three ships were in sight off the Point of Petropaulowski, the mirage transforming them into every imaginable shape. With light variable winds, assisted by our boats and a slight northerly current, we reached an anchorage in the entrance, in fifteen fathoms. This voyage occupied thirty-five days, and was only remarkable for the lightness of the winds, the fineness of the weather, and the almost entire absence of fog, twenty-four hours never having elapsed without our having obtained astronomical observations.

The three vessels we had noticed proved to be American whale-ships that had also towed into an anchorage. Captain Kellett boarded one of them, and was told that they had left the port the day before, but having lost some men, had returned to pick them up. From this vessel it was also learned that the Plover had not been to Petropaulowski, but that a report was current of a vessel having wintered somewhere to the northward. This information determined the Captain to go to the anchorage with the ship, and accordingly we weighed about midnight.

Nothing more picturesque can be imagined than the scenery of Awatcha Bay when lit up by the full moon. The cliffs standing out in bold relief, the conical volcanoes towering to the skies, and throwing long shadows into the valleys, the large expanse of water almost resembling an inland lake, all combined to impress the mind with lofty feelings: still this sight, however imposing, dwindled into insignificance before that which displayed itself when the sun arose behind the snow-capped mountains; the whole elevated land seemed to be a mass of fire, and the spectator remained as it were spell-bound, until the full appearance of daylight dispersed the illusion, and once more restored him to the sober thoughts of life.

In our passage up, the masters of the American whalers came on board to gain information relative to Behring's Strait; they informed us that, in consequence of the success of one vessel last season, a great number of American ships would pass through those straits this year. A paper by the Secretary of the United States Navy corroborates this account; and as the public attention has been ably directed to the importance of the whale-fisheries in the higher latitudes by Mr. A. Petermann, I shall give a few extracts: it says, "In the summer of 1848, Captain Roys, of the whale-ship Superior, penetrated the Arctic Ocean, through Behring's Strait, and encountered in his adventurous pursuit all the dangers of an unknown and Polar sea. He was successful in his enterprise, filling his ship with oil in a few weeks. Influenced by the report which he brought back as to the abundance of whales, owners in the United States fitted out a large fleet for those grounds, and in 1849 Captain Roys was followed by one hundred and fifty-four sail of whale-ships, each vessel (said to be) worth on the average, with her outfit, 30,000 dollars, and manned by thirty able-bodied seamen each. This fleet took that season 206,850 barrels of whale-oil and 2,481,600 pounds of bone. In the summer of 1850 there went up a whaling fleet of one hundred and forty-four American vessels, manned as above, and of a like average value. This fleet, in the course of the few weeks left for their pursuits in those inhospitable regions, took 243,680 barrels of whale-oil and 3,654,000 pounds of bone. In the current year (1851) there went up a fleet of about one hundred and forty-five American vessels; but their returns have not been received; partial accounts of wreck and disaster only have reached us; they are startling. The lives and property at stake there for the two years for which we have complete returns may be thus stated:—

"1849—Number of American seamen   4,650
         Value of ships and outfits ... 4,650,000 dollars.
         Value of oil taken 2,606,510   „
         Value of bone   814,112   „
                                      ————— 8,070,622
 1850—Number of American seamen   4,320
         Value of ships and outfits ... 4,320,000 dollars.
         Value of oil taken 3,761,201   „
         Value of bone 1,260,630   „
                                      ————— 9,341,831

         Total ships in two years   299
         Total seamen   8,970
                                      —————
         Value of ships and cargoes ..   17,412,453

"The losses during the year 1851 have been unprecedented, so far as heard from. No less than seven sail of this fine fleet of 1851, the Howqua, the New Bedford, the Arabella, the America, the Armata, the Mary Mitchell, and the Henry Thomson, have been wrecked there, and left behind as monuments of the dangers which meet these hardy mariners in their adventurous calling. There are reports of other losses and wrecks, these are certain; and though several of them were lost, not on shoals, but otherwise, yet these are enough to tell of imperfect hydrography, and to show the national importance of looking to it; for it may be so, that in case of loss in the ice, the knowledge of a sheltered anchorage near, and which a survey would give, would have prevented the exposure to the ice which induced the loss. All our commerce with what is called 'the East' is not so valuable as this was for 1849 and 1850. We see by the above statistics that in these two years more American seamen were engaged in that small district of ocean than are employed in our whole navy at any one time;

that in these two years these hardy mariners fished up from the bottom of the sea, and by their own energy created and added to the national wealth, the value of more than eight millions of dollars. And we moreover see that, owing to the dangers of the land and ice, the hidden rock, and unknown shoals, one vessel in every twenty, that went therein during the summer of 1851, has been left behind a total wreck, and that the lives of their crews, or of not less than one man for every twenty, engaged in that business, have been put in jeopardy, mostly from the want of proper charts. No protection that our squadrons can at this moment give to our commerce, with any of the States of Christendom, can compare with that which a good chart of that part of the ocean would afford to this nursery of American seamen, and to this branch of national industry. I learn that in lat. 64° 15' north, long. 178° west, Captain Middleton, of the bark Tenedos, of New London, discovered a shoal having only eight feet of water on it, and which was two acres in extent; that the ship Ajax, of Havre, was lost on a rock south of the Isle of St. Lawrence, ten miles from land; that 'the entire fleet of whalemen in the Arctic Ocean complain much that charts are wrong, that the coast is badly explored, but little known,' etc.; that 'several of our vessels have been near being wrecked by unexpectedly making land or rocks under the bows at night;' that they have found in the Arctic Circle low sand-spits, extending five or six miles out; that also 'in Ochotsk Sea there are hidden dangers;' that 'the Howqua, in 1851, was totally wrecked on a sunken rock in that sea.'"

Off Petropaulowski we found the Royal Thames Yacht Club schooner Nancy Dawson, owned and commanded by a Mr. Robert Shedden, formerly a mate in the Royal Navy. He informed us that his object was to go through Behring's Strait, and as far north as possible, in search of Sir John Franklin's Expedition. The schooner was last from Hongkong, having touched at the Loo Choo Islands, and was well stocked with provisions and instruments: her crew (the greater part of them Americans) were entered at Hongkong; they were a most disorganized set of men, and Mr. Shedden offered to place his vessel at Captain Kellett's disposal, and appeared anxious that he should send an officer on board.

As nothing had been heard of the Plover, we weighed on the 25th of June, in a calm, and towed out from the anchorage. We got a light wind from the southward, bringing with it a fog, though still not so thick but that both sides of the entrance could be seen. In beating out, and in making a stretch over to the eastern shore from Babouski Island, the fog closed down over the rocks, and deceived us as to their distance; we hove the ship in stays, but the whirls of the tide made her slack, and shot her on to the rocks, before we had time to bring up with an anchor. The stream-anchor and cable were laid out and hove taut, and at 2.10 P.M. the ship was hove off into deep water, having been nearly three hours on shore; fortunately, the water at the time was glassy smooth. The ship lay perfectly quiet, until a short time before getting off, when she lifted, and struck heavily by the bow two or three times, bringing away on each occasion small pieces of her false keel.

We remained at anchor during the night, and the next morning weighed with a light south-east wind, but, it being a calm, and a current setting directly on shore, we were obliged to anchor again in a very exposed position, near the island of Staritchkoff.

On the 27th a light north-east wind took us clear of the shoals off the entrance of Awatcha Bay, and almost immediately we entered a dense fog. Struggling with light variable winds and fogs, we did not sight Behring's Island until the 2nd of July. On the morning of the 13th we passed the carcase of a dead whale, and in the forenoon another; shortly afterwards we exchanged colours with one of the American whalers we had seen at Petropaulowski, and before twelve o'clock with the other two. Large flocks of the little crested auk were noticed about the ship. At noon the north-west end of St. Lawrence Island bore true east, distant twelve miles. Running during the night with a fresh south-south-west wind and thick weather, we hauled up for the Asiatic shore at seven A.M., and made the land near the northern point of St. Lawrence Bay, having experienced in that time a current of twenty-five miles to the northward.

Passing within three miles of East Cape, we shaped our course for Cape Espenberg, Kotzebue Sound, and sailing over the shoal spoken of by Captain Beechey, off Schismarief Inlet, found in seven fathoms the least water, and the sea at the time so high and hollow that it frequently broke into our main chains. Running along the low land off Cape Espenberg, which we passed shortly after midnight, we had uninterrupted daylight; the only difference between midnight and noon being as the light of a winter's day in England is to a summer's day. As we entered the Sound, the wind gradually lightened, and on the 15th, shortly after eight A.M., we made out a vessel at anchor under Chamisso Island, and at ten exchanged numbers with H.M.S. Plover. We reached the anchorage by one P.M., having run in fifty hours from the west end of St. Lawrence Island to the anchorage off Chamisso.

Commander Moore came on board, and we were glad to learn that the officers and crew were all healthy and in good spirits. The Plover, owing to her bad sailing qualities, did not reach the southern extremity of Behring's Strait until the latter end of October 1848, too late to press onward. She had therefore been compelled to pass the winter on the Asiatic side, in Ourel, a harbour accidentally discovered by her. During a detention of eight months, great hospitality had been experienced from the Tchukchis, who constantly visited the ship, and willingly exchanged for some beads and other trifles, their venison, fish, and furs. At last, in June, a passage through the ice having been cut, she succeeded in attaining the open water, and, touching at the Bay of St. Lawrence and other places, finally, and only one day previous to the arrival of the Herald, anchored off Chamisso Island. The principal instructions of the Plover were to search the north-west and north coasts of America, so as to connect the explorations of those parts with that of Sir John Richardson. These instructions were on the point of being carried out; indeed two boats, under the command of Lieutenant W. Lee, had already taken their departure from Chamisso Island for the Mackenzie River.

They were nearly out of sight when the Herald made her appearance, and the commander of the Plover deemed it necessary to cause them to be instantly recalled. The new arrival occasioned an entire change in the plan adopted. It was thought more prudent, considering the danger to which boats so heavily laden must be exposed, to despatch them from the highest possible north which the ships, without risking their safety, could attain.

We commenced immediately to coal and provision the Plover, removing officers, discharging objectionable men, and filling up their vacancies from our own complement. While this was going on, Captain Kellett went with Commander Moore, and his acting ice-master, to examine the different bays on the east side of Chloris Peninsula, for a wintering station for the Plover.

We were visited by baidars, carrying twelve men each; the latter were particularly tall, well-built, well-armed, and without either their women or dogs. At first they were rather shy, but as soon as our interpreter began to speak to them in their language they appeared delighted, came on board, looked all over the ship, and after we had made each of them some present, they returned, without attempting to pilfer anything. They belonged to Spafarief Inlet, and expressed their delight at being recognized by Lieutenant Cooper and others, who had been at their place last year, making presents to them without seeking a return. Captain Kellett and Commander Moore accompanied them to Chamisso Island, where, after hauling up their baidars, canting their bottom to the wind, the weather gunwale resting on the sand, the other raised about three feet, and supported by paddles, the space underneath covered with furs, they partook of several pipes with them.

Whilst they were engaged with their pipes, the boat's crew were employed in digging for the flour left by Captain Beechey twenty-three years before, in a position indicated by directions on a rock, which were as perfect as when first cut. We found this rock in 1848, but, supposing the flour to have been removed by the natives, did not dig for it. A considerable space was cleared round the cask, its chimes freed, only adhering to the sand by the two lower bilge-staves, yet still it required the united strength of two boats' crews, with a parbuckle, and a large spar as a lever, to free it altogether. The sand was frozen so hard that it emitted sparks with every blow of the pickaxe. The cask itself was perfectly sound, and the hoops good: out of the 336 lbs. of flour which it contained, 175 lbs. were as sweet and well-tasted as any we had on board; indeed afterwards Captain Kellett gave a dinner-party at which all the pies and puddings were made of this flour. The tin of beads was also found: those not of glass were much decayed; the cotton stringing was quite sound.

On the 18th of July we stood out of the anchorage. The Nancy Dawson yacht hove in sight at the same time; she accompanied us without touching at Chamisso Island; the Plover leading under all plain sail, the Herald keeping in company. On the following day we passed a ship, and at noon Point Hope bore N. 18° W. fifty-five miles. We experienced, contrary to expectation, in this run, a current setting S. 74° W. half a mile per hour. At six P.M. we exchanged colours with an American whaler, the Margaret, of Providence, whales at this time blowing in every direction round her; but the wind was too strong, and too much sea for her to attempt them. The fog was so dense that the Plover, although within speaking distance, could not be seen, and as we continued running to the northward during the night, we were compelled to keep company by gongs and bells.

On the 20th we nearly ran over the carcase of a dead whale that had been flinched. At noon, the wind having shifted to the northward, we had fine clear weather. At five P.M. we anchored off Cape Lisburne, with the Plover and yacht in company, and despatched two boats to examine the coast northerly, under the orders of Lieutenant Pullen and Mr. Parsons; a boat was also sent from the Plover a short distance to the southward. The Plover's boat returned after midnight, having landed in one or two places, and met with many natives, who were friendly and well-disposed. The weather was beautiful and clear, and at midnight the sun showed its semidiameter above the horizon, and nearly every person in the ship remained up to witness this phenomenon for the first time.

We weighed in the morning to follow the boats northerly. The Plover, being nearer in shore, was visited by two baidars, each carrying about twenty natives, men and women: a most miserable set of beings they were; they collected near this place for the purpose of catching birds and gathering eggs. Falling calm, we anchored at six P.M. north and east of Cape Lisburne, off shore about six miles, but weighed at midnight, with a light wind. The boats returned in the forenoon. Mr. Pullen had examined the inlet to the eastward of Cape Sabine without success; he was informed by the natives, through the interpreter, that none of the inlets on the coast would admit of a vessel entering them; that it was only a few of them at the early spring that their baidars could enter, and that they were closed when the winds began to blow from the eastward.

We experienced in the ship until six P.M. of the 23rd a tedious calm; the current fortunately set us north half a mile per hour. During this time we were visited by two baidars, with the same party of natives we had seen off Cape Lisburne; they came alongside fearlessly, and, for tobacco and beads, disposed of every article they had, the women selling their fur dresses, even to their second pair of trowsers. During the evening of the 23rd and the morning of the 24th, we were running to the north-east, with a moderate south-south-west wind, and a thick fog, clearing at intervals for a short time. Walruses, whales, and flocks of the eider-duck were seen.

On the 25th, as we were steering for Wainwright Inlet, the wind shifted to the north-west, and brought with it cold, but fine and clear weather. The vast number of walruses that surrounded us kept up a continual bellowing or grunting. The barking of the innumerable seals, the small whales, and the immense flocks of ducks continually rising from the water as we neared them, warned us of our approach to the ice, although the temperature of the sea was still high. We made the land about noon, ten miles to the northward of Wainwright Inlet, and anchored off its entrance, as the Plover and yacht had done before. In running down along the coast a post was observed on the higher land near the entrance of the inlet; shortly afterwards a man was seen to hoist on it what most of us supposed to be a flag. The Plover soon afterwards dipped her ensign (simply to clear it, as we afterwards learned): this was answered by the person at the post doing the same, and entirely removing it. Lieutenant Cooper was immediately sent on shore: he walked up to the post, and found it to be a native mark for a quantity of blubber and reindeer flesh, which had been buried there: the Eskimo had left.

Captain Kellett's reason for selecting Wainwright Inlet for despatching the boats, instead of proceeding as far north as the ships could go, was, that he considered it of the greatest importance that the Plover's wintering station should be known by the officer in command of the boat expedition. We commenced immediately to hoist out the boats, equip, and provision them; and while this operation was going on, Mr. Hill sounded the entrance of the inlet. He returned on board a little before midnight, reporting that the channel was very narrow and winding, that nine feet was the most water that could with certainty be carried in, and that even to ensure that depth the channel would require close buoying; that a fair wind, or a calm, so that a vessel might either sail or be towed in, was necessary, the channel being too narrow and intricate to warp through; but that, once in, there would be a sufficiency of water, and a convenient spot for the Plover to winter.

From this report Captain Kellett concluded that it was impossible for the Plover to enter Wainwright Inlet with the water found then, but as the entrance was encumbered with heavy pieces of ice aground, which during our stay were breaking up fast, he conceived it probable that, after they had disappeared, the channel might become more direct and deeper, and determined to return and make a closer examination of the inlet, so soon as he had seen the boats as far north as we could reach in the ships. The boats were therefore directed to visit Wainwright Inlet on their return, in case it should prove practicable for the Plover to enter, but that under any circumstance she would be found at Chamisso Island.

By midnight the boats were ready, and shoved off under three hearty cheers from the ships, which were as heartily returned by the boats. This little expedition consisted of twenty-five persons, and four boats, as follows:—Lieutenant Pullen, commanding Herald's 30-foot pinnace, fitted on board with the greatest care, thoroughly decked, schooner-rigged, and called the Owen, furnished with pumps, spare rudder, and a strengthening piece of 2-inch plank above her water-line. Two 27-foot whale-boats, covered in abaft as far as the backboard, but without either boxes or cases, the provisions being stowed, the bread in painted bags, and the preserved meats between tarpaulins; the men's clothes were in haversacks, capable of removal in a moment. Plover's pinnace, a half-decked boat, with cases for her provisions, etc., so placed as to resist pressure from the ice. There were in the boats seventy days' preserved meats for the whole party, all the other articles of provisions, except bread, to the same extent, being also soldered up in tins. In addition to these, the Owen had on board eight men's allowance of the regular ship's provisions. After she was stowed with this proportion, every corner that would hold a case of preserved meat was filled. The two larger boats carried in each of them five cases of pemmican, for the special use of Sir John Franklin's party.

The ships weighed in company with the boats, and ran along the land within about three miles, with a moderate off-shore wind. On the 26th, at four A.M., the ice could be seen in heavy masses, extending from the shore near the Seahorse Islands. At six, we were obliged to heave to, in consequence of a dense fog; this cleared off at 11.30; the Plover was close to us, but neither the boats nor the yacht were in sight. We both made sail, steering true north, and were at one P.M. in latitude 71° 5', where we made the heavily-packed ice, extending nearly as far as the eye could reach, from north-west-by-west to north-east. At this time we had soundings in forty fathoms of mud, the deepest water we have had since leaving the island of St. Lawrence. We continued running along the pack until eight P.M., when, a thick fog coming on, we ran two or three miles south, and hove to, wind blowing from north-north-east, and directly off the ice; we had run along it thirty miles. The pack was composed of dirty-coloured ice, not more than five or six feet high, except some pinnacles deeply seated in the pack, which had no doubt been thrown up by the floes coming in contact. Every few miles the ice streamed off from the pack through which the Plover sailed.

On the 27th, at 1.30, the fog cleared off; the pack was from north-north-west to north-north-east, distant about six miles. We made sail during the forenoon, running through streams of loose ice. At ten we passed more large and heavy floes; Commander Moore, considering them sufficiently heavy and extensive to obtain a suite of magnetical observations, dropped the Plover through between them, and made fast with ice-anchors under the lee of the largest.

Captain Kellett and Lieutenant Trollope landed on the floe*. The latitude, time, and variation were obtained on it, but the other observations were vitiated by its motion in azimuth, and by its constant breaking away; the level would not stand. We had twenty-eight fathoms of mud alongside it, and no current, and found the ice driving slowly to the southward, with the north-north-east wind then blowing fresh. Few walruses and but a single diver were seen. The general height of this floe was five feet, and about one mile in extent; on it were found pebbles and mud, which led Commander Moore to suppose that it had been in contact with the land, but the mud and pebbles may have been fecal remains of a walrus.

At three P.M. the Plover slipped from the ice, and both ships, with a north-east wind, made sail westerly until six o'clock, when we hauled up true north, having no ice in sight in that direction, and only from mast-head on weather-beam. It was a fine clear night, and we were running along six and seven knots; temperature of the water being 40°, depth twenty-one fathoms (increasing). At midnight the latitude was obtained by the inferior passage of the sun (72° 10′ 30″ N., altitude 1° 56′ 30″). At five A.M. the temperature of the water had fallen to 36°,

* See Frontispiece, Vol. I.

and almost at the same instant the ice was reported from the mast-head. Between this time and seven A.M., when we hove-to within half a mile of the pack, we ran 10·5, so that I consider eleven miles to be about the distance that packed ice in this part of the world can be seen in clear weather from a ship's mast-head.

The pack was of dirty-coloured ice, showing an outline without a break and five or six feet high, with columns and pinnacles much higher some distance in. Although the wind was off the pack, yet there was not a particle of loose or drift ice from it. Our soundings had gradually increased to thirty-five fathoms of soft blue mud. The only living things seen were a few birds. In the dredge we got mussels and a few bivalves common to these seas. We remained hove-to off the pack for an hour*. This position was our most northern one, lat. 72° 51' north, long. 163° west. The ice, as far as it could be seen from the mast-head, trended away west-south-west (by compass); Commander Moore and the ice-master reporting a water sky to the north of the pack, and a strong ice-blink to the south-west. It was impossible to gain this reported open water, as the pack was perfectly impenetrable. The pack we had just traced

---

* The temperature of the sea near the pack was—

Surface		36° Fahr.
5 fathoms		33
10 ,,		32
15 ,,		29
20 ,,		29
25 ,,		29
30 ,,		29
35 ,,		29·5

for forty leagues, made in a series of steps westerly and northerly; the westerly being about ten or twelve miles, and the northerly twenty.

We made sail at nine A.M., steering for the coast, a little to the westward of our track up; the wind, northeast, was gradually decreasing as we got southerly. At five A.M. it fell a dead calm, the sea was glassy smooth, and so transparent that a white plate was distinctly seen at a depth of eighty feet. This afforded us an opportunity of ascertaining the extent of damage the ship had received when on shore in Awatcha Bay. The forefoot was untouched, the false keel gone for about ten feet; beyond this she had sustained no injury that could be seen; the copper was broken, and excessively thin all over.

On the 30th of July we tacked in shore in eight fathoms, close to the northward of Blossom's Shoals. Commander Moore came on board, and proposed that, during the time the Herald was surveying Wainwright Inlet, he should go along the coast as far north as the ice would permit him, and endeavour to communicate with the larger boats, which we expected were somewhere about Refuge Inlet. With this intention both vessels started with a fine but adverse wind from north-east. The Herald worked in short tacks close along shore, the soundings, in muddy bottom, decreasing and increasing as she approached or receded from the land. We again anchored off the entrance of Wainwright Inlet, where not a particle of the ice seen on our former visit remained. We had not been long there when we observed the Eskimos carrying their baidars across the narrow neck between the inlet and the sea, and launching them. Captain Kellett, wishing to get as many of the natives as he could off to the ship, so as to have fewer to molest him on shore, detained the boats until two of them came alongside. They approached slowly, frequently resting on their paddles, the bowman each time invariably holding up his hands over his head at an angle of 45°, when lowering them passing them over his breast and stomach. Our boatswain did the same from the forecastle netting; they always waited for his answer before they recommenced paddling. We made them each a present of some tobacco and beads, and the ship's company began to trade with the natives for whatever they had to dispose of, consisting mostly of small figures and tools of ivory, bows, arrows, a few furs, sealskin boots, and pieces of reindeer flesh.

Captain Kellett went to examine the inlet; he had not been long on shore, before the natives left the ship and followed. Nothing could exceed their good-humour. When about to commence his observations, he ordered all trading to cease, drew a semicircle on the sand from water's edge to water's edge, and placed the boat's noses between its points. The natives seemed to understand the meaning of this line: not one of them attempted to overstep it; they squatted down and remained perfectly quiet and silent. When a stranger arrived they shouted to him, who no sooner comprehended the directions than he crept rather than walked to the boundary, and squatted among the rest. Afterwards they danced and sang, played foot-ball with the seamen (who however had not a chance with them), and displayed their skill in shooting at a mark; but after all their good behaviour they had been guilty of picking the pockets of two or three of our party: one lost a handkerchief, another a glove, and Commander Moore a box of percussion-caps.

The Plover anchored in company soon after noon, and Commander Moore went on shore, erected a mark, and buried a bottle with information of the boats. Captain Kellett had satisfied himself before his arrival that ten feet was the greatest depth that could be carried in, and that, short of taking the Plover's masts out, the vessel could not be lightened sufficiently to enter the inlet. Could it have been done with any partial lightening, it would have been attempted, being in every way so desirable a position.

On the 1st of August Commander Moore went up the inlet, and found some baidars that had just arrived with several reindeer cut in quarters. The natives were stowing the venison, with a considerable quantity they had already collected, in a hole dug on the sandspit off Point Collie, and they appeared annoyed at their stow-hole having been discovered. It was deep and lined with logs of wood, having a roof formed of the same material, about five feet above the ground, and covered with moss. For a small quantity of tobacco they sold us 800 lbs. of the meat. Learning from Commander Moore that they were willing to dispose of more, Lieutenant Cooper, Mr. Goodridge, and myself, went to purchase some. Seeing our boat pulling in fast directly for them, they got alarmed, and at length, before the boat touched the beach, a woman walked to the water's edge and held up a bottle one of our party had lost the day before, making signs to him when he landed that it had been picked up on the beach. It was in the same state as when he lost it, the cork never having been removed. They at least understand that stealing is an offence. At first they appeared rather sulky, and unwilling to part with any of their meat; after a few presents they resumed their former good-humour, and sold fourteen quarters, all of them of young animals; the meat was without a particle of fat, badly killed, but still was owned by most on board to be very sweet and tender.

In the afternoon a long westerly swell rolled in, with a very light wind still off the land. At six it shifted to the southward, with a threatening appearance. Both vessels immediately weighed and stood off the land in a thick fog, and with a falling barometer.

CHAPTER VII.

Separation of the two vessels—The Herald discovers a shoal and new islands—Cape Lisburne—Point Hope—Kotzebue Sound—Buckland River—Elephant Point—Departure for Mexico.

THE fine season seemed now to be past; heavy gales, rain, snow-storms, and dense fogs followed each other in quick succession, and led to the separation of the two vessels. The Herald, according to dead reckoning, was, on the forenoon of the 12th of August, in lat. 70° 20′, long. 171° 23′, and in eighteen fathoms. It was blowing very hard from north-north-east and afterwards from north-north-west, reducing us to treble-reefed topsails and reefed foresail. Shortly after noon our depth decreased to sixteen fathoms and the colour of the water became lighter, with a breaking sea all round. Our soundings decreased a fathom each cast until 1.30 P.M., when we wore in eleven fathoms, shingle, getting in wearing nine fathoms, then twelve fathoms; and when trimmed to go back, as we went on, had several casts of eight and one of seven fathoms; then suddenly got into fourteen, which gradually increased.

The sun came out, verifying our noon position, but until midnight it blew a strong gale. On the following day it was fine. We wore to stand back to the shoal; our water decreased to thirteen fathoms, and at ten we imagined we saw breakers on the lee bow. At midnight we passed over the tail of the bank, in eight fathoms, five miles north-west of our former position. We continued to stand to the eastward until we could weather the south end of the shoal; then tacked, passing in sixteen fathoms three miles south of our first position. When we bore up north to fix its western edge, a slight easterly current took us rather further in that direction than we intended; we confined it however within a radius of five miles. The weather would not allow of our anchoring so as to make a closer examination of this dangerous spot with our boats, and the sea was too heavy and hollow to attempt taking the ship herself into less water. In approaching the shoal the bottom changes from sand to fine sand, and when in the least water, coarse gravel and stones. We found nothing less than seven fathoms, but it is likely that a bank exists which would bring a ship up.

We experienced very strong variable and south-east breezes, with rain until midnight of the 14th, when the wind changed to the westward, and brought with it fine weather. We continued to stand to northward and westward until noon of the 15th, when, being in lat. 71° 12′ and long. 170° 10′, we bore up west-half-south, and passed several pieces of drift-wood. Our soundings increased as we left the bank (westerly) to twenty-five fathoms mud. On the 16th the wind was very variable in strength, and direction south-south-west to south-east. At midnight it blew fresh from south-south-east, and steering west-south-west, the depth of the water decreased to ten fathoms.

On the 17th, at three A.M., the temperature of the sea suddenly fell from 40° to 36°; the wind became light, and excessively cold. We shortened sail, supposing that we were near the ice. At five A.M. the wind shifted from the north-west in a sharp squall, with heavy snow. Shortly after eight, when one of these snow-storms cleared off, the packed ice was seen from the mast-head from south-south-west to north-north-west five miles distant. The weather was so bad that we bore up for Cape Lisburne; but as it suddenly cleared up we hauled our wind for the north-western extreme of the ice that had been seen.

At 9.40 the exciting report of "Land ho!" was made from the mast-head. In running a course along the pack towards our first discovery, a small group of islands was reported on our port beam, a considerable distance within the outer margin of the ice. The pack here was not so close as we had found it in other places; lanes of water could be seen, reaching almost up to the group, but too narrow to enter unless the ship had been sufficiently fortified to force a hole for herself. These small islands at intervals were very distinct, and were not considered at the time far off. Still more distant than this group (from the deck), an extensive and high land was reported, "which," says Captain Kellett, "I had been watching for some time, and anxiously awaited a report from some one else. There was a fine clear atmosphere (such a one as can only be seen in this climate), except in the direction of this extended land, where the clouds rolled in numerous immense masses, occasionally leaving the lofty peaks uncapped, where could be distinctly seen columns, pillars, and very broken summits, which are characteristic of the higher headlands in this sea,—East Cape and Cape Lisburne for example. With the exception of the north-east and south-west extremes, none of the lower land could be discerned, unless indeed what I took at first for a small group of islands within the pack-edge was a point of this Great Land. This island, or point, was distant twenty-five miles from the ship's track; higher parts of the land seen not less, I consider, than sixty miles. When we hove-to off the first land observed, the northern extreme of the Great Land showed out to the eastward for a moment, and so clear as to cause some who had doubts before to cry out, 'There, Sir, is the land, quite plain.'"

From the time land was reported, until we hove-to under it, we ran twenty-five miles directly for it. At first we could not see that the pack joined the island, but as we approached it we found the pack to rest on its shores, and to extend from them as far as the eye could reach to the east-south-east. The weather, which had been fine all day, now changed suddenly to dense clouds and snow-showers, blowing fresh from the south, with so much sea that we could not anchor as we intended. Captain Kellett left the ships with two boats: Mr. Maguire, Mr. Collinson, and I in one; Mr. Goodridge, Mr. Pakenham, and the Captain in the other. The ship kept off and on outside the thickest part of the loose ice, through which the boats were obliged to be very careful in picking their way on the south-east side, where we thought we might have ascended. We reached the island, and found running on it a very heavy sea. The First Lieutenant however landed, having backed his boat in until he got foothold (without swimming), and then jumped overboard. The Captain followed his example, hoisted the Jack, and took possession of the island with the usual ceremonies, in the name of her most gracious Majesty Queen Victoria.

After the unfortunate mistake in the Antarctic regions, it becomes a nervous affair to report a discovery of land in high latitudes, but in this case there can be no doubt that we had found an unknown country, and that the high peaks we observed were a continuation of the range of mountains seen by the natives off Cape Jackan, as mentioned by Wrangel in his Polar Voyages. That land, according to a belief current in Siberia, quoted by Cochrane, is inhabited by a people of whom we are at present entirely ignorant.

The high peaks we saw were afterwards called Plover Island,—a misnomer, or rather a compliment to the Plover, considering that that vessel did not assist in finding the group,—while the island of which possession was taken received the name of Herald Island. The latter is four miles and a half in extent east and west, and about two and a half north and south, of triangular shape, the western end being the apex. It lies in lat. 71° 17′ 45″ north, long. 175° 24′ west, is about 900 feet hight, and chiefly composed of granite. The rocks rise almost perpendicularly, rendering the island nearly inaccessible. Innumerable black and white divers find there a safe place for depositing their eggs and bringing up their young. Human beings, or any traces of them, we did not find, and all the plants collected amounted to seven species, common to these regions: a scurvy-grass (*Cochlearia oblongifolia*, DC.), a saxifrage (*Saxifraga rivularis*, Linn.), a wormwort (*Artemisia borealis*, Pall.), a grass (*Poa angustata*, R. Br.), two mosses (*Polytrichum sexangulare*, Hopp., and *Bryum lacustre*, Brid.), and a *Confervacea* (*Ulva crispa*, Lightf.).

We returned to the ship at seven P.M., and reluctantly made all the sail we could carry from this interesting neighbourhood to the south-east, the wind at the time allowing us to be just clear of the pack. On the 20th we sighted Cape Lisburne in a thick fog, and hauled off to await clear weather. Having on the 21st landed on that promontory, and finding no traces of the boat expedition, we steered for Point Hope, and there met the Nancy Dawson and two of the boats that had been despatched towards the Mackenzie River. They brought no information whatever respecting Sir John Franklin.

The boats, after leaving the Plover on the 25th of July, were detained a day or two by the ice, before reaching Point Barrow,—where the natives were most friendly and anxious to assist,—and arrived in Dease's Inlet on the evening of the 3rd of August. They were fairly away on the afternoon of the 5th, having with them one hundred days' provisions, besides ten cases of pemmican. This little expedition then consisted of two 27-feet whale-boats and one native baidar, manned with fourteen persons in all.

The Nancy Dawson, which accompanied the boats as far as Point Barrow, had many escapes: she was pressed on shore once, ran on shore on another occasion to the eastward of Point Barrow, when she was only got off by the assistance of the natives, who manned her capstan and hove with great good-will. On another occasion she parted her bower-cable, from the pressure of the ice that came suddenly down on her, and had a narrow escape of a severe squeeze. Mr. Shedden erected a mark on Refuge Inlet; he also intended to have left there some provisions, but the natives were too numerous for this to be done without their knowing. He found another small inlet a short distance south of Refuge Inlet, in lat. 71° 5′, where he buried from his own store a cask of flour and a cask of preserved meats. At Refuge Inlet he left information as to the position of these provisions. Nothing could exceed the kindness of Mr. Shedden to those in the boats, in supplying them with everything his vessel could afford, and in following them with considerable risk. His crew were unfortunately a most disaffected set; he had too many of them for so small a vessel.

The Herald, after experiencing several severe gales and very bad weather, which led to the separation of the schooner and the boats which accompanied her, reached Kotzebue Sound on the 2nd of September, where the Plover, Nancy Dawson, and boats were found at anchor under Chloris Peninsula.

After completing our water from the springs in Chamisso Island, our people assisted the Plover in preparing her winter-quarters. The boatswain with a party, and the carpenters, building a house.

Commander Moore having made up his mind to winter in Kotzebue Sound, and being desirous to visit some chiefs reported to live at a considerable place up the river, Captain Kellett determined to go there with a party sufficient to ensure respect. Accordingly, on the 9th, we started with the Owen, the Plover's decked boat, the Herald's cutter, and two gigs,—their crews, and several officers. The first night we bivouacked at Elephant Point, and the whole crew roamed over the ice-cliffs for fossils, but could not find many. The second night we stayed at an Eskimo encampment, of twenty-two tents and about a hundred and fifty people. We pitched our tents close to those of the natives, had our coppers, pots, kettles, axes, saws, etc. on shore, but although at times we had a third of their numbers about us, not an article was lost; and they were not troublesome when we told them we wished them to go away. They brought us wood and water, gave us fish and venison, and offered us whale-blubber and seal-flesh.

The natives were highly amused, and joined our crew in their sports of leaping and running. The shooting parties were always accompanied by some of them; they were greatly surprised to see some of the young officers killing the birds right and left. The moment our boats started, until we got far up the river, we were preceded by their little kayaks, sounding with their paddles, to the channel. We had pilots in each of the large boats, who remained constantly with us, and who showed great concern when they unavoidably got us on shore.

Their behaviour, on the visits of Captain Beechey and ourselves, was very different, and may perhaps be owing to our having an interpreter, who could inform them of our object in visiting them. The Russian settlement may also have been instrumental in causing this alteration in their conduct. We found many of them with shirts, handkerchiefs of gaudy colours, cotton printed with the walrus, reindeer, and other animals that they are in the habit of catching and representing in ivory, knives, and kettles; all these came from the Russian settlement. They were latterly very anxious to obtain muskets, and evinced no fear in discharging them.

The Buckland, from the mud and leaves hanging on the banks, showed that at some period of the year it was at least ten feet above its level at that time. On the 11th of September about noon we arrived at a part of the river thirty miles up, perfectly barred across with heavy rock, over which there was a fall of about eighteen inches. There the heavy boats were stopped; but, by unlading the lighter ones, we were enabled to haul them over.

Captain Kellett wishing to return to the ship, Commander Moore and Mr. Maguire, senior Lieutenant of the Herald, went on, to make a tracing of the river. The party returned on the 19th, and succeeded in penetrating about thirty miles beyond where Captain Kellett left them. In this distance they met with but two natives. They passed several places where they were obliged to unload, and haul the light boats over. They found also pine-trees, scattered about in twos and threes, a little distance from the bank, and in one place some fine basaltic columns.

While we were lying in Kotzebue Sound the Captain

gave permission for as many of the officers as could be spared, to make up a pleasure-trip for the purpose of examining the ice-cliffs in Eschscholtz Bay. As several were anxious to see a phenomenon so extraordinary, as well as being quite ripe for a day or two's fun of any kind that promised novelty or any relief from the monotony of ship-board, no sooner was the Captain's sanction made known, than a party of eight officers was formed, and two boat's crews speedily volunteered for the occasion. "Every precaution," says Mr. Edwin Jago, "having been made,—including the most rigid measures against any inconvenience likely to result from the total absence of those well-known and most useful institutions called hotels, taverns, or inns, as well as the contingency of our being wind-bound for a week,— we shoved off from the ship about nine o'clock in the morning, with a wind which promised us an early arrival at the place of our destination. The boat-sailing was to me by no means the least agreeable part of our time, for the two boats into which our party had distributed kept together within chatting distance, and I could fain have wished that the distance of six or seven miles we had to traverse could have been doubled or trebled.

"A couple of hours brought us well up with Eschscholtz Point; and now, as if to impress us with a lessened idea of the desolation of the place, and to afford us ample time for viewing it from the sea, the sun—whose warmth is rather to be desired in the Arctic Circle, even in the middle of September—shone out, and the wind gradually dying away, the weather became so beautifully serene that one was filled with amazement when reflecting that the black-looking cliffs were composed of huge and solid masses of ice. The most unobserving spectator however could not fail to distinguish indisputable signs that he was in no low latitude, for the yet-remaining patches of snow discernible in the ravines and the numerous flocks of wild-fowl too plainly represented to his imagination the rigorous aspect Nature would here assume on the passing away of a short-lived summer.

"About noon we arrived off the spit which juts out from Elephant Point,—the spit upon which we were to pitch our tent. We were not long landing, and, having previously agreed at what hour we should meet to dine, and leaving the boats' crews to erect the tent, and arrange sundry other little matters for the general comfort, we started off with our guns, each taking the direction his fancy led him. It was desirable that we should separate, as we thereby increased our chance of adding to our stock by shooting as many ptarmigans as possible. But after walking a long way without succeeding in this laudable object, I determined to go and take a preliminary look at the ice-cliffs. Arriving there I met several others of our party, and, after temporarily satisfying my curiosity, I again started off alone over the valleys. Seeing several flocks of ptarmigan, and getting occasionally nearly within shot, my anxiety to bag a few induced me to follow them from place to place. But all without success, for in every case they, in the most tantalizing manner possible, would be up and off just at the instant I began to feel sure of them, and to calculate how many I should get at a shot. This unsatisfactory kind of excitement lasted for some time, until I began to think of returning, and commenced retracing my steps for that purpose. Ascending a hill, and observing a point with a spit running off it, I, without considering, imagined it to be the one upon which we had landed, and was rather astonished to find I was no further off.

"As it was yet some time from the hour appointed for dinner, and entertaining as I do a disgust for waiting for it, I resolved to renew my efforts in chase of the birds. That pursuit I followed up with a similar want of success to within a short time of the prescribed hour. I now returned over the hill, where, imagine my surprise, upon a nearer approach to this spit I found that it was not the one. Hey-day! thought I, late I must inevitably be. So to take the quickest way, I determined to return by the beach. Half an hour's walk took me to the sands, and, recognizing the place, I concluded that in a similar time by walking fast I should accomplish the distance. With this prospect I tramped along, but soon found that, since my passing the same spot in the afternoon, the tide had risen so far as to render it impossible for me to proceed. Anxious not to lose more time than could be helped, I struck in for the hills, but in doing so I had to cross a marsh. I attempted it, and soon got up to my middle in water, but as I did not then find it deepen, and being within only a few yards of the dry ground I still persisted in my direction. Although it was, as I have said, only a few yards, yet these cost me more labour than I had calculated on, for the bottom suddenly changed into a soft mud, into which at every step I sank knee-deep, and found it most difficult to proceed at all. It was a crisis: I must either reach the rising ground in a few steps, or be left stuck fast in the mud. Not wishing to remain longer than I could help in such a position, I exerted my strength to the utmost, and at last reached *terra firma*.

"The fast approach of the sombre hues of evening warned me that to get back before dusk I had yet to exert myself, so having recovered my breath I commenced pushing my way through the dwarf trees, thick shrubs, and brushwood, to cross the ravine. This labour was anything but easy, and when I had at length reached the opposite hill another disappointment awaited me. I had yet at least one other ravine to cross. I was so fatigued that at times I was compelled to stop awhile, and actually retched from exertion. Repeated draughts from the cold streams that rippled through the valleys from the melting ice had the effect of keeping me up to the walking-point, and enabled me to proceed.

"The hill showed me no spit, but there was yet a higher summit before me; I however had now the advantage of firm ground, and the relief I felt from it was encouraging. Feeling assured that I could be at no great distance from the boats, and as it was fast growing dark, I discharged my gun several times with the view of making my proximity known to my companions, and with the hope of hearing an answer to direct my path. But no return came; so the resolution I formed was, that, if on reaching the greatest eminence the spit should not be in sight, I would give it up as a bad job for the night. This was soon achieved, when, hurrah! I should not be obliged to pass a night in a ravine, thinly clad, hungry and wet, which I had persuaded myself I should not have found pleasant in such a region—for there lay the spit before me, with the two boats and the tent.

"It was now all right, and, as is generally the case, and perhaps wisely so in this world, that a dilemma is thought lightly of after a favourable termination, I, instead of considering the best method of spending the night in the manner I had anticipated, began to think what a havoc I should commit amongst the viands at dinner, and fancied the hearty laugh there would be raised at my expense. As soon as I was perceived coming along the spit, a boat was sent ashore for me, and the moment after I got into the tent I was received by one of the party with a most expressive exclamation. But as on entering I had espied a bottle standing by the tent-pole, and was by that time ascertaining its contents, it was necessary to finish my drink to restore articulation before I could reply. He then explained that, feeling uneasy, they were about to light a fire, and send parties in quest of me, and, above all, that dinner had been put off on my account.

"We were soon on board the large decked-boat in the cabin of which we were to dine. Most of us possessed sharp appetites. There was one exception: poor Whiffin complained of sea-sickness. As the motion was very slight, I at first felt inclined to believe that it might have arisen from previous alarm for me, but I was first staggered in this belief by the entire want of sympathy he exhibited on my return, but latterly by hearing him give detailed directions for his dinner being taken to the tent, where it was arranged we should pass the night; I completely renounced the opinion, and settled down in the idea that sea-sickness was the complaint. The remarkably precise manner in which our friend gave his orders on this subject, while labouring under the disease, afforded a clear proof that in this case at least the mind was not much affected by the derangement of the stomach. We landed as soon as dinner was over, and being all much fatigued, our mirth was cut short by the allurements of Morpheus, and, warmly ensconced in furs and blankets, we were soon fast in his embrace.

"The next day was the one unanimously agreed upon for the inspection of the ice-cliffs, so immediately after breakfast all repaired thither. It was a lovely morning, and, with the exception of a few passing snow-showers during the forenoon, the weather was delightful. But few fossils were collected by our party, nor could it be wondered at when it was remembered that the place had been stripped of them by an expedition from our ship only the preceding summer, at which time a large amount was obtained, including some valuable specimens, upwards of twenty years having elapsed at that time since any previous visit. Our own party however did not return empty-handed,—some very fine molar teeth were found, which with other specimens tolerably well filled a large bag.

"This day was spent in a variety of ways, every one appearing to wish to make the most of his time, as it was agreed we should return to the ship on the morrow. The same jollity and mirth prevailed when we again met at dinner, and most of us, I believe, felt sorry that the next day had been fixed on for returning; some even expressed a hope that we might be wind-bound. We determined at all events to make the most of the present, and that night fully proved the possibility of spending a merry one in a tent,—toasts, songs, recitations, and jokes of all kinds were kept up until daybreak, when sleep was allowed by all to be absolutely necessary.

"On the following morning, after a good walk, we embarked, and for several hours were struggling against a foul wind; when, finding it impossible to reach the ship, we returned to the spit, where our tent was once more pitched for another night, not much to the regret of some of us, for our stay had not yet been sufficiently long to make us desirous of getting back to the vessel. Another jolly night was spent, and early in the morning we weighed in time to take the full advantage of a favourable tide. The wind at last became so strong as to be just as much as we could stand up under, and we watched with interest the efforts of the smaller boat to keep up with us, in which she succeeded till within a mile or so of the Herald, when she shipped a sea which half-filled her, and compelled her to bear up and run under the lee of Chamisso Island, there to spend a night by no means pleasant. We in the large boat were more fortunate, arriving on board by two or three P.M., only regretting that the rest of our companions were unable to participate with us in the comforts of dry clothes and a good dinner. They were however able to get to the ship early in the morning, and although the last night had in a great measure cooled the passion of some for Arctic pic-nics, yet I doubt if there is one who would not at the present time be only too glad to embark upon another such."

On the 26th all the Plover's wants were fully completed. She was not dismantled, nor did Commander Moore intend doing so until she was fairly laid up on the beach. In consequence of the illness of Mr. Shedden, of the yacht, and of Captain Kellett having previously removed his chief mate, Mr. Parsons (second master), of the Herald, was directed to navigate her to Mazatlan.

Early on the morning of the 29th of September we weighed from Kotzebue Sound, with a fair breeze from the north-east. At the time of our departure there was early snow on the low lands. The streams were still running; in fact, the whole month of September had been remarkably fine, generally with strong winds from the eastward. We experienced very bad weather on getting out of the Sound, and parted company with the yacht. We passed through Behring's Strait in the morning of the 2nd of October, in a heavy gale from north-north-west, and at midnight of the 11th, the Aleutian groups, by the Straits of Amoukhta, in long. 171° west. These straits are thirty-five miles wide, perfectly safe, and free from the races usually met with in the other straits of this chain.

On the 13th of October, in lat. 47° 30' and long. 167°, we experienced a heavy northerly gale, with an unusually heavy sea, which broke on board of us, and nearly swept our decks. On the 19th, in lat. 43° and long. 160°, we had another gale at south-south-east. Between this time and the 14th of November, when we anchored at the port of Mazatlan, there was nothing remarkable but the prevalence, in 41° north, of south-east winds, which forced us to the coast within a hundred miles of San Francisco before we got the north-west wind. At Mazatlan we found lying the Nancy Dawson, which had arrived the morning previous, and H.M.S. Amphitrite.

Mr. Shedden did not long survive his arrival at Mazatlan. Naturally of a weakly constitution, he had suffered greatly from the sudden change from a hot to a cold climate, and the arduous voyage on which he was engaged. While yet in the Arctic regions he was so ill that the navigation of the Nancy Dawson had to be entrusted to Mr. W. Parsons, of the Herald, and as the little vessel advanced towards the tropics the health of her owner became worse every day, until, on the 17th of November, his earthly remains were laid in the Protestant burial-ground at Mazatlan, his funeral being attended by the officers of the Herald and Amphitrite, as well as by the British Vice-Consul, and other residents of the port.

The Nancy Dawson will ever be remembered in the history of navigation as the first yacht that performed a voyage round the world, and penetrated to the eastward of Point Barrow; while the generous impulse which induced Mr. Shedden to search for his missing countrymen will always be appreciated by every feeling heart, and held up as an example to future generations.

CHAPTER VIII.

The Plover's Wintering in Kotzebue Sound—Mr. Pim's Journey to Michaelowski.

BEFORE following the Herald on her surveying operations in the Gulf of California, it may be as well to detail the proceedings of the Plover during the long Arctic winter, which fortunately I am able to do, from the excellent journal of Mr. Bedford Pim, who, until the 17th of July, 1849, had been attached to the Herald, when, in order to fill one of the vacancies caused by the departure of the two officers for the Mackenzie River, he was transferred to the Plover, and remained in her a whole year.

"The departure of the Herald," says Mr. Pim, "the prospect of a long winter, the loneliness and melancholy aspect of the adjacent country, all tended to increase a feeling which the sudden loss of companions and friends is always calculated to produce. The natives also, to whose passion for barter we had been indebted for large quantities of fish, venison, and berries, paid us a final visit, in their baidars, on the 9th of October, and we seemed now to be entirely excluded from all human intercourse. However, by degrees we became more and more accustomed to our solitude, and tried, by mental and bodily exercise, to make the time pass as agreeably as possible.

"The weather became cold and boisterous; snow-showers and gales of wind followed each other in quick succession, and about midday on the 17th, the temperature of the sea being 28° Fahr., the water thickened. Ice rapidly formed over the bay, and, thirty hours afterwards, it had assumed such a consistency as to enable the crew to drag a heavy boat some distance over its surface. A disruption however soon took place; at half-past four on the morning of the 20th a high tide broke up the whole field, and in two hours not a vestige of it was to be seen. But this change did not last long; the next morning a new crust had formed, and was as early as the 23rd sufficiently strong to allow a party to stand upon it for the purpose of freeing the ship from the ice. On the following day the thermometer fell to zero, and the winter had now fairly set in.

"These prognostics rendered the speedy housing-in of the ship imperative. A wooden frame, covered with canvas and tilt-cloth, served as a roof; several windows admitted the still remaining portion of daylight; three fireplaces and a Sylvester's stove, lit occasionally, diffused an agreeable temperature; in fine, as far as the internal arrangements were concerned, the dockyard authorities had so well provided for every want that a considerable degree of comfort was experienced. Those who enjoy all the luxuries of civilized society may perhaps smile at the assertion; yet, in a region where even a wretched Eskimo hut has charms, and where nature shows herself only in the most chilly and sombre aspect, the accommodation which the vessel afforded was fully appreciated.

"It was fortunate that the housing-in was so soon completed, as in October we had a constant succession of bad weather, accompanied by a low temperature. The ice towards the end of the month was three feet thick; it had however, before this time, owing to the meeting of the tides, been thrown up, occasionally to a height of twenty feet, forming hummocks, pinnacles, and walls, and presenting a most picturesque spectacle, which forcibly impressed an imaginative mind with the idea of extensive ruins. The *aurora borealis* also, in proportion as the temperature decreased, became more frequent, and displayed a greater degree of brilliancy.

"It was expected that as the cold increased few signs of animal life would be visible. Such however was not quite the case. Deer appeared in large numbers, and offered so great a temptation for hunting that several parties started for that purpose; but inexperience and haste prevented their killing a single head, and moreover so alarmed the herds that they never afterwards approached our immediate neighbourhood. Ptarmigans and hares were abundant, and the sportsmen frequently added these luxuries to the table. Wolves and foxes occasionally enlivened the scene, and the former, probably driven by hunger, sometimes ventured within musket-shot, where they commenced their dismal howlings. Bears appeared more scarce; only one was seen during the whole winter.

"Although November was drawing to its close, yet the sun continued to show its countenance, and a difference of 12° was perceptible when within the influence of its rays. The temperature still decreased; the change however, being accompanied by fine calm weather, was little felt, and every one was able to take exercise in the open air. A remarkably fine day seemed to offer a favourable opportunity of airing the men's bedding. The atmosphere however at this time is filled with particles of ice, which rapidly accumulate upon any object exposed; they are so minute as to be invisible to the naked eye, but their presence becomes at once evident when any heat has thawed them. The consequence was that the bedding, instead of being dried, had undergone an invisible process of wetting, causing several cases of catarrh, and showing that the measures conducive to health in one country may in another lead to opposite results.

"The natives began to renew their visits about the commencement of this month, walking from considerable distances, and coming more frequently as the winter advanced. They appeared almost different beings. Their light and filthy summer dresses had been exchanged for others which fitted more closely and were better made. They were no longer the apparently overawed people who, in their small skin baidars, paddled near the sides of our huge ships, but seemed conscious that they were moving in an element for which nature had admirably adapted them. Their step was firm, their movements graceful, their dread of the white man had vanished, and they appeared to communicate with us on the footing of perfect equality. Whenever they arrived their sledges were well laden with venison, fish, and furs. The latter were brought in great quantities, for the eagerness with which they were purchased led them probably to suppose that we were traders; even after they had comprehended the reason of our wintering in Kotzebue Sound, they continued to supply us with sable, ermine, beaver, fox, and other furs of more or less value. The fish were excellent in flavour, and occasionally of considerable size; one mullet, for instance, bought for an ordinary blue bead, was thirty-three inches in length, and weighed twenty-one pounds.

"Several natives were living on board, and it was learned from them that they frequently took long journeys. From this fact it was not unreasonably supposed that they must be in possession of information relative to more distant parts, and that, by freely mixing amongst them, some valuable hints, tending to further the object of our search, might be obtained. An excursion to the Buckland River was consequently determined upon. A party, composed of Commander Moore, Lieutenant Cooper, and Mr. Bourchier, taking advantage of the return of the visitors, left the ship with them. The two former officers were seated upon sledges, the latter walked. Contrary to expectation, the party came back a few hours after they had started, complaining of the churlish disposition of the natives, and their unwillingness to assist. The interpreter however gave a different version of their conduct: he had learnt that the Eskimos had been exasperated by the harsh treatment inflicted upon the dogs, and the practice of using the sledges as a seat. In subsequent expeditions we took advantage of this information, and at once enlisted their good-will.

"On the 5th of December three of the officers, Mr. Bourchier, Mr. Stevenson, and myself, accompanied a party of natives to their *yourts*, or underground huts, in Hotham Inlet, accomplishing sixty-three miles in forty-eight hours. For ten days we lived among them, which had the effect of increasing our confidence, so much so that several other journeys were undertaken to the same hospitable village. These excursions, short as they were, proved highly beneficial, preventing that dreaded enemy of seamen, the scurvy, and moreover keeping the mind in constant occupation by storing it with interesting information relative to the manners, customs, and language of these extraordinary people.

"In some instances however the confidence which we placed in the natives was abused. One man stole a saw, another a bayonet, and others, yet more daring, were discovered to have carried off three heavy ice-anchors. As the latter thefts had been committed by the Spafarief tribe, that community was always looked upon with distrust, and one day, being detected in the act, the whole were dismissed from the ship. Their old chief however was recalled: he presided over an extent of country from which the main supplies were obtained, and it was deemed politic to conciliate him.

"The end of the year was fast approaching, and manifested itself in the brief duration of light. On the shortest day, dawn commenced about ten A.M. and dusk as early as two P.M. The temperature continued to decrease, though not uniformly, being one day some degrees above, and perhaps the next as many below, zero. On Christmas-day the cold was bitterly felt, the thermometer standing 26° below zero. Notwithstanding, the usual festivities were celebrated: the ship's company dined on the upper deck; but, as the chilly atmosphere was not conducive to their comfort, they were glad to escape below as soon as the fish, venison, and plum-pudding had been consumed.

"The general state of health was excellent, and the Captain having given the officers leave to make excursions as their inclinations should dictate, the months of January and February passed away as quickly as, under these circumstances, could be expected. These excursions were directed to Spafarief and Hotham Inlet; they were more frequent in January, February being so cold that no one could venture into the open air without being well wrapped up, and even these precautions were very often not sufficient to prevent frostbites. Indeed, on the 12th of February the cold was so intense that the thermometer fell to 43° below zero, and both rum and quicksilver, upon being exposed to the atmosphere, became almost instantly hardened. We looked therefore most eagerly for milder weather, and hailed with joy the increase of daylight, as the forerunner of a more genial temperature.

"When the Herald visited Kotzebue Sound in 1848 she heard from the natives that some white men were travelling in the interior. This report, from want of confirmation, led merely to vague conjectures, and was almost forgotten, when, in November, 1849, another reached the Plover, stating that two ships had been seen to the eastward of Point Barrow. I had always entertained an opinion that much information might be obtained by travelling to Michaelowski, a Russian fort, which, though situated to the southward of Kotzebue Sound, had the advantage of communicating with several tribes. The report now received was calculated to strengthen this opinion, and induced me to make an offer to undertake the journey; owing however to various reasons, unnecessary to specify, it was for a time declined by Commander Moore.

"On the 10th of March, 1850, however, I received orders to carry my plan into execution, and to take with me Bosky, the interpreter. On the morning of the following day I started. The weather was beautiful, the temperature 17° below zero, with a light breeze from the south-west. Owing to the badness of the roads, and the heavy weight of the sledges, which contained fifteen days' provisions, arms, ammunition, and other travelling necessaries, little progress was made, and it took five days to arrive at a village near the source of the Spafarief River. At this place, beyond which none of the former visitors had proceeded, I parted from some officers, who had been surveying, and to whom I gave, in conformity with the Captain's orders, both sledge and dogs. The real difficulties now commenced. The natives were unwilling to part with their dogs, and, had it not been for the assistance of the chief, I could not have proceeded. He lent me a sledge and a dog, and induced some of his countrymen to dispose of four more of the latter, so that, with two of my own, the requisite number was made up. After much trouble one of the men agreed to serve as a guide, and, although the payment of his demands considerably impoverished my resources, yet I was ready to make any sacrifice. He informed me that in two days we should reach the shores of Norton Sound, and each evening a village, where food and lodging could be obtained.

"On the 18th of March we finally departed from the beaten track, taking a south-easterly direction. A very few miles however proved the worthlessness of the new dogs; it became necessary to let one go, another was too young, and a third too old to pull, and little progress could be made. When night was approaching a halt was called among some pine-trees, where a fire was kindled, and some tea and soup prepared. The scene of a winter bivouac is indeed curious. The travellers, grouped around the fire, are variously employed: one is melting the snow, another bringing fuel, while a third unpacks the sledge, spreads the deer-skin to sleep upon, or prepares the provisions for cooking. The dogs, secured to surrounding trees, strain their tethers to reach the scraps thrown to them, and occasionally send forth their long dismal howl, only to render the scene more dreary.

"On the following day, after much labour and fatigue, we arrived at the top of some high mountains, and, descending them, bivouacked late at night in a wooded valley. The next morning it became evident that the dogs could not drag the sledge any further, having now been three days without any food save the mere scraps from our meals, which, being composed of preserved meats and biscuit, were little indeed. One of them I was compelled to shoot, because it was weak and lean, and, if left on the snow, a lingering death must have been its fate. I also expected that the carcase would be an acceptable meal for the rest; but, although starving, not one would touch it. Under these circumstances it became necessary to leave the sledge behind. It was placed under some trees, and covered with some branches and snow, so as to hide it from sight. Cheered with the hope of recovering it through the assistance of the natives, we departed, taking with us our arms and two days' provisions. Our path lay through a thickly wooded country, the snow was consequently very soft, and it was well indeed that all were practised in the use of snow-shoes, or else the hardships of the march would have been more than doubled. Soon after dusk the dogs ran before and set up a dismal howling, signs sufficiently conclusive that the village was near. At length it appeared in sight; we hurried on, and found it deserted. Thus after three days' toil the place was reached, only to convince us how little reliance could be placed upon the assertions of the guide. We had now only one day's provisions left; not more than half the journey was accomplished, and there were yet eighty or ninety miles more to overcome.

"After passing a miserable night we made an early start, with the determination of reaching the next village. The country still continued woody, but did not afford a chance of increasing the provisions by any game. Towards dusk we obtained from a lofty ridge of hills a view of the shores of Norton Sound. The descent occupied some time, and it was about ten o'clock before the dogs gave indication of the proximity of human habitations. No response however was made, no natives came forth to greet us, and we were soon made aware that no living beings were to be found within the huts. A search was instantly commenced, but only a little train-oil rewarded the trouble, which, with a few scraps of leather, served as a meal for the dogs, and, scanty as it was, proved their salvation. Our own condition was by no means enviable, for when it is considered that twice the amount of food is requisite in these regions, and the daily labour we had to perform, our slight meal, from the remnants of the provisions, appeared meagre indeed. Hunger and fatigue however were soon forgotten; a large deer-skin found in one of the huts formed a most acceptable covering, and every one was soon in a sound sleep, the first enjoyed since leaving the Spafarief village.

"This place seemed to be the *ultima Thule* of our guide. True he knew that there was a village at some distance, and he was able to point out the direction, but beyond that he appeared ignorant. I was glad however that he remained with us, as his experience in travelling could not but prove useful. Just before starting it was discovered that the pocket compass was missing, so that we were compelled to launch upon the sea-ice, trusting in a great measure to chance. A bleak expanse of snow lay before us as far as the eye could reach, and mile after mile was passed without gaining a sight of the low land which joins Cape Denbigh to the main. It was already past midnight before we once more stepped upon firm ground, and, after a short rest, resumed our march, so that daylight found us across the low spit of land, on the opposite beach. We could now however drag our weary limbs no further, and, at the risk of being frost-bitten, were compelled to lie down.

"As the day advanced the guide declared that he could see a village. With great exertion we crawled to the hut, without however seeing any signs of life. Just as despair began to obtain the mastery, and induce an apathy as to our fate, a woman appeared, who inspired us with new life. We were soon esconced in the warm furs, and regaled with fish, train-oil, and berries,—to hungry men a most acceptable feast. The poor dogs, now in their sixth day of abstinence, were not forgotten; they were allowed an unlimited amount of fish, purchased with a clasp-knife which I happened to carry with me. Bosky at this place informed me that he was unable to walk any further. The scurvy was breaking out in an alarming manner; his legs were covered with ulcers, having been frost-bitten while he was resting the last time, and now presented a shocking appearance; moreover he had a severe fall on starting from the last village. Notwithstanding, he kept up with us during the two-and-twenty hours that we were on the journey, and I cannot sufficiently admire the quiet endurance with which he bore his sufferings.

"Late in the evening the men returned from a hunting excursion, and had been lucky in the capture of a deer. We were however too sleepy to participate in the feast, especially as the fish-sauce, *i.e.* train-oil, of the meal partaken did not agree with our stomachs. We now learnt with certainty that two days' journey would bring us to a small Russian outpost, where, Bosky assured me, every comfort would be cheerfully afforded. The next morning we started, and as the natives were going in the same direction, the interpreter obtained a seat on their sledge, and I occasionally shared the same advantage. In about six hours we arrived at a solitary hut, where we were hospitably received, and regaled by its inmates with dried salmon and their favourite train-oil and berries, neither of which was declined.

"A good night's rest greatly invigorated us, and parting with the guide, who, accompanied by another native, returned for the sledge, Bosky and I started on foot early the next morning for the Russian outpost, a distance of twenty-five miles. We expected to reach it by night, but had overrated our strength, and, although making frequent rests, my companion soon became unable to proceed. Coming upon the dead body of a deer, which it appears had been driven over the cliffs by the wolves, it was determined that he should remain by it while I endeavoured to find the outpost and send him assistance. As night was coming on I kept close to the beach, not liking to cross the bays for fear of missing the house. I passed several wolf-tracks, and their howl had often the effect of quickening my pace as imagination pictured one of them in full chase. Luckily I escaped interruption, and at last found the house, which, had I not closely traced the land, would have been passed. The inmates were asleep. I soon roused them however, and endeavoured to impart my story by signs, but began to despair of being able to make them comprehend Bosky's position, when the poor fellow himself appeared. The fear of the wolves had given him additional strength, and just enabled him to reach the house.

"Bosky's assertion regarding the hospitality of his countrymen was amply verified. Gregora, the master of the block-house, daily placed upon his table the best his stores afforded, the effects of which became soon apparent in the visible improvement of Bosky's health. As nine days had passed and the sledge not arrived, I determined to wait no longer; having despatched another man in quest of it I departed, placing Bosky on a sledge hired for the purpose. On the 6th of April, the twenty-sixth day since leaving the ship, we arrived at St. Michael's, and were received in the kindest manner by Andrea Gusef, the commandant.

"At first the interpreter appeared stupefied, but gradually recovered. Through him I learnt that some white men were living on the banks of a river called by the Indians 'Ekko,' and that the Russian trade had already suffered on that account. I naturally concluded that the people must be some of the Hudson Bay Company's officers; and suggested to Gusef that they were probably also in search of Sir John Franklin. Subsequent information induced me to alter this opinion. First, they were badly supplied with provisions, and had bartered their percussion guns in order to obtain food; as the Company only exchange flint guns, of which they have plenty in store, and as it is not likely that the officers would be compelled to part with their private weapons, it may fairly be supposed that the party had no connection with that body. Secondly, the spot where they were supposed to be, I am led to believe, is two or three hundred miles within the Russian boundary-line, and moreover up a river,—a most improbable place for any Englishman to penetrate in search of gain. Lastly, the party was said to consist of two officers and ten men, evidently the crews of two small boats, the departure of whom from the Mackenzie River I had reason to believe impossible. I therefore concluded that these people must be a portion of Sir John Franklin's expedition, and proceeded to obtain as accurate knowledge as possible of every circumstance relating to them.

" As the ice in Norton Sound was shortly expected to break up, I lost no time in coming to a determination of what was best to be done. I concluded that, destitute as I was of every necessary, it would be folly to undertake a journey in search of the party; I therefore prepared to set out for the ship to impart my tidings, and obtain the necessary supplies for a lengthened absence. As Bosky was too unwell to move, I arranged to take a half-caste, named Nekever, whose qualifications were somewhat similar to those of my former companion. Gusef also agreed to have a few necessaries, which his experience had proved to be useful, ready by the time of my return.

" In retracing my steps I lost no opportunity of purchasing meat for the dogs, and, during the three days of my journey to Gregora's house, succeeded in obtaining about three hundredweight—sufficient to supply them until arriving at the ship. The next morning the natives brought the sledge which had been left behind: the cover was much torn by the wolves, the bread devoured; nothing else was injured. Departing the ensuing day, I chose the old track, and had an opportunity of distributing some presents amongst my friends, who assured me of every assistance in their power on my return.

Wishing them good-bye we commenced crossing the large bay, the scene of our former sufferings,—not however without accident. The day was misty and rainy, and the possession of a compass did not prevent our travelling some distance out of the way, to seaward, where the waves were beating on the edge of the ice. Soon afterwards a view was obtained of the open water, strewed with drift-wood. Every exertion was used to leave such a dangerous locality, and towards midnight we found ourselves safe on *terra firma*. Had there been any wind at the time it is probable that we should have been carried to sea upon some of the broken pieces.

"We arrived the next evening at the deserted village, and found a family had established themselves there, from whom we obtained some fish and ptarmigan. The latter frequent in great numbers the bushes on the coast, and are easily caught by the natives; and we were able to shoot sufficient for use. Upon the elevated land the thaw had advanced with such rapidity that the streams were running several feet deep over the surface of the ice, and we experienced difficulty in crossing, of course wetting everything and having occasionally some narrow escapes. The Spafarief village was at last gained, on the 25th of April, and the ship reached on the 29th.

"In the interval the natives had brought several reports relative to white men, which, strange to say, coincided in the main points with those obtained from the Russians. I naturally entertained great hopes of being permitted to return to Michaelowski, in order to obtain more authentic data respecting the alleged proximity of a party. To my surprise, I was informed by Commander Moore that he did not consider any of the rumours of importance, and that, consequently, my project of exploring the interior could not be acceded to.

"During my absence, the survey of Eschscholtz Bay had been carried on, and, after a few days' rest, I was sent to assist in the operation. Thus reinforced the task was continued. It made little progress however, as the lateness of the season, the rapid thawing of the snow, and the accumulation of water upon the surface of the sea-ice, rendered travelling with sledges both irksome and difficult. The water daily increasing, and having apparently cut off all communication with the ship, it was determined, in conformity with the instructions of the Commander, to cross over to Elephant Point. The passage led through two streams, which, insignificant a few days before, had now almost assumed the appearance of rivers. The dogs had to swim over, while the party, wading up to their breasts, tried to hold up the sledges, and defend them from the drifting masses of ice. Thus, without experiencing any damage, except that of a thorough wetting of all our effects, the opposite bank was reached.

"On arriving upon the sea-ice, the difficulty of crossing the bay was found far greater than we expected. The water was in many places as high as the armpits, and it took twenty hours—from two o'clock in the morning until ten at night—to accomplish the distance of six miles and a half. At last, with the loss of a sledge and a delay of three days, the party, wet, cold, and hungry, gained Elephant Point. Every one was so exhausted that, without pitching a tent or taking any refreshment, he lay down and, wrapping himself in his blanket, was almost instantly asleep. Finding it impossible to continue the survey, I departed on the following evening to inform the Captain, and as quickly as possible returned with orders for the recall of the surveying party.

"The rapid approach of summer was everywhere apparent. At the commencement of June, the land, with the exception of heavy drifts which had accumulated in the deep valleys, was free from snow; a lively green began to overspread the landscape; geese and ducks since the first week in May had made their appearance, and every day additional flocks arrived; the golden plover, the snipe, and numerous other small birds enlivened the air with their notes, while the busy hum of the mosquito and the murmuring of rivulets gave evidence that winter was past, and summer fairly set in.

"As the lanes of water rapidly widened and seemed to offer a means of moving the ship, all sail was set, and an attempt made to force a passage, but the vessel had hardly advanced a few yards when she became fixed, and remained in that position several days.

"On the 18th of June some natives came over the ice, leaping with great dexterity from piece to piece. They brought a few skins for barter, and said that the bay would be too encumbered to admit of moving the ship for the next fortnight. They had been fortunate in the capture of several white whales and seals, numbers of which had been observed sporting in the open water. As the ice still remained open, all the officers, with the exception of the Captain and Lieutenant, went on a shooting excursion to the Buckland River. The passage was accomplished without any greater difficulty than occasionally having to haul the boat over intervening masses of ice. On the 1st of July the party returned well rewarded with quantities of wild-fowl.

"In the meantime the ship had received several severe shocks from large floes of ice which bore down upon her, fortunately without inflicting any serious injury. An idea may be formed of the pressure from the fact that the vessel, although riding with one hundred fathoms of chain, and in only three fathoms water, was forced on shore on Chloris Peninsula. Although becoming every day less entangled, yet it was not until the 14th of July that the ship could be moved to her anchorage off Chamisso Island, and even there a good look-out had to be kept for the large pieces which floated out of the Sound, and were occasionally driven against her bows.

"As the summer was now far advanced, every one looked forward to the arrival of the Herald, and all eyes were constantly turned in the direction whence the ship was expected."

We must leave for awhile Mr. Pim and his enterprising companions, and resume the narrative of the voyage of the Herald at the time when that vessel had reached the port of Mazatlan.

CHAPTER IX.

Mazatlan—Surveying operations—San Jose—Guaymas—Islands and Ports of the Gulf of California.

How great was our mortification when, on reaching the port of Mazatlan, we received the intelligence that the cholera was ravaging the place! After a voyage of such long duration we met, instead of the much-needed amusement and recreation, death and mourning. One could scarcely pass a street without observing before the open window two or three corpses, surrounded by flowers, burning candles, and all the decorations that the customs of the country dictate. In the houses of the natives numerous prayers were addressed to the Virgin and Saints, and in those of the foreigners a depression of spirits and a dullness prevailed which gave a signal proof of the terror that had seized all classes. If a conversation was commenced, whatever the subject, it invariably turned to the topic of the day—the preservation of health, the necessity of abstaining from vegetable food, and the importance of avoiding as much as possible the night air. Indeed the latter precaution seemed to be observed with more than usual caution. Darkness had hardly set in when the streets were deserted by all save a few watchmen, or people who attended the fires, which, with the view of purifying the atmosphere, had been kindled in various parts of the town. On some evenings however the monotony was every moment interrupted. Torches and lanterns, a priest, and the image of some favourite saint, borne on the shoulders of negroes, were seen advancing, the whole followed by a crowd of people, chiefly women, who were muttering prayers, and kneeling occasionally to receive the sacerdotal benediction.

The theatre was closed, and the bull-fights discontinued, to prevent the spreading of the disease, yet, strange anomaly! rejoicing and festivity prevailed in many a private house to celebrate—what? the death of a child! In most countries parents are inconsolable when deprived of their offspring; not so in Mexico. A child, if it dies while innocent, *i.e.* below the age of puberty, is thought to proceed direct to heaven, and to become an angel, without having to pass through the much-dreaded purgatory. Its death is therefore regarded by many rather as a special favour of the Almighty than as a misfortune, and we hence find in many instances an almost entire absence of those sacred feelings which nature has so wisely established between parent and child. The event is celebrated in the most frivolous manner. No tears are shed, no lamentations heard, all is gaiety and festivity; and the stranger, on seeing polkas, waltzes, and contra-dances follow each other in quick succession, fancies he is looking on some bridal scene, when, in fact, he is all the time witnessing a funeral ceremony.

A Protestant can hardly imagine the extent to which this belief is carried. I was once present at the house of a European family when a woman of the neighbourhood came to say that her youngest child was at the point of death. "My dear lady," she said, "my *angelito* (little angel) is dying, and I am come to ask whether you could oblige me with a box for burying it." The lady informed her that, if possible, she would comply with her request, when the unnatural mother continued, "We are to have such a ceremony! The godmother is going to send the Padre, with full music, to administer extreme unction, and she has also promised to pay for the musicians and the fireworks when my *angelito* is taken to the *camposanto* (burial-ground), so I am in a great hurry to make the necessary preparations, that nothing may be wanting when it pleases Our Lady to call my *angelito* to heaven." The child expired the next day, and during the whole of the following night dancing and festivity were seen in a house which ought to have been filled with mourning.

The funeral itself is in many instances equally revolting. The corpse of the child, dressed in great state, is placed erect on a board, by means of a pole, and, thus standing, is carried on men's shoulders through the streets, giving at every step a nod with the head, which is most disgusting to behold. A band of musicians lead the train; then follow the priest, the mourners—if I may call them by that name—and several men, who throw up rockets and crackers, to the great delight of the multitude. In some parts of Mexico deceased children are actually attired as angels, with a pair of goose or pelican wings, suspended by a rope between two trees, and thus swung in the air, while the friends and relations dance around it, like a herd of savages.

We remained in the port of Mazatlan a few days in order to recruit our health, which had suffered severely from the protracted voyage, frequent change of climate, and salt provisions. Several cases of scurvy had made their appearance among the ship's company, and even some of the officers began to experience the unpleasant swelling of the feet and legs which is generally the forerunner of that malady, so that a few days more at sea would have augmented the sick list considerably. Fresh vegetables were in great demand; unfortunately Mazatlan was at this time ill-supplied, the inhabitants, from fear of the cholera, would not purchase them, and the country-people, finding no market, had ceased to send their produce.

As the intelligence brought by the Herald from the Arctic regions was likely to cause changes in the plans adopted by the Lords of the Admiralty for the relief of Sir John Franklin's expedition, and the co-operation of our vessel might still be required, Captain Kellett resolved to occupy the time necessary for the interchange of despatches with England by surveying a portion of the Californian Gulf, while I, thinking that the sterile nature of that district and the advanced season would offer but little inducement to accompany the ship, determined to make a journey into the interior of Mexico.

Cortez was the first explorer of the Gulf of California. Several expeditions sent in that direction having failed, he determined to accompany one himself, and for that

reason the Gulf of California is sometimes called the Sea of Cortez. Diego Hurtado, Grijalva de Cordova, Vasquez de Coronados, and Ferdinand de Alarchon discovered the Colorado River and the island of Cerros, or Cedros; but Francisco de Ulloa was among the foremost of the discoverers. The last-named traveller commences his journal in that strain of exalted piety which so fearfully contrasts with the blood-stained and ferocious acts of the Spaniards of those days, making us say with humility, Alas, poor human nature! Knowing that these men were the companions of Cortez and Pizarro, and of those warriors who effected such changes in these regions, one reads such a passage as the following with a shudder:—
"We embarked in the haven of Acapulco on the 8th of July in the year of our Lord 1539, calling upon Almighty God to guide us with his holy hand to those places where He might be served, and His holy faith advanced; and we sailed from the same port by the coast of Zacatula and Motosi, which is sweet and pleasant, owing to the number of trees which grow there, and the rivers which pass through those countries, for which we often thank God their Creator." But while remembering with unmixed displeasure the actions of Cortez and other Spanish warriors, we must express admiration for the exalted piety of the Roman Catholic missionaries, who, in these countries, inhabited by human beings in the lowest state of degradation, endured poverty and misery in all forms, to win the Indians to better habits and a purer faith. Although they have left little to mark their path in the world; although their efforts seem to have been ploughed on the water and sown in the sand, still

their patient virtues must ever shine as a bright page in the blood-stained history of Spanish America. The name of California is for ever united with the unselfish devotion of the Franciscan friars. Putting aside the prejudices of nation, of sects, or of education, let us admire, wherever we find it, unselfish devotion, patient perseverance in well-doing, and heroism in facing physical dangers, which would do honour even to veterans whose trade has been war.

"H.M.S. Herald," says Mr. Henry Trollope, "sailed from Mazatlan on the 3rd of December, 1849, in company with the yacht Nancy Dawson*, and after a long passage of five days—the distance being only 180 miles—she anchored in the Bay of San Jose del Cabo, as it is called, to distinguish it from other places of the same name,—for San Jose seems to have been a great favourite among the Spaniards. The road of San Jose is open and exposed; water is obtained with ease, wind and weather permitting, but at times, when north-west winds prevail, there is such a surf upon the beach that landing is impracticable.

"The river of San Jose gives an air of fertility to the valley unusual in California. The village is straggling and ill-built, and took its rise during the last war with the United States; it is not likely to increase much, although the produce of the country in a district so generally barren as California must always render it of some importance. The vicinity is studded with craters, cones, and table-lands, so remarkable that volcanic agency is

---

* The Nancy Dawson, under the command of Mr. J. Hill, sailed from San Jose del Cabo on the 9th of December, 1849, and arrived in England in June, 1850.

evident. Horses are in plenty, and we got better bullocks than we had had in any part of the coast.

"The authorities at San Jose, being in dread of the cholera, and fearing that we might be infected, coming from Mazatlan, intended to put us in quarantine; but an impudent Yankee came galloping down to the beach, informing us that he was despatched from the Governor to offer us supplies, etc. We communicated, and the mischief, such as it was, was done. It was afterwards found that this man had no authority, and was in every respect a bad character; he was, we understood, sentenced to receive a hundred lashes on a certain part which would render riding unpleasant to him for some time to come.

"Having surveyed the bay, which is, to say the least, an exposed and wild anchorage, we proceeded on our voyage, working up against the prevalent north-west winds on the Californian or western side of the Gulf. This shore is studded with islands, and is most extraordinary in its formation: castles, towers, peaks, pyramids, massive lines of fortification, appear here in all the grandeur of nature. Returning, we carried a survey of the side of the Gulf down to Cape San Lucas, but at this time made the best of our way to Guaymas, a port off which we arrived on Christmas Day.

"Guaymas is remarkable for its formation; it is, as it were, a crater hollowed out of a peninsula, on the north side of which the town is placed. A curious object, consisting of two peaks, called by the Spaniards Tetas de Cabra (teats of a goat) stands to the north-west of the town, and it is desirable to make these on approaching the land, as the prevailing winds and currents are then favourable for making the port. Cape Haro, a bold bluff headland, rising like a tower, four miles south of the entrance, will next be descried, and keeping the land on the left hand, Pajaros Island, steep and rugged like the adjoining coast, forms a breakwater before the mouth of the harbour, running between it and the main. The harbour opens out like a mountain lake, with islands on its surface, and the straggling ill-built town in the distance.

"Guaymas is a place of some trade; it has increased considerably since 1833, but, although still a depôt for English and French goods, it has again declined. The nearest town is Petic, or Hermosilla, which was visited by Mr. Billings and Mr. Hutchinson. The country in the neighbourhood is extremely barren; in the valleys there are few trees, and occasionally a peak is covered with brushwood, but in general the land seems to defy the labour of man; drought is the great enemy against which agriculture has to contend. It has been called the finest country in the world for an astronomer, and the worst for a farmer. The cactus is the most prominent of all plants or shrubs; it flourishes in undue luxuriance, I was going to say, but that its extraordinary structure, being in fact one mass of succulent matter, would appear to be a bountiful provision of nature in such an arid soil. Wherever a stream exists the land teems with fertility. There is not a building in Guaymas worthy of being described; it is an ill-built, straggling, half-ruined town, containing between 2000 and 3000 inhabitants. But as a natural harbour Guaymas is unique in its kind: the land seems thrown out from the main expressly to form the harbour, which is however shallow for the larger class of ships, it having barely more than fifteen feet even in its entrance; this defect however is comparatively of little moment, for the anchorage between Pajaros Island and the main is perfectly secure.

"We were very gay during our stay. The inhabitants behaved in a cordial manner, and our young people— in fact, old and young—fully entered into their dancing propensities. Tertullias, balls, and *petit soupers* were the order of the day. We gave a grand ball on shore in the Punta de Arena, where a spacious tent and supper-room was fitted up, and dancing kept up from nine o'clock in the evening until three or four in the morning. I cannot say much for the beauty of the damsels, but they were young and good-humoured, and enjoyed dancing excessively: they never seemed tired. Our young people left their hearts behind them for twenty-four hours, or some of the more impassioned and constant I think for forty-eight.

"After a month's sojourn, and having refitted and painted our vessel, we left the place on the 1st of February, 1850, and visited San Marco and the Bay of Mulegi, surveyed the islands of Santa Ineza, and the bays under Point Pulpito, aptly named, and Point Mangles, famous on the coast for its valleys, well supplied with wood of a superior quality. From Point Mangles we proceeded to the Coronados Islands, surveying the Bay of Lloretto, Carmen, the Danzanti Isles, and Puerto Escondido. On Sunday, the 24th of February, a party consisting of Mr. Hull, Mr. Anderson, and myself, with the whaler and the Owen, were detached on this duty, while the ship proceeded to the opposite shore and examined the low and dangerous island of Lobos. This work done, they rejoined us at Salinas Bay, Carmen Island, on Saturday, the 2nd of March. Lower California, although sterile, is from its formation highly interesting. When the shades of evening have closed around, or before the daylight breaks, nothing can exceed the beauty or the magnificence of the barren peaks and cactus-crowned rocks. The castles of feudal ages come before the mind in contemplating these extraordinary shores, and although visiting them and knowing them to be the work of nature alone, yet one can hardly believe that they are not the creations of man.

"On the 4th of February a small schooner came into the bay and landed a party to collect salt. These people are obliged to bring provisions and water, for none is to be found in the neighbourhood of these salt lakes, whence the name Salinas Bay is derived. There are on San Jose Island similar lakes, but they are not so large; they have a peculiar aspect, white as the drifted snow. Proceeding with our survey, the Owen, with Mr. Hull, fixed the position of Santa Cruz, the south point of Ceralbo Island, while the ship examined the Farallon de San Ignacio, a steep tower-like islet on the opposite shore, and then returned to Ballena Bay, in the island of Espiritu Santo. After examining this we landed on a rocky patch almost four miles north of Ceralbo Island, leaving which we ran for the Bay of San Jose del Cabo, and returned to Mazatlan on the 22nd of March, where we found H.M.S. Inconstant."

CHAPTER X.

Journey into the interior of North-western Mexico—Old Mazatlan—San Sebastian—The Sierra Madre—Copala—Santa Lucia—Durango—Santa Teresa—Return to the Port of Mazatlan.

OF all the states composing the Republic of Mexico none are less known than Sinaloa, Durango, and Chihuahua. Partly from fear of savage Indians, partly from want of pecuniary means, they have been avoided by most travellers; and those who have given a general description of the country have treated them vaguely, or confined themselves to the enumeration of the obstacles which prevented them from visiting this interesting portion of the Confederation. To botany, and natural history in general, the north-western states are an unexplored field. Few naturalists have investigated them, and those specimens that have been transmitted by amateurs have mostly proved new to science.

Encouraged by such prospects I lost no time in making preparations for starting, and having completed my arrangements, I left the port of Mazatlan on the 23rd of November, 1849, accompanied by two Mozos, and an equal number of baggage-mules. The lagoons and mangrove-swamps that surround the town, their abominable smell, and the unhealthiness which they spread over the adjacent district, made the first four leagues of my journey unpleasant. When this distance had been passed, the road ascended slightly, a purer air began to prevail, but the country became hardly more interesting. It being the dry season, most plants were leafless, all the herbage was burnt up, and, although here and there a few evergreen fig-trees, acacias, and arboreous cactuses, or some white blossoms of the Palo blanco (*Ipomœa arborescens*, Don), might be seen, yet they were so isolated that they failed to impart life or gaiety to the landscape.

About noon I reached the river Mazatlan, crossed it without difficulty, and entered the old town of the same name, which, by way of distinction, is called El Presidio de Mazatlan*. Formerly in a flourishing condition, it is now, since the port has risen to such a degree of importance, and all the wealthier inhabitants have repaired thither, a mere ruin. There are some beautiful old edifices built somewhat in the Moorish style, having long colonnades, with arches, and stone pillars, and fine open court-yards, but they are every year becoming more decayed, and even the church has been kept in such bad repair that nothing remains standing save the walls; the bells, following the roof, have long since fallen, and are now hung on a scaffold, where they are chimed every evening to remind the inhabitants of the hour of vespers.

* The name is derived from the Aztec words *mazatl*, deer, and *tlan*, country, and signifies *country of the deer*,—an appellation which is appropriate, as there are plenty of deer to be met with in the district.

There is a mesòn, or inn, offering accommodation for travellers and beasts, but my guide, having probably gained respecting it an experience which was in store for me on my return, avoided the place, and conducted me to the house of his *compadre* (godfather). The host proved to be a schoolmaster, who was just then dismissing his pupils; he received us with great politeness, informing us at the same time that his house was entirely at our service. Having given a sufficient quantity of *sacate* (maize-straw) to the beasts, and taken ourselves some dried beef (*tasajo*), eggs, and plantains, we continued our journey, and reached about dusk the town of San Sebastian, or La Villia, as it is sometimes called.

Having visited the place in 1848, in company with Mr. Robert Pakenham, one of my fellow-voyagers, I repaired at once to the house of a former acquaintance, Don Alejandro Bueso. This gentleman and his family gave me a hearty welcome, embracing me in the Mexican fashion, and shaking hands repeatedly. It took me some time to answer the numerous questions which my host, his lady, and daughters addressed to me. However, having at last satisfied them, they began to give me their little "odds and ends," which, being narrated in the sweet tongue of Castile, and with that frankness for which Spaniards are so distinguished, could not fail to interest me. After supper I had a long conversation with Don Alejandro, in the course of which he informed me that, in conjunction with a German merchant at Mazatlan, he had undertaken the working of one of the copper-mines of Malpica. From the warmth with which he spoke on the subject I soon found that a chord had been touched which never fails to vibrate in the breast of every Spanish-American; for mining operations and sudden riches are to them identical.

San Sebastian is situated about 1000 feet above the sea, and has on that account a more healthy climate than Mazatlan. It has two churches, and three hundred private buildings; the number of inhabitants amounts to nearly 1000, who carry on to some extent the cultivation of maize and *maguei* (*Agave*), and extract from the latter *aguardiente de maguei*, a highly stupefying beverage. Cutting logwood (*Hæmatoxylon Campechianum*, Linn.), or Brasil, as the Mexicans call it, is another source of employment. The wood, especially that of the stem of the tree, which obtains double the price the branches do, is carried in large quantities to Mazatlan, and is, except specie (chiefly dollars), the only export of that place. The logwood-tree is of middle size, and has deep natural furrows, which are a favourite retreat of snakes; how completely these reptiles thus conceal themselves may be gathered from the fact that they are frequently caught after the wood has been cut, carried on the backs of mules to the coast, loaded and unloaded, and stowed on board the vessels which are to take it to foreign countries.

The first part of the road from San Sebastian was monotonous, passing through *maguei* plantations, remarkable for their stiff and uncouth appearance. Towards the afternoon I came into a more varied landscape, to the foot of the Andes, on Sierra Madre, as they are here called. The oppressive atmosphere of the coast was less felt at every step, the air became cooler and more agreeable to European constitutions, and, although the excessive dryness continued, a few stragglers of oak and fir showed themselves. In the evening of the 26th of November I reached the village of Copala, and on the following day that of Santa Lucia.

I met every day numbers of emigrants, who had come by land from the United States, and were proceeding by way of Mazatlan to California. They were mostly in companies of twenty or thirty. Some of them were decent people, but a great number seemed to be the mere scum of society, who robbed the Mexicans whenever they had a chance, taking away the maize, killing the poultry, and refusing to pay after articles had been handed over to them. The natives had in many instances been compelled to hide their provisions and live-stock, and it was only after long persuasion that I could induce them to sell me the articles I required. As a large sum was charged in Mazatlan for a passage to California, and the finances of many of the emigrants were not in a very flourishing condition, a considerable number of them, previous to their embarkation, had, in order to supply this deficiency, taken part in the guerilla against the Comanches and Apaches, for which they were well paid by the Mexican Government.

Of all the places I have seen in Mexico none has pleased me more than Santa Lucia. Situated about 4000 feet above the sea, enjoying throughout the year a temperate climate, it lies in a romantic valley, encircled by mountains which admit a view of the Pacific Ocean. The houses of the Indians, scattered over an undulating surface, are surrounded by that beautiful vegetation in which the graceful forms of the tropics are harmoniously blended with the flora of the temperate zone. The acacia stands in company with the oak, the fir, and hardy *Umbelliferæ;* and *Compositæ* are mixed with *Alstrœmerias, Cupheas, Lobelias,* and *Lophospermums,* from which humming-birds suck the nectar. Nearly every hedge is overgrown by a splendid creeper, the *Ipomœa Schiedeana,* Ham., the flowers of which are so large (from four to five inches across) and so close together that the whole plant resembles a blue sheet, whence the vernacular name, *Manto de la Virgen,* or cloak of the Virgin. There is another plant of great beauty in these parts, the *Noche buena,* or Catalina of the Mexicans (*Poincettia pulcherrima*), now common in Europe; an extract from its bracts, mixed with lime-juice, gives an excellent scarlet dye.

Leaving Santa Lucia I passed Ocotes—a place deriving its name from the *Ocote,* a fir from which pitch is made—and reached, on the 1st of December, the rancho of Guadalupe, situated about 6000 feet above the sea. Oaks and coniferous trees form the principal part of the vegetation. In ascending towards the summit of the sierra the temperature had gradually decreased, but fortunately not fallen to the freezing-point. On proceeding however everything assumed a wintry aspect, and I became aware that my principal harvest was over. At 8000 feet the evergreen oak disappeared, the fir being the only tree. Of herbage nothing remained but brown leaves; and the little streams, which at a lower elevation gave variety to the sylvan scene, were covered with ice one to two inches thick. The nights were bitterly cold, and in vain did I try to get a few hours' sleep: it was impossible, even near the fire.

The settlements in the Sierra Madre are few, and, on account of the indolence of the inhabitants, badly provided with the comforts of life. Maize, beans, and chili (*Capsicum* sp.) is all the traveller is able to obtain. From the Indian corn little cakes are baked, known by the name of *tortillas*, or *gordas de maiz*, in the preparation of which the women spend nearly the whole day; indeed so much time is wasted in making them, that in towns and on large estates the wealthier people keep a *tortillera*, a person who does nothing else but make these cakes. Beans may be termed the national dish of Mexico; they conclude every meal of both rich and poor, and without them a Mexican would no more think of having made a good dinner than a Hawaiian would without his *poi*, or an East Indian without his curry. There is however only one particular kind which they eat; it is brown, and is called by the Aztecs *Yetl*, by the modern Mexicans *Frijol*, and by botanists *Phaseolus Hernandezii*. The eating of *tortillas* and beans savoured with chili was customary before the conquest of Mexico, and is probably of ancient date. As you approach the western coast provisions become more abundant; but even at Mazatlan, where there is always a ready market, by the numerous ships frequenting that port, and almost any price might be obtained for fresh vegetables, the people are too indolent to cultivate the fields. There are only a few sweet potatoes, bananas, cabbages, and tomatoes. *Verdolaga* (*Portulaca oleracea*), which grows wild in the vicinity, is brought on the table as greens. More productive in fruit and vegetables, though far inferior to either Panama or Guayaquil, is San Blas.

I continued my journey over large plains, passing Cayotes, El Salto, Llano Grande, Navios, Los Miembres, and Rio Chico, all miserable huts. To cross these elevated plains during winter is not without danger. The sky, always of an azure blue, suddenly becomes cloudy, snow begins to fall, and in a short time the traveller is prevented from proceeding. If he is near a hut he may be safe; if not, which is very often the case, as human habitations are from twenty to forty miles distant from each other, he and his animals are exposed to great hardships. It would be well were these the only difficulties; but there are others of a more serious nature. In nearly every mile of the road you observe one or more heaps of stones, on the top of which are wooden crosses: each of these monuments marks a spot where people have been slain by robbers. In some parts they are so numerous that the places look almost like burying-grounds. In other countries, if people meet on a solitary road they are pleased—" Similis simili gaudet;" but here, directly parties descry each other, they count forces, and prepare for an attack. They draw near in silence, the one measuring the other with suspicious eyes, until somebody makes the usual salutation, and they proceed to their respective destinations. It is a lamentable state of society when you must look upon every fellow-creature with distrust, and can never move a step without being armed.

When I arrived in the city of Durango several foreign residents invited me to stay with them. Mr.

Washington Kerr, an American merchant, to whom I had a letter of introduction from Mr. Talbot, the British Vice-Consul at Mazatlan, having been the first who made me the offer, I took up my residence in his house. Of the hospitality shown me by that gentleman, as well as by other foreigners, I cannot say too much; they treated me with the greatest attention, and I shall always remember their kindness with feelings of gratitude. During my short sojourn I became acquainted with three persons who were of more than ordinary interest to me. The first was a niece of Bolivar, a highly accomplished lady, who could speak five European languages with the greatest fluency, and who is now married to a German merchant, Mr. Lehmann. The second was a descendant of Montezuma, the Emperor of Mexico, who on this account was generally called by the inhabitants El Emperador; he filled an office at the Mint, and I fancied I could discern in his physiognomy a certain resemblance to that which the face of his great ancestor is said to have expressed. The third was Don F. Ramirez, the historian, well known by his Spanish translation of Prescott's admirable 'History of the Conquest of Mexico,' to which he has added a volume of notes and additions. Ramirez possesses a profound knowledge of the Aztec picture-writings, and intends to publish an account of the early history of the tribes of Anahuac, their origin, migration, and ultimate settlement on the plains of Mexico. He has a very extensive library, including every book which has the least reference to his favourite study, from the gigantic work of Lord Kingsborough down to the smallest pamphlet.

The city of Durango is situated in a large plain, about 6000 feet above the sea, and is built in regular squares. It is sometimes called Ciudad de los Alacranes, because the place is infested, especially during the summer months, with scorpions, which are considered extremely venomous, and are said to have caused the death of a great many people. They are so plentiful that the Government has been compelled to offer premiums for their destruction. Whether a single bite of a Durango scorpion is really fatal I have not been able to ascertain, but I was assured by a gentleman, upon whom I have reason to rely, that he once saw a boy dying from a number of bites. The boy having collected some scorpions in a bottle, and placed the vessel under his shirt, on his breast, began playing with other lads, fell down, and broke the bottle; the scorpions immediately attacked his naked breast, and infused their venom; the poor boy died the following day.

The houses are built somewhat in the Moorish style, with fine colonnades, arches, and court-yards; the latter are generally planted with orange and pomegranate trees, and are occasionally used as ball-rooms, after being covered with canvas, and carpeted for that purpose. Among the public edifices, the churches and convents are the finest; there is also a theatre, which however is in very bad order, and a Plaza de Toros, where nearly every Sunday afternoon bull-fights take place. The principal promenade is the Alameda, a square planted with poplars, willows, ash-trees, and roses, and furnished with a number of stone seats. It is kept in very nice order, and in the afternoons, especially on Sunday, nearly everybody, rich and poor, makes it a point of proceeding thither, either on foot, on horseback, or in a carriage.

The climate is, like that of the greater part of the Mexican highlands, dry but agreeable. The extremes of heat and cold are unknown. Towards the end of February the night-frosts cease; the spring commences; poplars and willows begin to get green; peaches and apricots put forth their blossoms. But the temperature alone, though fast increasing during April and May, is not sufficient to awaken nature altogether. The fields remain dry until, in the latter end of May or the beginning of June, the vivifying rains set in, which continue until the first week of September. In a few days everything has started into life, and the vegetation proceeds with extraordinary quickness. There is no severe winter; in October the night-frosts recommence; snow seldom falls, and never remains long on the ground.

The vicinity of Durango is arid and thinly wooded; indeed there are but seven species of indigenous trees, viz. a willow, an *Acacia*, a *Prosopis*, a *Cratægus*, the *Taxodium distichum*, *Casimiroa edulis*, and *Yucca aloifolia*. These, together with a few shrubby *Acanthaceæ*, *Compositæ*, *Scrophularineæ*, and *Cacteæ*, and the everywhere prevailing *Agaves*, constitute the principal portion of the flora. The round *Cacteæ*, called *visnágas* by the natives, are extensively used to make a sweetmeat sold in the streets of the city by the name of *dulce de visnagas*. In the north of the town, about a mile distant, lies the Cerro de Mercado, an iron mountain, overgrown with opuntias. In the gardens, besides the native productions, nearly all European fruits and vegetables are grown. This however has only been done of late years, and principally by foreigners, especially Dr. L. Kegel, who have introduced a great number. The peach and vine succeed well, and of culinary vegetables none excel the cauliflower, which attains such a size that a single head measures eighteen inches to two feet in diameter, and makes a donkey-load. The gigantic cauliflower is not distinct from our European species, but is solely produced by a cultivation which necessity has dictated. Being one of the northern vegetables that degenerate, or bear no seed, if not annually procured from Europe, it is propagated by cuttings. After the heads have been gathered, the stubs are allowed to throw out new shoots, which are again planted, and have to grow two years, producing in the second the enormous heads. The principal indigenous fruits are the *Tejocote*, or *Texocotl* (*Cratægus Mexicana*, DC.), and the *Zapote blanco* (*Casimiroa edulis*, Ll. et Lex.), an *Aurantiacea*. The latter is a tree which has a remarkable tendency to accommodate itself to different climates: it grows from the coast-region up to an elevation of 7000 feet, producing everywhere an abundant harvest of delicious fruit. It was well known to the Aztecs, who termed it *Iztactzapotl*, and also *Cochitzapotl*; the former name is composed of the words *iztac*, white, and *tzapotl*, Sapota. *Tzapotl*, from which comes the Spanish corruption *zapote*, and the English *Sapota*, signifies a succulent fruit containing large hard seeds, as, for instance, that of *Lucuma, Anona, Achras*, etc., a word for which our present botanical terminology has no equivalent expression. The second name, *cochitzapotl*, is derived from *cochi*, to make sleepy, and *tzapotl, Sapota,* as the fruit when eaten acts as a soporific*.

My original plan was to visit Chihuahua. The principal reason which induced me to alter the route was the season. I had seen the destructive effect the winter produced upon the vegetation of the highlands, and was therefore obliged to abstain as much as possible from proceeding further northward. Another was the great risk which every one incurs who now ventures to Chihuahua. The tide of civilization, pressing hard from north and east, is driving all the Indians into the corner formed by the states of Chihuahua, Sonora, and Durango. The Mexicans, too weak to oppose, are fast retreating, and thus it is that during the last few years the above-named states have been depopulated and ruined. The savages spare none: every white man who falls into their hands dies a cruel death. So great is the terror they inspire, and so daring their courage, that they have ventured into the streets of Durango—a place of 22,000 inhabitants—killing and robbing in every direction. The Mexican Government is well aware of the danger. They have formed several guerilla parties, composed of North Americans and other foreigners, who make attacks upon the Comanches, and are paid for every head they bring 200 dollars; but the Indians are so numerous that little effect has at present resulted from the terrible measure.

I therefore took a south-western direction, the road to Tepic. Departing from Durango on the 2nd of January,

---

* Hernandez, in his 'Historia Plantarum,' lib. ii. cap. 142 (edition of Madrid, 1790), gives a fair account of the tree and its economic and medicinal properties.

1850. I reached, on the 5th instant, Mesquital, a considerable village, whose inhabitants, as the name indicates, occupy themselves by preparing mesquital from the agaves. In proceeding, I crossed the river Mesquital, the banks of which were shaded by huge trees of *Taxodium distichum*. This tree, called in Spanish *Sabino*, in Atzec *Ahoehoetl*, always grows near running streams, like the Cedro de la Sierra (*Chamæcyparis thurifera*, Endl.). Often have I rejoiced when, after having sought a long time for water, the tops of some sabinos were descried: I had found the object of my search. As far as Mesquital there are several large estates, but, having passed that place, you enter a desolate district. There are no houses, no people. The road becomes mountainous and very badly marked, as it is only trodden by a few Indians, the principal communication between Durango and Tepic being carried on by way of Guadalajara. I collected however a good many specimens, the vegetation not having suffered so much from frost as in that part of the Sierra Madre which I crossed when coming from Mazatlan.

On the 12th of January I reached the village of Santa Teresa, two days distant from Tepic. This village is surrounded by oak and pine forests, and inhabited by the Coras, a tribe of Indians whom the Jesuits converted to Christianity during the last century. There were only three persons in the place who could speak Spanish, all the rest talking a language of their own. The inhabitants seem to be an honest people, and I rather offended them by sleeping in the tent and not coming to their houses; several times they tried to make me understand that they were not like the Apaches, and had no communication with the Comanches.

I remained five days in Santa Teresa, proceeded to within a day's distance of Tepic, and then returned to Durango, taking a different route, which conducted me to a place called Guajolote. The Indians of Guajolote and the Cora tribe in general boil and eat the flowers of *Yucca aloifolia* and several *Agaves*. What wonderful plants the agaves are! There is not a particle of them that is not used in some way or another. In Ecuador I found the people using the spongy substance of the flower-stem instead of tinder, and in all the schools the green leaves instead of paper. A punishment among the Aztecs was introducing the spiny points of the leaves into the s'.in, as may be seen from their pictorial writings.

In Durango I made the acquaintance of Mr. Henri Herz, the celebrated pianist and composer, who had made a professional tour through Mexico, and was on his way to California. In every town through which his journey had led him, he had been received with distinction,—a king could not have wished for greater honours. He had composed for the Mexicans a 'Marcha nacional,' which has become so popular in the country that the Government had solicited M. Herz to compose also a national anthem. He acceded to the request, but it was a long time before suitable words could be procured; heaps of poems were sent in, but none of them were calculated to inspire a composer, until at last a young Englishman residing in Mexico wrote the desired lines, which at once were set to music.

Hearing that I was to proceed to Mazatlan, M. Herz asked leave to accompany me, and I was only too glad to augment my forces, for the road to the western coast was rendered insecure by the Comanches, who had already killed several of the rancheros. We left Durango on the 13th of February. Several of the places we passed through were either burnt down by the wild Indians or deserted. Thank God, we did not meet with any of the savages, and on the 22nd of February arrived safe at Mazatlan, where we were hospitably received by the house of Lomer, Melcher, and Co.

CHAPTER XI.

Departure from Mazatlan—Third voyage to the Arctic regions—Honolulu—Aleutian Islands—Kotzebue Sound—Cape Lisburne—Arrival of H.M.S. Investigator—Norton Sound—Grantley Harbour—H.M.S. Enterprise—The Herald returns to the Sandwich Islands.

THE Herald left Mazatlan on the 4th of April, 1850, sighted the island of Clarion on the 20th of the same month, and anchored in the inner harbour of Honolulu, Oahu, on the 16th of May. She remained in that port fifteen days, making preparations for her third northern voyage, and awaiting the arrival of H.M.S. Enterprise and Investigator, which after their return from the eastern side of Arctic America had been despatched from England under the command of Captain Collinson and Commander M'Clure, to continue the search after Sir John Franklin's Expedition on the western. But on the 24th of May, the necessary arrangements being completed, and the expected vessels not arriving, the Herald quitted the Sandwich Islands, and made a very fair passage up to the Aleutian Islands, where she encountered for several days a fresh north-north-east wind and much rain.

On sighting the coast of Kamtchatka (June 23rd), we found it covered with snow, with every appearance of its having been a severe winter. Passing to the eastward of Behring Island we were favoured with southerly winds, with clear weather, which carried us up to St. Lawrence Island by the 10th of July. In running across the Bay of Anadyr, we spoke a whaler, the America, of New Bedford, and learnt from her that about two hundred sail were in this sea and through the Strait. Passing westerly of St. Lawrence, we met winds from north-west to north-north-east, and, what is of unusual occurrence, beat through Behring's Strait with moderate and beautifully clear weather; being able to see at the same time Asia, America, and the Diomedia Islands, all clear of snow, with the exception of the patches in the valleys which never thaw, and, in standing close under East Cape, found the coast perfectly clear of ice. Several native baidars boarded us; they were aware of the Plover's having wintered in Kotzebue Sound, mentioning Commander Moore's name; these people had known him when wintering on the Asiatic side in 1848.

In running into Kotzebue Sound, we observed off Cape Krusenstern an extensive pack of ice, and found the Sound itself so encumbered with heavy floes, through which we threaded our way, that at midnight, seeing no opening, we were obliged to retrace our steps; the pack appeared to extend from shore. Being in sight of Chamisso Island at the time, and within twelve miles of the anchorage, we fired a gun in hopes that the Plover might have heard it. Next morning, close to the edge of the ice, and distant twenty-five miles from Chamisso

Captain Kellett despatched a cutter, with Mr. R. Maguire, first lieutenant, to endeavour to communicate with the Plover. She passed a barrier of five miles through openings between the floes, occasionally unable to see her way, and then got into open water near Chamisso Island, where she found that vessel in readiness to depart so soon as the ice would allow. her.

Fortunately the weather remained fine; had it been thick, and blowing a south-westerly gale, we should have run, and more than probably have got ourselves into difficulties; never having suspected the possibility of any ice being in this sound so late in the season. While becalmed it was curious to observe this extensive field breaking up and disappearing before its great enemy: the temperature of the water was 50°, and the air 60° Fahr. A fresh north-westerly wind afterwards sprang up, with which the Herald worked out to the entrance of the sound (July 16th, 6 A.M.). Having no ice in sight, we bore up for Chamisso to pick up our boat, intending to anchor as close as the ice would permit; to our astonishment, the vast mass, which had but thirty hours before opposed a perfect barrier to our entry, had vanished; even all the shores within view were perfectly clear.

We found the Plover outside, having weighed the evening of our boat's arrival; she followed us into the anchorage under Chamisso Island. We were glad to learn that her officers and crew were in good health; although during the winter serious apprehensions had been entertained, as symptoms of scurvy had appeared. On the breaking up of the ice the Plover had many escapes, and at one time, fearing that something serious might happen, provisions had actually been landed. The officers were frequently detached, exploring the country, and adding to our geographical knowledge in these regions.

Captain Kellett received from Commander Moore two communications, acquainting him with Eskimo reports which he had obtained from the natives of Hotham Inlet relative to the encampment to the northward of a number of white people (in the vicinity of Point Barrow it is supposed), and requesting permission to ascertain the truth of these rumours. Having completed the Plover with the provisions she most needed, Captain Kellett immediately despatched him on this service, fearing it might have been Commander Pullen and his party, who, in attempting to return, had been obliged to winter on the coast; the natives having reported that the party they spoke of would be fallen in with further south, as they had been endeavouring to get that way.

On the 21st of July the Herald left Kotzebue Sound for the north, and on the 24th sent two boats on shore at Cape Lisburne to erect a mark and bury information for Captain Collinson; this promontory and Point Hope being the two rendezvous appointed. We then, with a north-east wind, stood to the northward, and made the ice, heavily packed, at noon on the 26th, in lat. 70° 18′ north, long. 167° 48′ west, fifty miles further south than we encountered it in 1849. Working easterly we again made it on the 29th, in lat. 71° 19′ north, long. 162° 57′ west, and a third time within twenty miles of Wainwright Inlet. Having established the position of the pack, we bore up for Cape Lisburne, running over in our passage south the Plover's three rendezvous without meeting her, to endeavour to fall in with Captain Collinson's Expedition. On the 31st of July, Cape Lisburne south fifty, east twelve miles, we met with H.M.S. Investigator. She had made a surprising passage of twenty-six days from Oahu; left it on the 4th of July; cleared the Sandwich Islands on the 5th; passed the Aleutian Group by the Strait of Amoutka on the 20th; Behring's Strait on the 27th; saw Plover on the 29th, and Herald on the 31st; she steered a straight course and carried a fair wind the whole way.

From Commander M'Clure we learnt that Mr. Pullen had arrived at the Mackenzie River, and that he had been ordered to proceed on another expedition. Commander M'Clure being three men short of complement, we filled up the vacancies with volunteers from our crew, all excellent men and healthy. Captain Kellett wished the Investigator to take from us some provisions, but she was full; having at the time vegetables on board, and the last bullock had been killed a few days before; the men were in excellent health and high spirits. "I went over the ship," says Captain Kellett, "and was highly pleased with the comfort and cleanliness; everything appeared in its right place. Commander M'Clure did not much extol her sailing qualities, but spoke in high praise of her capabilities for taking the ice. He parted from me at midnight, with a strong north-east wind, and under every stitch he could carry, and he was seen again by the Plover, on the 5th, in lat. 70° 44', long. 159° 52', steering to the north with a strong south-west wind; the two vessels could only communicate by exchanging numbers."

We continued to cruise off Cape Lisburne, expecting daily to meet the Enterprise. On the 13th of August the Plover hove in sight, with Commander Moore, whose legs were so swollen that he was but just able to hobble on board the Herald.

The reasons for not acquiescing with him in sending another boat expedition to the Mackenzie (to follow up and investigate these reports) were, because Captain Kellett was of opinion that these reports had been created by the anxiety of all on board the Plover to gain information, which caused the natives to be fully aware of the subject upon which the strangers wished to obtain correct data. The Eskimos are quick, and, where it is likely that their natural cupidity would be gratified, ever ready, can they but get a lead, to exercise their ingenuity by inventing a story. It was *after* Commander Moore had made the chief of the Hotham Inlet tribe understand the object of the Plover's wintering in those regions, that the majority of the reports were received; only one, on which not the least reliance was placed at the time, had been reported previously; every American ship which passes through these straits is furnished with instructions relative to the missing Expedition; in fact the whole of the small extent of coast accessible to ships was at that moment " alive with native reports."

At Wainwright Inlet, although Commander Moore made every inquiry after the missing ships, he could get no intelligence; the natives followed him along from the inlet, and at Point Barrow they had the story ready. From the chart made by the woman in Kotzebue Sound, it was supposed that the Kopak, of which the Eskimos had spoken, was either Point Hope, Wainwright Inlet, or Point Barrow, all of which places were visited this season. The natives at Point Barrow told Commander Moore that they had not seen either the ships or the graves, but that they had learned the story from some natives who come from the Kopak, with whom they meet to barter at a place distant from Point Barrow, ten sleeps or days' journeys (about twenty-five to thirty miles each). From this Commander Moore inferred that the Kopak must be situated a little to the westward of the Mackenzie; but, as all these reports refer to the autumn of 1848, Commander Pullen must have unravelled them in 1849.

The Lords of the Admiralty had directed, that should no position be found south of Wainwright Inlet,—into which place eight feet was all that could be carried this year,—the Plover was to be placed in Kotzebue Sound. But Commander Moore declaring that "he could not winter there without almost certain destruction," Captain Kellett ordered the Plover to proceed to Grantley Harbour, the only place south of the strait in which she could be of assistance as a depôt.

After despatching the Plover on the 15th of August we continued to cruise off Cape Lisburne, where we placed further information for Captain Collinson. The natives had removed our first deposit, but we knew that had another vessel arrived they would have presented the paper to her; all of them are now aware of the value of paper, and are anxious to be possessed of some, invariably looking to see if it contains writing.

On the 25th we landed at Point Hope, where we found, untouched, the bottle deposited by the Plover on her passage north; we erected a more conspicuous mark, and buried a bottle with further information. Being thoroughly convinced that the Enterprise had passed, we made sail for Behring's Strait with light northerly winds, with the intention of going to Michaelowski, Norton Sound, to investigate the reports brought from that place by Mr. Pim during the last winter.

When thirty miles off East Cape, on the 27th, we communicated with the American whaler Margaret Scott, of New Bedford, a full ship, bound southerly, and sent Mr. W. Billings, the assistant surgeon, on board to visit her sick. We passed the Strait in a moderate gale, and next evening were becalmed within ten miles of Sledge Island, and arrived off Egg Island (Michaelowski) on the morning of the 31st. It being calm, the Captain left the ship in a cutter, accompanied by the late Mr. Woodward, Mr. Pim, and myself.

On our arrival at the redoubt we were excessively disappointed to find that the chief and his second, those who gave Mr. Pim the information, had both left for Sitka, taking with them every paper and letter. The present chief was unacquainted with the country. On asking him what he knew of the reports promulgated by his predecessor, he told us that he knew of none; that he was not aware of any white men being in the country; and that none of their people were killed last year; in fact, that Gusef, the former chief, had left him without any information whatever relative to them. We interrogated our former interpreter, who, having been

Mr. Pim's medium of communication, replied that Gusef had received a letter from Derabin subsequent to Mr. Pim's departure, but had not heard that it contained anything particular. On asking him concerning the double-barrelled gun, said to have been bartered by the Indians, he replied he knew an Indian who had seen one, and some clothes.

On our former visit to this place in 1848, a report, obtained through the same interpreter, was current, of six white men being in the interior; and among the Eskimos of Kotzebue Sound, the same year, a similar one was in circulation. We could only account for the Russians spreading them by the belief that some one must be in their vicinity purchasing furs, the quantities annually brought to the fort having during the last two years diminished more than one-half. They could not be persuaded by Mr. Pim but that the Plover was trading; these suppositions were however set aside by our visit. It is possible that the Plover may have interfered with their trade,—the natives finding they could obtain from her all they wanted for fish and venison, articles much more easily obtained than furs, and disposed of without going so great a journey. On relating to the chief the account brought by Mr. Pim, he informed us that he had not heard nor did he know anything of this, but that he had received instructions from the Governor-general at Sitka to render every assistance to any officer or men employed in searching after the missing ships, and endeavour by every means to obtain information of them and relieve them. We had rendered into German the notice from the Arctic papers, offering a reward for any positive information in expectation of getting it translated into Russian by Kukuff. He told there was however a man at Derabin who would be able to do so. Captain Kellett also gave the chief a letter from Baron Brunow, addressed to the governor of the Russian colonies; this document settled all doubts; he told us that he was going to Derabin as soon as the frost set in, and that if there should exist any reports with sufficient foundation, he would send an expedition to unravel them; and that he would also communicate with the Plover in the spring.

The redoubt of Michaelowski supplies annually two forts and one or two fishing-posts in the Sound with goods. The most distant and most northerly fort is Derabin, situated near the head-waters of the Ko-ikh-pak, which falls into Norton Sound, a short distance to the west of Michaelowski redoubt; its position in latitude and longitude is unknown. A launch leaves Michaelowski in the spring with goods; it takes her thirty-five days to reach this fort, and fifteen to return; by winter travelling it may be reached in six days from a fishing establishment called Gregora. The other fort is called Kalmakosskoi, and is situated to the south-east of Michaelowski, five days' journey on another river falling into the sea west of the redoubt. These are the only places supplied by the fort; they knew nothing of any post on the Yucan, nor of any establishment in or near Kotzebue Sound.

From Bosky, our former interpreter, and also from the one at present on board the Plover, both of whom have been to Derabin, we learned that the Lek-kho is the actual head-water of the Ko-ikh-pak, and not, as was previously supposed, a river on the other side of the mountains, falling into the Arctic Sea. It is however difficult to get any of these interpreters to perform their office faithfully; they will neither propose the questions you wish, nor return the exact replies.

We sailed from Michaelowski the same evening, and arrived at Port Clarence on the 5th of September, where we found the Enterprise and the Plover. The latter was already inside Grantley Harbour, preparing a house for the reception of her provisions; the former was on shore, having grounded in attempting to enter Grantley Harbour. With every assistance we could give her they failed in getting her off that evening or the next morning. They commenced lightening her, which was done before the evening tide, of more than a hundred tons, when she went off without damage of any kind. They were obliged to heave her astern, and with the bower-chain, as she had no stern-holes; some difficulty and delay would have been experienced in doing this had it not been for the ready resource of Mr. Skead (her second master), who placed a small anchor in the port, the arms and shank making a perfect lead for the cable.

The Enterprise had been at Cape Lisburne on the 14th of August, and although a party effected a landing there, neither the marks erected by the Herald and Plover, nor any other traces of our vessels, had fallen under her observation. This statement would almost appear inexplicable, had not upon that very day the Herald, while communicating with the Plover, been drifted thirty miles off the land. The accident, trifling as it may appear, proved of great importance, as to its consequences must be ascribed, if not the total failure of this year's expedition, at least one of the most serious impediments to the further progress of the Enterprise. The state of that vessel must be fully understood in order to justify her movements. Since parting with the Investigator in the Strait of Magellan, she had not met with any of the ships composing the Relief Expedition, and, ever since leaving Oahu, remained in total ignorance of their operations. Nevertheless, expecting to fall in with one or the other, she steadily continued her course towards the north, entered the ice, rounded Point Barrow, and succeeding in reaching as far as 73° 25′ north, 152° 40′ west, being thirty-two miles higher than the position attained by the Herald in 1849. But her troubles seemed to increase; huge masses of ice impeded all further progress, and although soundings of 130 fathoms with no bottom gave encouragement to proceed, and revived hopes that the actual passage could be effected, yet, being uncertain of the position of the Investigator, Plover, or Herald, and consequently having no resources within reach, Captain Collinson resolved to return to the southward. With some difficulty the vessel extricated herself from the ice, and, touching at Point Hope, obtained from the natives a scrap of paper containing the intelligence that the Plover and Herald were to be found at Port Clarence. A few days' sail brought her thither, where however but one of those vessels, the Plover, had as yet arrived. Thinking Grantley Harbour, the inner basin of Port Clarence, suitable for winter-quarters, an attempt was made to enter, but she approached too near a shoal, and had the misfortune to run upon it.

The Enterprise being re-stowed, she sailed on the morning of the 14th of September, but, being unable, from the strength of the north winds, to pass through the Strait, anchored under Cape York on the evening of the 16th. The wind moderated on the 17th, and on the 18th she had a fair wind through.

All hands were now employed in erecting a storehouse, landing provisions, removing the officers and men considered by the medical officers as unfit to remain in the Plover on her extended service, of whom the greater part had, during the last winter, showed symptoms of scurvy. Her complement was augmented to forty persons (including the interpreter), with volunteers, many of the the best men, and all the healthiest from our ship, as Commander Moore considered his crew should not be further decreased; the natives in Grantley Harbour being numerous, certainly not so trustworthy, and more independent in their manner than those of Kotzebue Sound. We were visited by a great number of them; on these occasions many acts of pilfering were committed. Their principal establishment, which is said to occupy a large space on the banks of the river Kanyekt, falling into Grantley Harbour, is called Kavyiak, distant a day's journey from the place were the Plover was to winter.

On the 21st of September, the Plover's house being finished, her provisions landed and stowed, and the ship herself dismantled, we endeavoured to get away, but being becalmed we were obliged to anchor. On the 22nd we again tried; and finally, on the morning of the 23rd, left Port Clarence with an increasing breeze from the northward, which reduced us to close-reefed main-topsail, and compelled us to heave-to fifty miles north of the east end of St. Lawrence Island. Next day at noon we passed the east end of the island, with light northerly winds, which shifted during the night to the eastward; by the morning it blew a gale, rendering it necessary either to heave-to or scud; we chose the latter.

The following morning (26th), the gale having lightened, we had just made more sail, when Charles Kennedy, A. B., fell overboard from the main rigging, striking the chains, it is supposed, in his fall; the ship at the time was running eight knots. The life buoy was immediately let go, sail promptly shortened, the ship rounded to the wind, but all was of no avail; neither man nor buoy could be seen. To have lowered a boat in the sea then running would have been to sacrifice her crew. Independent of the gloom which the loss of a man invariably spreads throughout a ship, it was the more distressing, as in a period of nearly six years, in all our gales, this was the first fatal accident that had happened to us.

On the 28th we passed the Aleutian chain by the Strait of Amoukta, and on the 16th of October reached the anchorage of Honolulu, Oahu. Thus we completed our third and last voyage to the Arctic Ocean. We had used every endeavour to rescue the unfortunate navigators, but were mortified to find that, after all our exertions and hardships, we had failed in accomplishing the grand object of our mission.

CHAPTER XII.

Historical Summary of the five years' search after Sir John Franklin, from the 1st of January, 1848, to the 1st of January, 1853, enumerated according to the dates on which the Expeditions left the British shores.

THE reader would probably feel disappointed if I were to conclude the narrative of an Arctic relief expedition without affording him a view of all that has been done to rescue the gallant Franklin and his brave companions. The question has now become so complicated, and the materials bearing upon it are so much scattered about in narratives of voyages, pamphlets, periodicals, and "Blue Books," that probably the best service a writer can render to the public is by presenting a concise account of the various attempts made to determine the fate of the missing voyagers, and the results which have attended these meritorious endeavours. The great difficulties however that surround the subject made me anxious that this account should be written by one more competent than myself, and applying for that purpose to my friend Mr. Augustus Petermann, he responded to my wishes by sending the following sketch, which, it may be interesting to know, was not finally printed until it had been submitted to various Arctic authorities, who kindly pointed out whatever inaccuracies they detected in the statements.

On the 26th of May, 1845, H.M.S. Erebus and Terror, under the command of Sir John Franklin, and carrying a total of 138 men, sailed from the Thames for the purpose of making once more the attempt to discover the North-west Passage. Their last despatches were from the Whalefish Islands, dated July 12th, 1845, and the vessels themselves communicated last with the Prince of Wales whaler, near Melville Bay, on the 26th of the same month. As the third winter was passing by without any intelligence of Sir John Franklin reaching England, anxiety for his safety began to prevail, and his vessels began to be spoken of as the "Missing Expedition." In the following year it was considered necessary to despatch expeditions in search of the missing one, and on the 1st of January, 1848, the first of these vessels left England. Five years have since passed,—expeditions after expeditions in the cause of humanity have unceasingly left these shores,—the British Government has spared no expense, private individuals of England and America have materially assisted,—the whole world has taken an intense interest in the fate of the 138 brave men who gallantly set out to solve one of the greatest geographical problems; but no tidings have been received, no clue to the mystery has been obtained, and the only indirect intelligence respecting their fate consists of traces found at Beechey Island, indicating their winter-quarters in 1845-46.

First Series of the Searching Expeditions.

The first Searching Expeditions sent out by the Government were admirably planned. Bearing in mind that Franklin's route lay in the direction from Lancaster Sound to Behring's Strait, the Admiralty determined on three expeditions: one to proceed to Behring's Strait, to *meet* the ships, another to Lancaster Sound, to *follow* them in their supposed track, and a third down the Mackenzie River, to search the Arctic shores of North America, in the event of Sir John Franklin having been forced to make for that coast. It was reasonably hoped that one of these expeditions would succeed and fall in with the missing one.

The Behring's Strait Expedition, 1848 *and* 1849*.— This consisted of the Herald and Plover, surveying vessels. The latter ship, commissioned by Commander Moore, sailed from the Thames on the 1st of January, 1848, to join the former under Captain Kellett, but being a slow sailer, she did not reach the Sandwich Islands until the end of August, 1848, too late in the season for commencing any search in Behring's Strait. She wintered in the Bay of Anadyr, whence she sailed on the 30th of June in the following year, and on the 14th of July, having passed Behring's Strait, anchored off Chamisso Island in Kotzebue Sound, the appointed rendezvous. The next day she was joined by the Herald and

---

* The Expeditions are enumerated according to the date when they left the British shores.

the yacht Nancy Dawson, commanded by Robert Shedden, who, hearing in China of the object of the expedition to Behring's Strait, nobly resolved to aid in the search for his imperilled countrymen. On the 18th of July the three vessels left Kotzebue Sound, and, after keeping pretty near the shore as far as 70° north, they stood out to the north-west. On the 29th of July their further progress was arrested by an impenetrable pack of ice, which forced them to return southwards. The highest latitude gained was 72° 51′, long. 163° 48′. The Herald tried a second time to push northwards in a more westerly direction, but again her progress was arrested, and she returned to Cape Lisburne on the 20th of August, reaching Kotzebue Sound on the 31st. There the Plover wintered, while the Herald returned to the coast of Mexico, arriving at Mazatlan on the 14th of November, 1849, almost simultaneously with the Nancy Dawson yacht, the gallant commander of which died at that place.

On this expedition, although the coast was carefully searched, and frequent communication held with the natives, yet no trace or tidings whatever of the missing vessels were obtained. The geographical discoveries made however are among the most important which have resulted from the various searching expeditions, for the southern extremity of the Polar Land, so long spoken of by the Russians, was discovered and fixed on the map. It was on the 17th of August, when in lat. 71° 20′ north, long. 175° 30′ west, that Captain Kellett landed on an almost inaccessible island of granite, named after the Herald, rising about 900 feet above the sea. Beyond this isle, to the west and north, an extensive high land was seen, "where the clouds rolled in numerous immense masses, occasionally leaving the very lofty peaks uncapped, where could be distinctly seen columns and pillars." The position of this land very nearly corresponds with that described by Admiral Wrangell, off Cape Yakan, and is no doubt connected with it, and probably the same as that said to have been reached by Andreyew in 1762, called Tikigen, and inhabited by a race named Kraïhaï.

The Plover, when off Wainwright Inlet (lat. 70° 20') and on the 25th of July, 1849, despatched an expedition consisting of four boats, commanded by Lieutenant Pullen, and having for its object to trace the Arctic coast of North America as far as the Mackenzie. Finding considerable difficulty in proceeding with the four boats, the two largest returned to Behring's Strait, whilst the others continued the voyage. After a perilous navigation of thirty-two days the latter arrived at the mouth of the river, having obtained no clue or intelligence of the missing expedition. The party went up the Mackenzie, some wintering at Fort Simpson, some on Great Bear Lake. In the following year Lieutenant Pullen resumed the coast search, tracing the shores from the mouth of the Mackenzie east as far as Cape Bathurst, from the 22nd of July to the 10th of August, 1850. He intended to push towards Banks Land, but being baffled in this attempt returned up the Mackenzie to his previous winter-quarters, and in the following year, by way of York Factory, to England.

No geographical discoveries were made by this branch

expedition, but a good deal of information respecting the country and its inhabitants was obtained. Lieutenant Hooper especially collected many words of the Eskimo language between Point Barrow and Cape Bathurst.

2. *Land Expedition under Sir John Richardson and Dr. Rae*, 1848 *and* 1849.—This party left England on the 25th of March, 1848, by the mail steamer for New York, and proceeding from Montreal in four boats to Cumberland House, and by the Methy Portage down the Mackenzie, they reached the sea on the 4th of August. The coast was searched east as far as Cape Krusenstern without obtaining any traces or tidings of the missing expedition. Having arrived at that promontory, the winter was felt to have set in with rigour, compelling the party to make the best of their way overland to their winter residence on Great Bear Lake. They set out on the 2nd of September towards that point, whence, after spending the winter, Sir John Richardson returned to England, while Dr. Rae in the summer of 1849 proceeded again to Cape Krusenstern, in order to cross thence to Wollaston Land, and to push on towards Banks Land. But all his attempts at effecting this project were baffled; the ice entirely barred the progress of his boat, and compelled him to abandon the enterprise.

In this expedition no traces were found; but a very valuable mass of information was collected by Sir John Richardson respecting the physical features of North America, particularly that portion visited by him, and given to the world in the narrative of his voyage.

3. *The Barrow's Strait Expedition, under Sir James C. Ross and Captain Bird*, 1848 *and* 1849.—This expedi-

tion, consisting of the Enterprise and Investigator, left England on the 12th of June, 1848, and reached Barrow's Strait late in August. The heavy ice did not permit the vessels to push beyond Leopold Island, and on the 11th of September they entered Leopold Harbour to winter. In the spring of 1849 sledge-parties were organized, the most important of which, that headed by Sir James Ross, traced the northern shore of North Somerset and its western shore as far as lat. 72° 38' north. He returned to the ships on the 23rd of June, his party being much worn out by fatigue. Sir James Ross resolved on examining Wellington Channel, but he was unable to move his ships out of their winter harbour until the 28th of August, and then his intentions were completely frustrated by the heavy ice. It was a matter of congratulation to be so fortunate, after great danger in the ice, to make their way homewards out of the pack. On the 29th of September, 1849, the expedition safely reached the Orkney Islands.

No traces or tidings of Sir John Franklin were found; a comparatively small extent of coast on the western side of North Somerset were all the geographical additions resulting from the voyage.

4. *Auxiliary Voyage to the Barrow's Strait Expedition, North Star*, 1849.—This vessel, under the command of Mr. J. Saunders, sailed from the Thames on the 26th of May, 1849, freighted with provisions for the missing Expedition, and with orders and supplies for that under Sir James Ross; she was to proceed at once to Lancaster Sound for that purpose, and, after the completion of this service, to examine the great sounds at the

head of Baffin's Bay. Her progress was very slow, and she only reached Melville Bay, in the northern part of Baffin's Bay, on the 29th of July, the place where vessels generally cross the latter over to Lancaster Sound. The North Star however was beset in an ice-field and drifted helplessly about. On the 29th of September, having been sixty-two days in the ice, without being able to reach either Lancaster Sound or the head of Baffin's Bay, she took up her winter-quarters in Wolstenholme Sound, a little to the north of Melville Bay, and it was not until the 1st of August, 1850, that she was able to leave her retreat. She reached Lancaster Sound, and saw and spoke most of the vessels of the various Government and private expeditions despatched thither; left provisions in Navy Board Inlet, at the entrance of Lancaster Sound, without making any of the vessels acquainted with the fact*; and returned home on the 9th of September, arriving at Spithead on the 28th of the same month.

Of all expeditions, none probably was so unfortunate as the North Star; she was prevented from carrying out any of her instructions, and from making any additions of moment to our geographical knowledge of the Arctic regions.

The first series of the searching expeditions, so well planned, fell far short of their proposed limits. Their principal result however was that they afforded negative evidence that the missing vessels could not have been near Barrow's Strait, Behring's Strait, nor any part of the American shores from Behring's Strait to the Copper-

* Sir Edward Belcher's squadron, looking for these stores, has nowhere found them.

mine River. Indeed, when it is considered that between the regions searched on North Somerset by Sir James Ross, and the American shores to the south-west, examined by Richardson and Rae, a region of only 450 miles of extent intervenes, there was scarcely any ground for supposing that Franklin could have been arrested in a lower latitude than Parry Group, without being able to find his way to some of the points visited by the searching expeditions. It might safely be asserted that Franklin would scarcely be found at a less distance from the American continent than three hundred miles, or five degrees of latitude.

Second Series of the Searching Expeditions.

These expeditions were despatched in 1850, and were on a still more extensive scale than the first, the basis of the plan remaining unaltered in the main. No less than six different expeditions, consisting of fourteen vessels, were sent forth to the icy regions, and all these, with the exception of the three Behring's Strait vessels, were accumulated upon Lancaster Sound and Barrow's Strait. Three of the expeditions were fitted out by Government and three by private means.

1. *The Behring's Strait Expedition, under Captains Collinson, M'Clure, Moore, and Kellett*, 1850, 1851, etc. —This expedition consisted of the Herald and Plover, to which were added the Enterprise and Investigator, employed in the previous expedition under Sir James Clark Ross. The latter two vessels sailed from Plymouth on the 20th of January, 1850. The Enterprise penetrated some distance to the north and east of Behring's

Strait, but found it impossible to get through the ice, and was consequently forced to return and pass the winter at Hongkong. She departed a second time in May, 1851, and the last accounts report her having quitted Port Clarence, in Behring's Strait, on the 10th of July, 1851, for the purpose of carrying on her explorations to the north-east.

The Investigator made her way to Point Barrow, to the westward of which she was last seen by the Plover on the 4th of August, 1850. She was then steering to the north, with a strong south-west wind, and had an open sea ahead for some distance. Captain M'Clure's intention was to pass on to the eastward as far as Cape Bathurst, where he purposed wintering. From that point he would endeavour, in the following summer, to make the best of his way north-east to Banks Land, and in a letter dated the 20th of July, 1850, he states, "No alarm need be felt should the Investigator not be heard of until 1854."

The Herald, under Captain Kellett, departed from the west coast of Mexico for Behring's Strait in April, 1850, to make another start for the north, but met with less success than in the previous voyage, and in the autumn of that year she bade adieu to the Arctic regions, arriving at Spithead in June, 1851.

The Plover, under Commander Moore, was refitted from the Herald, and stationed, as a reserve or store ship to the Enterprise and Investigator, at Port Clarence, Behring's Strait, where she was to stay until the autumn of 1853. In 1851, a further addition of stores, provisions, clothing, and fuel was sent to the Plover, completing her to December, 1853, with an additional supply of six months' provisions and warm clothing for sixty men. These stores were taken up by the Dædalus under Captain Wellesley, from Valparaiso. Commander R. Maguire left England on the 2nd of February, 1852, to supersede Commander Moore, of the Plover, and to take up further stores. Up to the 7th of September, 1852, no intelligence of any traces of Sir John Franklin had been received at Port Clarence, and no communication respecting the progress of the Enterprise and Investigator under Collinson and M'Clure. Upwards of four years' endeavours and many attempts from that direction have therefore been fruitless. No geographical discoveries were made in those regions in the years 1850 and 1851.

The Barrow's Strait Expeditions.

2. *Captain Penny's Expedition,* 1850 *and* 1851.—Of the five Barrow's Strait expeditions this was the first that left the British shores. The difficulties of navigation in Baffin's Bay, and especially in the northern portion from Melville Bay to Lancaster Sound, having become apparent by the previous expeditions, the Admiralty, in their desire to render the expeditions this time as complete and effective as possible, decided on adding to the power of the navy the experience of a whaling captain. Accordingly, they appointed Captain Penny—who had had much experience in the icy seas, having been engaged in the whaling trade since his twelfth year—to the command of two vessels, in addition to the great expedition under Captain Austin. These vessels, named the Lady Franklin and the Sophia, sailed from Aberdeen on the

13th of April, 1850, the command of the Sophia having been entrusted to Mr. Stewart. It was intended, previous to entering Lancaster Sound, to examine Jones's Sound, but the accumulation of ice prevented it. Captain Penny now shaped his course towards Wellington Channel, at the entrance of which he arrived on the 24th of August. Having heard of the traces found by Captain Ommanney at Cape Riley and Beechey Island on the 23rd of August, he landed on the eastern side of Wellington Channel, with the view of examining those parts more closely than had been done before. On the 27th of August unquestionable traces of Sir John Franklin were discovered on Beechey Island, and it was clearly ascertained that that spot was the site of his winter-quarters in 1845–1846; but, notwithstanding a most careful search in every direction, no written document could be found. In Captain Penny's opinion the traces showed marks of a hasty departure on the part of Sir John Franklin, who—he further believed—had gone up Wellington Channel on the sudden opening of the ice. Captain Penny intended following up that channel, but was frustrated by its being blocked up with old land-ice. On the 9th of September he directed his course westward; but the ice became packed, and he was forced, on the 12th of September, to take up his winter-quarters in Assistance Bay, situated near the south-western extremity of Wellington Channel. The winter having passed, Captain Penny's sledge-excursions to the north were commenced on the 13th of April, 1851. At the point where Wellington Channel trends to the west, where it is interrupted by several islands and takes the name of Queen Victoria Channel, Captain Penny's progress was arrested by open water, extending twenty-five miles to the west, with decayed ice, and a water-sky to the north. Shortness of provisions forced the various travelling parties to return to the south, after having performed a distance equal to 2000 miles. Having failed to obtain from Captain Austin's squadron one of the steamers for the purpose of following up his discovery of the open water beyond Wellington Channel, Captain Penny shaped his course homewards on the 12th of August, where he arrived about the middle of September, 1851.

Whether Captain Penny's voyage is considered with reference to discoveries made in connection with the missing vessels, or to discoveries in a geographical point of view, or whether the comparatively small expenses of the voyage, and the short time in which it was accomplished (only eighteen months), be taken into account, it has been by far the most successful and important of all the searching expeditions that have till now been completed. This opinion must have prevailed in the minds of the authorities when subsequently they determined to concentrate their energies in following up the discoveries of Captain Penny,—unfortunately however not until a year had elapsed. Penny's discoveries form as yet our only means for conjecturing with some degree of probability which route from Barrow's Strait Sir John Franklin may have taken. In a geographical point of view they prove the existence of a sea of considerable extent and depth beyond Wellington Channel, and in close contiguity with the labyrinthic region which has hitherto frustrated all attempts at effecting the so-called "North-west Passage." The discoveries also indicate that that sea leads into either the Siberian or the American Polar Sea,—probably into the latter, as some pieces of drift-wood of American origin are said to have been found.

3. *Captain Austin's Expedition*, 1850 *and* 1851.—This expedition, consisting of the ships Resolute and Assistance, and the screw-steamers Pioneer and Intrepid, commanded by Captains Austin and Ommanney and Lieutenants Osborn and Cator, was, in respect to equipment, the most complete and effective that had ever left the British shores for the Arctic seas. A transport-ship was despatched in advance as far as Whalefish Islands, and the squadron itself departed in the beginning of May, 1850. On the 15th of August the vessels parted company off Cape Dudley Digges, the plan being that the Resolute and Pioneer should examine the south shores of Lancaster Sound, and the Assistance and Intrepid its north shores. Captain Ommanney, in the Intrepid, reached Cape Riley and Beechey Island on the 23rd of August, and had the good fortune to be the first to find positive traces, at both places, of the missing expedition. Captain Austin, in the Resolute, did not get to those places until the 28th, when he joined Captain Penny in the examination of the remains of Sir John Franklin's winter-quarters, discovered by the latter. Being baffled in the attempt to push up Wellington Channel, he changed his course towards the west. But in spite of all endeavours very little advance could be made, and Captain Austin was soon obliged to relinquish

the effort. He took up his winter-quarters, on the 13th of September, at Griffith Island, a little to the west of Assistance Bay,—those of Captain Penny. Several travelling parties were despatched as late as the 2nd of October, but they were compelled soon to return. The winter was passed in good health and spirits, sledge-parties on an extensive scale being organized towards the spring. These were all despatched in a westerly direction, to explore the regions surrounding the winter-quarters in a semicircle, from north to south through west. By far the greater number started on the 15th of April, 1851, consisting of fourteen sledges and one hundred and four officers and men. The different parties returned between the 27th of April and the 4th of July, with but few casualties, although having been out from six to eighty days, and having travelled from forty-four to seven hundred and sixty miles. The greatest distance, in a direct line, was travelled by Lieutenant M'Clintock, who reached one of the western points of Melville Island, distant from the winter-quarters three hundred and fifty miles, which it took eighty days, going and returning, to accomplish. No trace whatever of Sir John Franklin having been found by any of the sledge-parties, Captain Austin concluded that the missing expedition had not been to the southward and westward of Wellington Channel. As soon as Captain Austin was released from his winter-quarters, on the 12th of August, he left Barrow's Strait, passed the entrance of Wellington Channel, and shaped his course out of Lancaster Sound, with the intention of examining Jones's Sound, but after having entered it a little way, a barrier of ice arrested further progress. No traces were there found, and on the 6th of September the expedition proceeded to make the best of its way out of Baffin's Bay, passed Cape Farewell on the 16th, and arrived at Aberdeen on the 26th of the same month.

In this expedition the first traces of the missing vessels were found. With regard to geographical discoveries, but slight additions were made, when considering the magnitude and resources of that expedition, as well as the great exertions of the sledge-parties over the ice, a considerable part of the coast-line traced by the latter having already been discovered by Sir Edward Parry thirty-two years previously.

4. *Expedition under Sir John Ross*, 1850 *and* 1851.— While the three preceding expeditions were fitted out by the Government, the other three were effected by private means. The Arctic veteran, Sir John Ross, volunteered his services to proceed in the search of Franklin; the region however to which his proposal was directed being already provided for by the expedition under Captain Austin, the Admiralty declined his offer. Signally persistent in his endeavours, he prevailed upon the Hudson's Bay Company and the public to enable him, by subscription, to realize his scheme. Accordingly Sir John Ross, accompanied by Commander Phillips, left the west of Scotland on the 23rd of May, 1850, in the Felix, accompanied by the Mary, as a tender. He arrived at Beechey Island on the 27th of August, and inspected the traces of the winter-quarters discovered by Captain Penny's expedition. The Felix did not get across the Wellington Channel till the 9th of September,

and took up winter-quarters in Assistance Bay on the 12th, simultaneously with Captain Penny. Commander Phillips made an excursion during the summer of 1851 on Cornwallis Land, a laborious task, owing to the advanced period of the season. On the 12th of August, 1851, having been released from his winter-quarters, Sir John Ross, seeing no prospect of being able to get up Wellington Channel, commenced his homeward voyage, passed Godhaven on the 30th of August, and arrived on the west coast of Scotland on the 25th of September, 1851.

This expedition was attended with no results, either as to the missing vessels or to geographical discoveries. But a cruel report, which for a time increased the anxiety of the public mind, was got up by an Eskimo, one Adam Beck, who served as interpreter to the ships. When off Cape York, in the northern part of Baffin's Bay, Sir John Ross held communication with five poor harmless wretches of Eskimos, who made a communication which was interpreted in this meaning, "that two ships had been destroyed by fire in Wolstenholme Sound, and their crews massacred by the Eskimos." It happened that chance had collected the whole force of the searching squadrons near this point, so that the startling report could be deliberated upon. It was found to be without any foundation whatever, and, in the opinion of those best qualified to judge, "so preposterous and so repulsive to common sense that one cannot help smiling, in spite of the painful feeling which is aroused by allusion to such an atrocious deed." Captain Inglefield, in his voyage up Baffin's Bay, moreover, has set the question finally at rest by visiting and closely examining the very place where the massacre was alleged to have occurred.

5. *The United States Expedition*, 1850 *and* 1851.—
In the spring of 1849 Lady Franklin made a touching appeal to the American nation, which was generously responded to by a noble-hearted citizen of New York, Mr. Henry Grinnell, who stepped forward, and at his expense fitted out and despatched two ships to the Arctic regions. These two ships, the Advance and Rescue, left New York on the 25th of May, 1850, under the command of Lieutenant De Haven, who was instructed to proceed first to Wellington Channel and Cape Walker. They arrived at Beechey Island just at the time when Captain Penny's expedition had discovered Franklin's winter-quarters. Their movements thence were much like those of the other expeditions; baffled in their attempt to get up Wellington Channel, they made their way out of it to proceed in the direction towards Cape Walker. On the 10th of September the American vessels, with the entire searching squadron, were concentrated about eight miles south of Griffith's Island, the furthest westing attained by the former. While the English vessels now took up their winter-quarters, the American commander, though he was provisioned for three years, decided on proceeding homewards. His vessels however became imbedded in pack-ice, opposite Wellington Channel, and were helplessly drifting during the ensuing winter through Lancaster Sound and along Baffin's Bay, beyond Cape Walsingham, where, after much exposure, trial, and danger, they were at last liberated, on the 10th of June, 1851. The commander, nothing daunted, determined

to return northward, but was unable to reach beyond Melville Bay, whence he once more steered for New York, where he arrived on the 30th of September, 1851.

In one respect this is the most extraordinary of all searching expeditions, namely, in its being exposed to the drifting in the ice from the middle of September, 1850, to the middle of June, 1851, an occurrence altogether unprecedented. Such were the dangers of the situation, that the men had their knapsacks and sleighs ready, in order to save themselves over the ice should their vessels be crushed. But although the vessels were thus imprisoned for no less than nine months, during the worst part of the year, and drifted a distance of upwards of a thousand miles,—and though they were lifted up by the stern more than six feet, they escaped but little damaged, and the expedition returned without the loss of a single man, though all had been attacked by the scurvy. The case of these two vessels, of only 144 and 91 tons, is alone sufficient to inspire us with the hope that those of Franklin would—at all events—be not so easily destroyed by the ice.

6. *Captain Forsyth's Voyage*, 1850.—This was a fifth expedition to the same region as the preceding four. It was thought that Regent Inlet ought to be minutely searched, although this sea is so near Baffin's Bay that even whalers occasionally descend it to a considerable distance south. Accordingly the Prince Albert, a clipper of about 90 tons, under Captain Forsyth, left England on the 5th of June, 1850, on that special service, which cost nearly £4000, the greater part of which was contributed by Lady Franklin, the rest by public sub-

scription. Captain Forsyth went along the western side of Regent Inlet as far as Fury Point, where the ice compelled him to return. Before however steering homewards he sailed as far as Wellington Channel, where he met the other expeditions. He arrived at Aberdeen on the 22nd of October, 1850, after an absence of about four months.

Captain Forsyth brought the first news of the discovery of the traces on Beechey Island to England, which excited great interest.

Third Series of the Searching Expeditions.

This series consists of expeditions despatched in the years 1851 and 1852. Though likewise accumulated upon the American side, they were not confined to one particular spot, as were the greater number of the preceding ones. Their chief result, as far as is known at present, is that they have more fully confirmed the opinion that Sir John Franklin must have penetrated to a considerable distance beyond the known Polar regions of America, towards Behring's Strait and the Siberian shores.

1. *Dr. Rae's Journey to Wollaston and Victoria Lands,* 1851.—Dr. Rae, having been unsuccessful in his attempts in the summer of 1848 and 1849, to reach Wollaston Land in a boat, determined on a journey over the ice in sledges in the spring of 1851. Leaving Fort Confidence, on Great Bear Lake, on the 26th of April, accompanied by four men, with three sledges drawn by dogs, and a small sledge drawn by the men, he reached the coast near the mouth of the Coppermine River on

the 2nd of May; thence he crossed, in three days, over the ice to the southernmost point of Wollaston Land, and tracing from that point the coast to the east as far as 110° of longitude, and to the north-west as far as long. 117° 17′, he returned to his starting-point on the coast on the 4th of June. On the 5th of July he departed again, but this time in boats, to explore Victoria Land. Keeping along the northern shores of the American continent as far as Cape Alexander, and thence crossing over to Victoria Land on the 27th of the same month, he traced the coast to the east and then north, reached the latitude of 70° 14′, his furthest point, on the 13th of August, and came back to the Coppermine River on the 29th of August.

Though no traces of Sir John Franklin were found by this expedition, yet, in a geographical point of view, it is of some interest, as a considerable extent of new coast, connecting Wollaston and Victoria Lands, was discovered, which are probably separated from Banks Land and Prince of Wales Land by a channel, through which the drift-wood makes its way to the eastern side of Victoria Land.

2. *Mr. Kennedy's Voyage*, 1851 *and* 1852.—On the 22nd of May, 1851, the Prince Albert was again despatched to continue the search in Prince Regent Inlet, this time under the command of Mr. Kennedy, accompanied by Lieutenant Bellot, of the French navy. In the first year Mr. Kennedy did not get further than Batty Bay, on the western side of Prince Regent Inlet, where he took up his winter-quarters. Mr. Kennedy and his party made excursions to Fury Beach, in the

south, as early as January, 1852, with no other light than that of the moon, and thence started, on the 29th of March, with the intention of exploring Regent Inlet to its southern extremity. But discovering at Brentford Bay a channel trending to the west through North Somerset, they followed it, crossed over to Prince of Wales Land, and advanced in a westerly and then northerly direction as far as Ommanney Bay, whence they shaped their route towards Cape Walker. Shortness of provision compelled them to return from that point to Port Leopold, where they arrived on the 5th of May. On the following day Mr. Kennedy proceeded to Beechey Island in the Prince Albert, and having there received communications from the North Star, one of the vessels of Sir E. Belcher's squadron, he shaped his course homewards, and arrived at Aberdeen on the 7th of October, 1852.

On this voyage no traces of Sir John Franklin were found. A small extent of new coast however was discovered, and it was also ascertained that North Somerset is an island, divided from Boothia Felix by a narrow channel, which has been called Bellot's Strait.

3. *Captain Inglefield's Voyage*, 1852.—On the 6th of July, 1852, Captain Inglefield sailed from the Thames in the screw-steamer Isabel, for the purpose of examining the head of Baffin's Bay, and its western shores as far as Labrador. He reached Wolstenholme Sound, Greenland, on the 23rd of August, which he closely searched, and finally determined that there was no truth in Adam Beck's story. From the 25th of August to the 1st of September Captain Inglefield explored the most northern por-

tion of Baffin's Bay, from Whale Sound to Jones Sound, but finding no traces whatever of the missing expedition, he abandoned a further search in that direction, and steered for Beechey Island, where he received communications from Sir Edward Belcher's expedition, after which he examined the western shores of Baffin's Bay, from lat. $72\frac{1}{2}°$ to $71°$, until, on the 14th of October, the lateness of the season forced him to relinquish a more extended search, and direct the ship's head homewards. He arrived at Peterhead on the 10th of November, exactly four months from the day he sailed.

This, of all the terminated searching expeditions the last, was, like the greater number of the previous ones, unsuccessful in ascertaining the fate of the missing vessels or finding any traces of them. In a geographical point of view the results of this voyage are highly interesting; they establish, among other features, the existence of an extensive sea beyond and in connection with what has been hitherto called the "head" of Baffin's Bay, and into which Whale Sound and Smith Sound are the chief entrances. There are however many reasons for believing that this sea is neither connected with the great Polar Sea, generally called the "Polar Basin," nor that beyond Wellington Channel. Captain Inglefield also attained the latitude of $78° 35'$, the highest ever reached on the American side of the Arctic regions, but which falls far short of those at all times attainable on the opposite side, where Sir Edward Parry, in the great Polar Sea to the north of Spitzbergen, reached the latitude of $82° 45'$, and probably $83°$, in small *open boats*.

Searching Expeditions remaining in the Arctic Regions.

1. *The Behring's Strait Expedition.*—It has already been seen in the foregoing that the Investigator, under Commander M'Clure, had pushed on to the north of Behring's Strait, and was last seen by the Plover near Point Barrow, on the 4th of August, 1850. Commander M'Clure's intention was to pass on to the eastward for Cape Bathurst, where he purposed wintering. From that point he would endeavour in the following summer to make the best of his way north-east to Banks' Land.

The Enterprise, under Captain Collinson, left Port Clarence in Behring's Strait on the 10th of July, 1851, for the purpose of proceeding also in a north-easterly direction. Neither this nor the former vessels have been heard of since. As a relief and store ship the Plover, under Commander Maguire, is stationed in Behring's Strait, with instructions to advance to Point Barrow, or beyond; and the Rattlesnake, Commander H. Trollope, has been directed to co-operate with these vessels.

2. *The Barrow's Strait Expedition, under Sir Edward Belcher.*—This is the most extensive expedition as yet despatched in the search, consisting of five vessels, the Assistance, Resolute, North Star, Pioneer, and Intrepid. On the 21st of April, 1851, these vessels sailed from England direct for Wellington Channel, Beechey Island, at its entrance, being intended as the head-quarters. The despatches brought home by Captain Inglefield made us acquainted with the progress of this expedition up to the 7th of September last. On the 11th of August Sir Edward Belcher had reached Beechey Island, and soon

after he proceeded in the Assistance and tender up Wellington Channel, while Captain Kellett with the Resolute and tender went towards Melville Island, where the latter was to deposit provisions for the use of Captain Collinson and Commander M'Clure, who are supposed to have reached that island. The North Star remained at Beechey Island as a depôt store-ship.

Conclusion.

Such are the noble efforts which have hitherto been made to rescue Sir John Franklin and his companions. But now that nearly eight years have elapsed without tidings of them, even the most sanguine must begin to feel anxiety about their safety. If, as is very probable, they have not perished from the want of food, but have been eking out an existence by means of certain Arctic animals, their number must have greatly diminished, and those who may still be alive would doubtless, from their long confinement and severe trials, have their strength so reduced as to be unable to extricate themselves from their prison, or make much locomotive progress. In any efforts therefore that may yet be made for their relief, *time* should form a chief point of consideration, as every week may cut off some from the number yet living. It is now satisfactorily established that they must be looked for far beyond the American shores,—indeed far beyond Melville Island,—namely, opposite the shores of Siberia, in a region extending from the land discovered by Captain Kellett to the eightieth parallel, and from the meridian of Point Barrow on the American side to that of the Kolyma on the Asiatic. This is just the region which has been, and is still, altogether unprovided for in the search, except by the Assistance and her tender under Sir Edward Belcher, who has gone up Wellington Channel, where most probably the missing expedition has preceded him. But although Sir Edward Belcher found an unusually open season, enabling him to push his way up that channel, it is not very likely, considering the time that would be lost in looking for traces, that he would overtake Franklin in less than three years by following him on a route which has occupied the latter six years. For it must be remembered that Sir John Franklin in 1846 was in exactly the same position as Sir Edward Belcher now is, if he then did get up Wellington Channel; and surely his expedition was as effective as that of the latter, and his crew not inferior.

While it is evident that the relief expeditions hitherto have been too much concentrated on one side of the Arctic regions—in summer, 1850, no less than eleven vessels were accumulated in one spot—it is not too much to say that the search on the track of the missing vessels has only now commenced, by Sir Edward Belcher's having sailed up Wellington Channel.

The rest of the searching vessels at present in the Arctic regions, the Investigator and Enterprise, as well as those under Captain Kellett, are only directed to Banks Land and Melville Island, a region probably far away from Sir John Franklin's position. "The fearlessness and tameness of the animals in Melville Island," says Lieutenant M'Clintock—the best authority on this point—"was almost in itself a convincing proof that our countrymen had not been there;" and indeed, it may be added, not anywhere within five hundred miles. If Sir John Franklin had wished to retreat to any known region on the American side, nothing could surely have hindered him from doing so. It is well known that sledge parties have travelled distances of nearly one thousand miles during one winter, and Sir John Ross, after four years' imprisonment in the ice, and with a force of only twenty-four men, greatly reduced by hardships and trials, travelled at least five hundred miles, partly by land and partly by water, from the point where he abandoned his vessel to that where he was released.

The fact that no less than fifteen expeditions, consisting of thirty vessels besides the boats, had failed in their main object, prompted me a short time back to draw attention to a portion of the Arctic regions which has remained entirely neglected, and to suggest a plan of search through the Spitzbergen Sea, that great ocean between Spitzbergen and Novaya Zemlya. I adduced reasons to show that that sea would probably offer the best route, and demonstrated that its exploration was a most important desideratum in a commercial and geographical point of view. As my plan is already before the public*, it is unnecessary to detail it here. If

* The various communications in connection with my plan, an outline of which was first submitted to the public in the 'Athenæum' of the 17th of January, 1852, are as follows:—

1. The Search for Franklin. Illustrated by a Polar Chart. London, Longmans. (May 15, 1852.)

2. Notes on the Distribution of Animals available as Food in the Arctic Regions. (Journal of the Royal Geographical Society of London, 1852, vol. xxii.)

3. Sir John Franklin, the Navigableness of the Spitzbergen Sea, and the Whale-fisheries in the Arctic Regions. (A paper read at the

the searching operations are to be based on a comprehensive and exhaustive system, my scheme cannot possibly be left unconsidered and neglected. The commercial interests of the country likewise demand an early exploration of the region to which I have drawn attention, and science looks eagerly forward to the solution of one of the most interesting of geographical problems. Moreover, when it is considered that five years' increasing efforts from one side have hitherto proved complete failures, the other side, so promising as regards an easy and speedy access with the aid of steam, should no longer be neglected. As yet the missing voyagers may not all have perished, but a further delay of one or two years may not leave one of them to tell the woeful tale of their sufferings, and may repeat the fearful case of Sir Hugh Willoughby's Expedition, where the stiff and frozen corpses only were found on the dreary shores of the Arctic regions.

A. P.

meeting of the Royal Geographical Society, November 8, 1852. See abstracts in the 'Times,' November 12, and 'Athenæum,' November 13, 1852.)

4. On the Whale-fisheries in the Arctic Regions. ('Times,' November 8 and 11, 1852.)

5. Baffin's Bay and the Polar Basin. ('Athenæum,' December 11, 1852.)

6. Letter addressed to the Lords Commissioners of the Admiralty, dated November 29, 1852. (Parliamentary Papers, 'Arctic Expeditions,' ordered by the House of Commons to be printed, December, 1852.)

CHAPTER XIII.

Continuation of the voyage of the Herald—Honolulu—King Kamehameha's Levee—Commencement of our homeward voyage—Arrival in Hongkong—Visit to Canton.

CONSIDERABLE improvements had been made in Honolulu since our last visit: a market-hall had been built, an aqueduct to supply shipping with water from the mountains had been constructed, and a great many private houses had been added to the town. The harbour was crowded with vessels, and the streets enlivened by vast numbers of strangers, who were either on their way to California or had returned from that country. Trade was in the most flourishing condition, and fresh cargoes of goods arrived daily from China, Australia, North America, and Europe; indeed signs of prosperity and progress were everywhere visible. Agriculture had also received its due share of attention, and an association had been instituted under the title of the Royal Agricultural Society of the Hawaiian Islands. The King had become the patron, and in August last, when the Society was formed, delegates from the different islands assembled in Honolulu, each bringing the various productions of the group, and thus constituting, though on a diminutive scale, the first agricultural exhibition ever witnessed in Polynesia. The young society displays great activity: a volume of its Transactions has appeared, funds have been liberally subscribed, and vessels have been sent to China in order to introduce labourers.

During our stay King Kamehameha held a drawing-room, at which Captain Kellett and several of our officers were presented. Mr. Whiffin, who formed one of the party, has written an interesting account of the ceremony, which, although the style differs materially from that adopted in this work, I shall without hesitation submit to the reader:—

"'Who is for the levee?' shouted the boisterous midshipman of the morning watch, as he rattled down the after-ladder into the steerage, where the majority of his messmates were trying, by the application of cold water and the friction of coarse towels, to restore to their cheeks that freshness which bad diet and long service in the tropics had destroyed.

"'What levee?' inquired one of them.

"'Why *the* levee,' rejoined the first. 'The Captain has sent off word that the King holds a drawing-room to-day, and that any of the officers who wish to be presented, must be on shore at the Consul's in full dress at half-past two.'

"'I would hardly go on deck to see the King; full dress indeed! pshaw; why he only wore a clout a few years ago, and the ladies of the court would n't have blushed much had he been without even that unassuming covering.'

"This is a specimen of the conversation which prevailed in our berth after his Hawaiian Majesty's pleasure had been made known. Fortunately all were not of the gentleman's opinion who communicated the intelligence, and many, myself among the number, fancied that it might be an interesting spectacle to witness how a people but lately emerged from barbarism would conduct the pompous ceremonies of a regal court; even, we argued, should it prove a farce, the laugh which we should subsequently have, would fully compensate for the trouble of going there.

"Our party was soon completed. After breakfast, eight or nine of our officers ordered their costly state garments to be released from the musty obscurity in which, since we departed from Guaymas, they had been buried, while I, leaving most of them to dress at their leisure on board, hastened on shore, with a small boy and a large parcel, to finish my extensive toilet. On reaching the lounge—a small tenement hired by our mess as being more convenient than the hotel for dressing and refreshing—I found it was locked, and vainly despatched several messengers around the town in quest of the native youth charged with the key and the care of the house; but he came not, so I philosophically pocketed my vexation, and, much to the amusement of the inmates, retired into an adjacent hut to wash, and assume the habiliments proper for the occasion.

"The hour appointed had passed by some minutes before my arrival at the house of our Consul, General Miller, where my disordered, bewildered, and perspiring condition astonished and amused the Captain and officers already seated there. Luckily a conversation succeeded, sufficiently long to allow me to cool and recover breath before starting.

"The palace is not more than three hundred yards from the General's house, but considering the stately manner in which we progressed, the walk occupied us fully ten minutes. A small look-out house is erected over the palace gates, which on this occasion was used to give warning of our approach; the sentries on either side performed the usual 'click click' salutation with their muskets as we passed through, while a company of Hawaiian infantry drawn up in the square went through a similar manœuvre on our ascending the steps.

"We were received in the porch by a number of officials, of whom some were white and the others the native chiefs, who politely escorted us into the spacious reception-room where King Kamehameha and his suite were assembled. The King was plainly dressed in a blue coat and white waistcoat, with a broad red riband extending diagonally across his chest; he was seated in a carved oaken chair, or throne, slightly elevated above the floor, cushioned and backed with red velvet; on his right was George Young, the prime minister, and the descendant of the celebrated John Young, at first the prisoner, and subsequently the firm and tried friend of the first Kamehameha, with whose history his name is closely interwoven. Mr. Armstrong, the Minister of Education, occupied his Majesty's left, and officiated as interpreter; while the rest of the seats on that side of the room were filled by the principal native chiefs, men of immense proportions, whose fine figures well became the handsome uniforms in which they were attired.

"How different were the ideas and feelings with which they welcomed us, to those with which they received the gallant Cook and his officers but seventy years before; in whose person they fancied they recognized their dreaded and long absent god Lono, and whom they would have accordingly killed, had they not considered it more politic to propitiate! That generation has scarcely passed away, and we find the Hawaiians in the midst of civilized splendour and commerce, and worshiping the same God as ourselves.

"As the Consul approached, the King rose from his chair, and, after an exchange of greetings, the business of the day was at once commenced by Captain Kellett being presented to him. His Majesty received him with an easy, graceful air, and recognized in him an old acquaintance. All of us who, until now, had been remaining in the background, were each in turn presented, according to his rank. Kamehameha did not however honour any of us with any little exchange of sentiment; we merely passed close by him from one side of the room to the other, pausing, when we got him transit, to make our most stately bow: he acknowledged our salutations in a modest easy way, which the most accomplished courtier could not have surpassed. Five or six gentlemen of different nations were next presented by the Consuls for their respective Governments; this completed the formal part of the ceremony. The King then sat down, and motioned all in the room to follow his example.

"A lively conversation, in couples, ensued throughout the room; the King and Captain Kellett had a long talk through the medium of Mr. Armstrong, whose assistance, from all I can hear, was little needed, the King being well acquainted with both the French and English languages. Great trouble has been taken by the missionaries in his education, and his former tutors still possess a considerable ascendency over him. From his looks I should judge him to be a man about thirty-five, powerfully built, with a good-humoured, interesting, though certainly not a handsome, countenance. In height he does not nearly equal the average stature of the other chiefs, who are mostly upwards of six feet. He appears to have but little love or aptitude for business, and is very much under the control of his counsellors, the majority of whom are seceders from the American Mission. Occasionally, the extreme moral restraint in which they hold him becomes intolerable, and he then breaks out, leaves the palace, repeals the pledges previously taken to abstain from strong drinks, and in one of his small country cottages engages in all kinds of unholy and immoral practices. One of these naughty freaks immediately preceded our visit, and the ministry had need of their greatest address to get him to return to the paths of virtue, or even to take any part in this day's proceedings.

"To the politeness of Mr. Bateman, an English gentleman filling the office of Attorney-General, I am indebted for the relation of many little incidents. By having the good fortune to be seated next to him, I was also made acquainted with the names of the principal chiefs and personages present, of whose identity I should otherwise have been ignorant.

"The room in which we were seated was a large square

apartment, stylishly furnished and richly carpeted; the walls were neatly embellished with gold, and were hung around with portraits of individuals connected with the history of the Hawaiian Islands subsequent to their civilization; among the rest I noticed George III., Louis Philippe, and Admiral Thomas; the latter especially was beautifully executed. Altogether the decorations were appropriate, modest, and consistent.

"About a quarter of an hour was pleasantly passed in chatting, and the King then making a motion to withdraw, we all retired into the adjacent chamber to register our names and inspect a piece of furniture intended as a present for her Britannic Majesty; this was a circular table, elegantly designed, and made from indigenous woods, principally of the Koa (*Acacia heterophylla*, Willd.); in the centre were inlaid the royal arms, well developed with the native woods of the appropriate colours.

"This apartment, though not so extensive as the former, was furnished with equal taste. On one of its walls I was attracted by the portrait of the 'Egbert of the Sandwich Islands'—the good, shrewd, and intrepid Kamehameha I., to whose policy and determination is imputed the sudden change of this people from a state of barbarism to civilization. The painting is roughly done. The King is represented in red waistcoat and shirt-sleeves; his face is tattooed, and his hair grey. The portrait must have been executed but a short time prior to his demise; it is the same from which Jervis has copied his engraving in the 'History of the Sandwich Islands,' where, speaking of him in his more vigorous days, he styles him 'in form and stature a herculean savage, in abilities and character a man that any country might have been proud to acknowledge.'

"While the rest of the officers were taking leave of the chiefs, one of the gentlemen afforded me a peep at the two small cottages at the back of the palace, in which the King and Queen separately reside; in these small places they spend most of their time in a very humble style, eating their *poi* and fish, as in days of yore. A billiard-room is built near the palace, to put a stop to the derogatory practice of royalty having resort to the hotel tables for that amusement. Of the exterior of these buildings there is nothing to remark, further than their being plain, substantially built, and well adapted to the purpose for which they were designed.

"The same guard presented their arms as we left the palace-yard; the words of command were given in English by one of the chiefs—our old friend Captain Rio, who had charge of the troop; since our last meeting him however at the bowling alley he had gone through an entire mutation in his apparel, his usual sombre dress being now replaced by a splendid scarlet uniform, similar to that of a captain in one of our line regiments, though the bucket-like head-covering worn by most of our infantry officers under the rank of field-officer was in him eclipsed by a smart cocked hat and plume, which on recognizing us he gracefully lifted.

"The afternoon was far advanced by the time we got back to the Consul's house, where Captain Kellett and some of us returned to partake of a slight refreshment preparatory to changing our dresses for riding. I felt much pleased with my morning's visit, and gratified with the unassuming way in which the entire ceremony had been conducted; the King had performed his part in a modest, dignified manner, without the least approach to display. I left the ship fully prepared for something comic; I came away convinced that I had seen but little which a sensible observer would ridicule.

"The position which the King now holds is certainly a high one, and with his present title people in general would infer that he had arrogantly adopted it, and assumed an authority, in imitation of our European monarchs; but it is not equal in actual importance to that of the rulers of the various islands prior to Cook's visit. No greater despots could have existed than those who ruled this group at the conclusion of the last century, in whose shadow it was sacrilege, and almost certain death, for a plebeian to tread. However the condition of the people may have been improved by their social intercourse with civilized nations, the awe and reverence they entertained for their King and aristocracy has certainly diminished."

On the 30th of October, 1850, the Herald fairly commenced her homeward voyage by bidding adieu to the Hawaiian Islands, shaping her course towards China. Wafted along by the north-west trade-wind, she arrived, on the 19th of November, in sight of the Island of Assumption, passed Formosa and the Bashee Group, and, after experiencing in the neighbourhood of the latter a series of severe gales from north-north-west, reached on the last of November (or rather 1st of December, for she had lost a day), the harbour of Victoria, Hongkong.

Several of us went once to Cowloon, on the mainland, in the Chinese territory, where a great part of the vegetables consumed in Victoria, and *Bœhmeria nivea*, for making grass-cloth, are grown. It is now universally regretted that the little peninsula of Cowloon was not selected for the British settlement, in preference to the unhealthy locality in which the present town of Victoria is built, for after all the enormous expense to which the Government has been subjected in order to carry out the great public works, drainage, canals, bridges, etc., the salubrity of Hongkong is but slightly improved, and the annual mortality continues to be considerable.

The view from Victoria Peak, a mountain nearly 2000 feet high, is beautiful, and amply repays the exertions even of him who ascends it merely for the sake of the surrounding scenery. The spectator may discover more than thirty islands, and a vast number of Chinese and European ships; he has a complete panorama of the town of Victoria, its magnificent edifices, roads, bridges, canals, and other public works which have been constructed since the occupation. The peak itself, as well as the whole ridge of the Hongkong mountains, is destitute of woody plants; but on the slopes, in the little groves and valleys, a mass of shrubs, chiefly evergreens and a luxuriant herbage, are met with. In some of the rivulets of the mountain I found a number of gold-fishes (*Cyprinus auratus*, Linn.); several of them were safely carried down to the town and deposited in a jar.

In the evening of the 2nd of December there was a meeting of the China branch of the Royal Asiatic Society, when the secretary read a paper by Dr. H. F. Hance, advocating the establishment of a botanical garden. It appears to be the general wish that such an institution should effect a twofold object—be useful to science and serve as a public promenade. Yet such is the peculiarity of the ground and climate that great difficulty will be experienced in choosing an appropriate place. If a situation unprotected from the wind is selected, a single typhoon may destroy within a few hours the most valuable collection; and a sheltered position, adapted for a botanical garden, is hardly to be found in the vicinity of the town. Little hope remains therefore of seeing both objects accomplished; but, as has been observed, the advancement of science should be the primary, and promenading the secondary, aim of the institution.

Being desirous of visiting Canton, I started, accompanied by Mr. John Anderson, midshipman, on the morning of the 11th of December, in a river steamer. Our voyage was first through a group of islands, and then up the river, passing the town of Whampoa. The high state of cultivation, the number of villages, the tall pagodas, the gorgeous temples, the great mass of ships, and the thousands of boats loaded with human beings, are truly worth seeing, and only to be met with in China. If a thoroughfare in the city of London is called crowded, I am actually at a loss what term to apply to the mass of boats and people seen at Canton: it is almost beyond belief. We reached our destination towards the evening, and were kindly received by Mr. W. Pustau, a German merchant, whose establishment at Victoria had already been placed at my disposal, and who here gave another proof of his hospitality.

Foreigners are peculiarly situated at Canton. They are only allowed to enter the suburbs: the actual city is not open to them; and as the streets of the former are very narrow and filthy, the sole place for walking is a small garden in front of the factories, on the banks of the river. Formerly this garden, which contains some fine palms, fig-trees, and flowers, and is kept very neatly, was divided by a wall into two portions, the smaller of which—containing a neat church, raised by general subscription of the Protestants—belonged to the English, the larger to the other foreign merchants; but now, after years of deliberation and many a warm discussion, the division has been pulled down and the grounds are united, forming a very nice promenade.

It is generally the ambition of those who visit Canton to go to the so-called heights of the city. As this expedition, if undertaken by single individuals, is not considered safe—some Europeans having occasionally been murdered, others beaten or pelted with stones—a party was formed. After about two hours of uninterrupted walking through the crowded streets of the suburbs we reached the outside of the walls, without being subjected to any insult except that offered by a lot of boys and girls, sometimes amounting to more than a hundred, who constantly followed us with the annoying cry of "Foreign devils! foreign devils!" From the hills we obtained a full view of the city—a mass of buildings so closely crammed together that it was almost impossible to detect either street, square, or other division; the whole presenting, if not a beautiful, at least a grand and curious spectacle.

The flora of the surrounding country was very scanty.

A few isolated pine-trees (*Pinus Chinensis*, Lamb.) grew on the heights; near the water, *Ficus nitida* and some bamboos; on the great city walls, *Bœhmeria nivea* and *Ficus stipulata;* while spreading over hedges was seen a hop, which differs so much in aspect and size from *Humulus Lupulus*, that on a closer comparison it may possibly prove a new species. Among the cultivated plants, except the *Sagittaria Chinensis,* which was grown in great quantities in swamps, there was nothing peculiar. The rice and most vegetables had not yet been sown, for it was still winter, which, though not to be compared with ours, is sometimes sufficiently severe to convert during the night the surface of the stagnant water into a crust of ice.

In approaching one of the twelve gates a number of Tartar soldiers came towards us, who, with the greatest politeness, told us that we had better return whence we came. But I had made up my mind that I would go inside the walls of Canton, so, stepping boldly through the gate, I walked a few steps forward, followed by my companions, and then turned back. The soldiers understood perfectly well for what the odd manœuvre was intended. They laughed heartily, and, after we had presented the pig-tailed warriors with some cigars, we all parted as friends.

The people of Canton seem to attach great value to the virtues of plants. In the principal streets are stalls where medicinal herbs, roots, barks, and other vegetable substances are sold. At one of these places I counted more than fifty different drugs. There is generally, especially if a cure is performed, a man puffing up and extolling the extraordinary properties of his wares, in doing which he indulges now and then in a piece of witticism, which occasions among his gaping audience great merriment. I have never regretted so much being ignorant of the vernacular tongue as here, for whatever may be the quackery connected with the Chinese practice of medicine, a great deal no doubt is sound science, dearly purchased by experience. In this respect we have yet much to learn from them. The great work of Li-shi-chin, called the 'Pun-tsau-kang-muh,' or *Materia Medica*, is a valuable compilation, of which Europeans know but little, and which has never been translated into any language. It consists of no less than forty closely-printed octavo volumes, and contains several hundred figures of minerals, plants, and animals. True, the representations are imperfect, but they are in most instances not inferior to the woodcuts adorning the pages of the old 'Kräuterbücher' and Herbals published in Europe shortly after the invention of printing. To identify the names and figures given by Li-shi-chin with scientific appellations, will be an interesting study to those who occupy themselves with Chinese natural history, and, judging from the few extracts which have lately been published, the labour of translating the whole would be amply repaid by a vast amount of curious and useful information.

It has been asked by Sir William Hooker, in Sir John Herschel's 'Manual of Scientific Inquiry,' whether, in the northern provinces of China, indigo or any other vegetable dye is used in colouring green tea. Whether different processes of dyeing are pursued in the north from those of the south I cannot say, but it is certain that around

Canton, whence great quantities of green tea are annually exported, it is dyed with indigo, turmeric, and gypsum, all reduced to fine powder. The process is well described by Sir John F. Davis ('The Chinese,' vol. iii. p. 244 *et seq.*), who however falls into the strange mistake of supposing the whole proceeding of colouring to be an adulteration, and leaves his readers to infer that it is only occasionally done in order to meet the urgency of the demand, while it is now very well known that all the green tea of Canton has assumed that colour by artificial dyeing. I had heard so much about tea—copper plates, picking of the leaves, rolling them up with the fingers, boiling them in hot water, etc.,—that I became anxious to see with my own eyes the process of manufacture, of which the various books had given me such a confused idea. One of the great merchants conducted me not only to his own but also to another establishment, where the preparation of the different sorts was going forward. There was no concealment or mysterious proceeding; everything was conducted openly, and exhibited with great civility; indeed, from all I saw in the country I am almost inclined to conclude that either the Chinese have greatly altered, or their wish to conceal and mystify everything, of which so much has been said, has been exaggerated.

The tea is brought to Canton unprepared. After its arrival it is first subjected to cleaning. Women and children are employed to pick out the pieces of twigs, seeds, and other impurities with which it happens to be mixed. The only sorts which may be called natural are those gathered at different seasons: the rest are prepared by artificial means. Without entering into a description of all these processes, it may suffice to take one as an example. A quantity of Bohea Soushung was thrown into a spherical iron pan kept hot by means of a fire beneath. These leaves were constantly stirred about until they became thoroughly heated, when the dyes above mentioned were added; viz., to about twenty pounds of tea, one spoonful of gypsum, one of turmeric, and two or even three of indigo. The leaves instantly changed into a bluish-green, and, having been stirred for a few minutes, were taken out; they, of course, had shrivelled and assumed different shapes from the heat. The different kinds were produced by sifting. The small longish leaves fell through the first sieve and formed Young Hyson, whole those which had a roundish granular shape fell through last, and constituted Choo-cha, or Gunpowder.

The 13th of December I devoted to visiting the great temple of Honang, so admirably described by Sir John F. Davis, and also some Chinese gardens. One of the latter, being the property of a rich nurseryman, and entirely devoted to his private amusement, was kept in beautiful order. It was adorned with summer-houses, and artificial ponds filled with numerous plants of *Nelumbium speciosum*, bridges, rock-work, and thousands of dwarf shrubs and trees, cultivated in glazed pots, the walks being lined with sweet-smelling *Olea fragrans*. The whole was on so grand a scale that it must have cost a great sum: if the old nurseryman made all the money by his trade, gardening must be a more profitable employment in China than it is in more civilized countries. In the different nurseries there existed very little variety among the potted plants. Rows and rows contained nothing save oranges, roses, *Celosia cristata*, and Chinese chrysanthemums of many different sorts, but inferior, I thought, to those cultivated in European gardens. *Serissa fœtida* was also plentiful, and generally trimmed into various figures,—pagodas, junks, animals, etc. I observed several imitations of the deer; the antlers and every part of the animal so nicely grown that I could not help admiring them.

After a few days' stay in Canton I returned to Hongkong, and found the Herald was making preparations for her departure; I shall therefore, before resuming the narrative of the voyage, afford the reader a general view of the physical features of the island of Hongkong, which I am able to do from a series of notes supplied by my friend Dr. H. F. Hance, who resided in that colony seven years, and who has given so many proofs of his high scientific acquirements, and his successful study of natural history.

CHAPTER XIV.

The Island of Hongkong—Its geographical position—Geological formation—Climate and meteorology—Botany—Zoology.

HONGKONG, a corruption of Hiangkiang, "the fragrant streams," is the name of one of a number of islands in the China Sea, at a short distance from the mouth of the "River of Pearls," on the left bank of which stands the city of Canton, and from which it is divided by a narrow strait called Kap-shui-mún* (*vulgò* Cap-sing-moon) or "Swiftwater Passage," running between the mainland and a continuous chain of small islands of similar character and aspect to itself. The island is situated between lat. 22° 9′ and 22° 21′ north, and long. 114° 6′ and 114° 18′ east, and is distant from Canton about eighty-five miles, and forty from the Portuguese settlement of Macao on the peninsula of Hiangshan. At the narrowest part of the Lai-i-mún passage to the eastward, it is only about half a

* By a very natural error, I find, in nearly all systematic works, plants gathered about this locality noticed thus:—" HAB. in Cap. Syngmoon," or " Crescit ad Prom. Sing-moon;" the first word being understood as an abbreviation of *Caput*.

nautical mile from the mainland. It resembles in general form a scalene triangle, of which the apex is towards the west, but is of very irregular and sinuous outline, especially on the southern coast, which forms the longest side of the triangle, having an area of 29·14 square miles, while it is not quite twenty-seven miles in circumference.

It consists of a long and precipitous mountain-ridge running east and west, in some places gradually sloping down towards the sea, where it is met by extensive level beaches of fine clear white quartz-sand; in others terminating abruptly in frowning perpendicular cliffs more than a hundred feet in height, perforated at their base by caverns, into which the waves dash with a hollow sound, throwing up clouds of spray. From this ridge spurs diverge at different angles. The peaks vary in altitude; the loftiest, Victoria, being about 1860 feet above the sea-level. The prevailing rock is syenite (extensively quarried and used for edifices), which is found in immense blocks imbedded in a soil composed of the same rock in various stages of disintegration and decomposition (laterite), or piled up in fantastic shapes on the hill-summits. The constituents of this rock also occur more or less separate: felspar in its normal condition or changed into a pure white or pinkish clay,—hornblende cropping out on the surface in deep black lustrous crystals,—and quartz traversing the laterite in dykes of variable thickness. Masses of trap are also met with, translucent crystals of carbonate of lime not unfrequently found in the centre of the blocks of syenite, and the beds of ravines afford fragments of laminated mica. No signs of stratification or of volcanic action are discoverable. At the base of the primary ridge, in those places where it terminates at some distance from water-mark, and between the various spurs, patches of alluvial soil are found consisting exclusively of decomposed vegetable matter washed down by the rains and mingled with the laterite. These are sedulously turned to account by the natives for agricultural purposes. The numerous ravines by which the flanks of the hills are cleft, furnish a never-failing supply of water, remarkable for its extreme purity, and a little below one of the loftiest peaks a considerable spring arises. During the summer season these streams become greatly swollen, and the spectator sees the angles of junction of the spurs and main range distinctly traced out by lines of foam indicating the course of these turbulent cascades.

The temperature is subject to a variation of from 47° to 93° Fahr.* The daily range rarely exceeds fifteen

* The following table is based on observations made during six consecutive years, and is, as well as the other meteorological ones, extracted from an almanac published in the colony.

Months.	Maximum.	Minimum.	Mean.
January	73°F.	49°F.	61·65°F.
February	78	50	63·5
March	80	49	65·7
April	87	49	72·7
May	88	68	78·3
June	92·5	75	83
July	92	80	85
August	92	78	83·5
September	93	78	82·9
October	90	67	80·3
November	85	57½	72
December	77	47	63·6

degrees. Once only during the years 1844–1851 did the thermometer sink as low as freezing-point.

Towards the end of October or the commencement of November the north-east monsoon sets in: the atmosphere is wonderfully serene, the air cold, bracing, and dry, and the transition from an atmosphere saturated with moisture is marked by the warping and splitting of tables and other wooden articles of furniture, accompanied by considerable noise, and the curling up of papers, as occurs in this climate when they are placed in a heated room: this is the winter, which lasts until about the middle of February, during which scarcely any rain falls and vegetation is burnt up and scanty, a few *Compositæ* being nearly all that can be found flowering. Gradually the temperature becomes higher, the atmospheric deposits greater; the dry, discoloured leaves of the myrtle, *Melastoma,* and *Emblica* fall, and are succeeded by a tender vernal green, and innumerable flowers spring up from the turf; until, about May, summer is heralded by the advent of the south-west monsoon. This season is characterized by a most intense and oppressive heat, which causes the greatest languor to European residents; rain falls for a week or ten days together, rather in sheets than drops; the swollen torrents rush roaring down into the sea, which they often discolour for a quarter of a mile from the shore; terrific thunderstorms reverberate amongst the hills; which are hidden in a dense veil of cloud and mist, and such is the excessive humidity of the atmosphere that articles of wood or Russia-leather, or covers of books, even if washed over with alcohol or a solution of some essential oil, become in the course of a night covered with a thick blue mould. The rain will then cease for a few days; the heavens remain unclouded, though always more or less hazy, and lit up in the evening by almost unintermitting flashes of sheet-lightning; not a breath will agitate the air, tremulous with the heat radiated from the ground, and the silence is alone broken by the unceasing, loud, and monotonous chirping of the *Cicadæ* hidden in the grass. At this period vegetation is at its height and is developed with wonderful rapidity; a few days suffice to perfect the blossoming of the richest flowers.

About the beginning of September the rain becomes much less frequent, though the heat is still excessive, and, as a natural consequence, the flora assumes a more sober and less attractive habit; this period may be considered equivalent to our autumn. It is now that the island is occasionally visited by typhoons*—those terrible circular storms which traverse the Indian Ocean and China Sea,

* There is much diversity of opinion respecting the origin and consequent orthography of this word, some deriving it from the Chinese *tà fúng*, literally *great wind*, which is however not the name they themselves apply to these hurricanes; whilst others with more probability deduce it from the monster Typhon, Typhaon, or Typhœus, names which, although, as occurs in innumerable instances throughout the whole of heathen mythology, sundered and misapplied in various ways by ancient authors, seem originally to have represented one being. Typhœus is described by Hesiod as the father of the adverse or malignant-winds, as opposed to the favourable or genial ones. Typhaon, his son, he personifies as a terrific hurricane, and the parentage of Cerberus, Hydra, Chimæra, and the Sphinx, ascribed to him, sufficiently denotes the mythical signification of his character. It is to be observed that a brother of Osiris bearing this name was also considered by the Egyptians as the author of all evil. (Cfr. Plut. de Isid. et Osirid.)

and when they meet with the land in their course unroof houses, tear off and carry away doors and venetians, drive vessels from their anchorages, prostrate trees, blight and destroy nearly all vegetation, and cause wreck and devastation wherever they pass. Finally, the temperature decreases, the rains cease, and the vegetable world remains dormant, seeking repose after its late activity, and recruiting strength for that of the succeeding year: winter has again returned, and the cycle of the seasons is completed*.

To a stranger landing or regarding the island from the sea, the aspect of Hongkong is very unpromising, conveying the idea of almost absolute sterility. The hills are covered by a mantle of coarse grass, amidst which rise masses of bare blackened rock, while the monotonous scene seems only varied by a few bushes or a solitary tree studded here and there, and by scattered groves of

* The following tables afford interesting meteorological data respecting the climate of Hongkong:—

Range of Barometer (deduced from six years' observations).			
Months.	Maximum.	Minimum.	Mean.
January	30·28	29·71	30.004
February	30·26	29·69	30·
March	30·19	29·66	29·94
April	30·04	29·65	29·857
May	29·95	29·58	29·767
June	29·88	29·46	29·655
July	99·85	29·35	29·65
August	29·84	29·27	29·596
September	29·94	29·10	29·713
October	30·16	29·56	22·84
November	30·17	29·80	29·987
December	30·25	29·80	30·03

the *Pinus Sinensis* clothing some of the declivities. As remarked by Meyen, there is no doubt that this tree was at one time far more common, and originally formed dense woods on the flanks of the hills of all the islands hereabouts; but it is used very extensively by the Chinese for burning, and plantations being seldom or never formed, it thus decreases rapidly. On a closer inspection however the botanist is gratified by finding that the first impression is very deceptive, and indeed it is pro-

Months.	Average No. of days in which rain falls.	Number of inches of rain.			
		1840.	1845.	1846.	1847.
January	5			0·25	5·12
February....	5			0·705	2·110
March......	12			7·925	1·950
April	10			5·07	7·35
May	17			12·92	8·45
June.......	18			21·68	11·60
July	16		7·565	11·85	10·14
August.....	21		14·	15·07	12·05
September ..	14		7·	21·6	7·3
October	15		13·20	1·80	1·70
November ..	8		1·60	6·93	1·80
December ...	18	0·65		6·275	

The rain table is based on observations of a far too superficial and unconnected character to be accepted as of particular value, for assuredly both the quantity of rain and the number of days on which it falls in December could never on a general average afford the results therein given. Those of the two last years are however probably to be depended on, and the anomaly referred to would doubtless disappear in a series of protracted observations, which are always necessary in investigations of this nature. We are unfortunately altogether destitute of any psychrometrical data; but considering the great quantity of rain and the number of days on wh'ch it falls during the summer months, it is tolerably certain that the dew-point does not differ materially from the ordinary temperature, at any rate during that season.

bable that, whether as regards the number of species or the variety of new and interesting forms comprised in its flora, the island is for its size and geographical position entitled to a very high rank. Of course in a limited spot like Hongkong, where the altitude of the mountains is not sufficient to exercise any very material influence, zones or districts of vegetation, such as occur in Java and other neighbouring islands, are altogether unknown.

The *normal* or characteristic species—those which are most widely distributed, most numerous, and which most clearly strike the observer as constituting the peculiar and distinguishing character of the flora—are, amidst a thick but rather coarse turf consisting of species of *Cyperus*, especially in damp localities, *Paspalus, Chrysopogon, Andropogon, Anatherum, Digitaria, Lycopodium cernuum*, etc.; *Myrtus tomentosa*, with its gay rose-coloured flowers and sober green leaves, clothed beneath with a close white down, which is met with everywhere, and may be considered the commonest plant in the island, and the fruit of which, when ripe, has a resinous and not unpleasant taste, somewhat resembling that of the black currant, and is eaten by the natives; *Melastoma calycina* and *M. macrocarpon*, covered with magnificent purplish-pink blossoms; *Ancistrolobus ligustrinus*, a pretty compact shrub, with dark blood-coloured flowers smelling like our St. John's-wort; and *Callicarpa tomentosa* and another, with branches hidden in a velvety fulvous down, lovely bright green leaves, farinose beneath, and dense bunches of small reddish-lilac flowers. An *Emblica*, very common on the low grounds, is among the first to put forth its delicate green leaves on the approach of spring; two *Clerodendra*, the neat myrtle-like *Rospidios vaccinioides*, *Strophanthus divergens*, with its trailing branches, dark glossy foliage, and curious reddish-yellow caudate corollas, two pretty *Uvariæ*, *Helicteres augustifolia*, *Desmodium triquetrum*, *Dicerma elegans* (to which may be referred without a doubt the *Æschynomene heterophylla* of Loureiro, hitherto undetermined), and *Melanthesa Chinensis* are almost equally common. *Alpinia nutans* elevates its gorgeous racemes of flowers of a light flesh-colour, streaked with the intensest gold and scarlet, by the water-courses; *Ameletia subspicata* in some parts clothes the flat moist meadow-like turf with so thick a verdure that when in blossom it looks at a distance like a field of thyme; the silvery foliage of the graceful *Rhus succedaneum* flutters in the breeze; *Smilax glabra* straggles over the rocks; *Lygodium Japonicum* and the leafless parasitical intertangled *Cassyta filiformis* climb over all shrubs indiscriminately, the latter perfidiously abstracting the sap with its cup-like suckers from those plants from which it claims support; and the abundant pectinated *Gleichenia dichotoma*, with *Pteris nemoralis*, *Adiantum amœnum*, *Nephrolepis tuberosa*, and other ferns, spring up among the herbage.

The most noticeable feature in the flora of this island is the mixture of Asiatic and European forms, especially conspicuous in the vernal vegetation of the hill-summits: in this respect it appears to approach closely to that of Cashmere. Its connection with that of Australia is very slight, being merely indicated by such genera as *Stylidium* and *Philydrum*, the last of which is exclusively confined to Cochin-China, the south of China, and parts of

New Holland. Tropical plants identical with or intimately allied to those of the Indian Peninsula and the Malayan Archipelago are not infrequent; and *Anthurium, Chirita, Æschynanthus, Sponia, Piper arcuatum*, etc. etc., may serve as examples, but they by no means represent the normal character of the flora, which is perfectly *sui generis*. The only three indigenous palms are a dwarf stemless species (perhaps a *Seaforthia*), *Zalacca*, and *Rhapis*. The cocoa-nut tree is occasionally planted, but does not thrive, the island of Hainan being its most easterly station in these seas, and even there it is said to perfect fruit sparingly. The most obvious relationship of the flora is however with Japan, as evinced by the presence of a new oak, half-a-dozen genera of *Ternströmiaceæ*, and some Hamamelaceous forms (adopting the late Dr. Gardner's views of affinity), as *Eustigma, Liquidambar*, and *Rhodoleia*, both families being peculiarly characteristic of those islands. How far a resemblance may hereafter be traced between the vegetation of Japan, the south and south-east of China, and some districts of Upper India, it is at present impossible to predict, but we may here refer to the distribution of *Abelia* and *Adamia*, and observe that a new *Helwingia* has been detected at Darjeeling, and two species of *Corylopsis* in the Bootan Mountains.

Amongst *cultivated* plants the sweet potato (*Batatas edulis*) holds the first rank; it is very largely consumed by the Chinese, even its boiled leaves being used as greens; beside this, we must notice as edible vegetables, yams (*Dioscorea* sp.) and *Colocasia*, several species of *Sinapis* and *Brassica, Basella rubra*, employed as a substitute for spinach, various species of *Dolichos, Soja*, and *Phaseolus*, egg-apples (*Solanum Melongena*), our common potato and pea, water-melons and other *Cucurbitaceæ*, ground-nuts (*Arachis hypogæa*), a little barley, grown exclusively for pearling, cassava (*Manihot utilissima*), *Allium fistulosum*, rice, millet, *Setaria*, sugar-cane, maize, *Abelmoschus longifolius*, the immature viscid capsules of which are brought to table; and, as fruit, pomeloes (*Citrus decumana*), oranges, loquats (*Eriobotrya Japonica*), papaws (*Carica Papaya*), wangpis (*Cookia punctata*), *Nephelium Litchi* and *N. Longan*, mangoes, bananas, pine-apples, *Averrhoa Carambola*, guavas, and *Jambosa Malaccensis*. The farinaceous fruits of *Trapa bicornis*, those of *Canarium album*, preserved with salt and much resembling an olive in flavour, the crimson papillose acid drupe of a species of *Elæagnus*, pears, plums, and peaches of exceedingly bad quality, and the amygdaloid nuts and fleshy root of *Nelumbium speciosum*, are brought to market, and are all grown in its vicinity, though not in the island itself. *Gossypium herbaceum, Bœhmeria nivea, Piper Betel*, and a species of *Indigofera* are cultivated for economic purposes other than esculent. *Ficus nitida*, the claims of which as a true native are considered doubtful, is planted around the villages; the fields and garden-patches are surrounded by hedges of *Pandanus fœtidus, Euphorbia nereifolia*, or *Curcas purgans*.

The fauna of the island is not of great extent; it comprises a small species of deer—very rare, if not extinct at present,—foxes, a manis, two bats, rats, and several other small *Muridæ*; a vulture, gulls, two or three species of king-fishers, partridges, jungle-fowl, quails, snipes, sandpipers, curlews, cormorants, minas, shrikes, Java sparrows, magpies, house-sparrows, a swallow, two owls, etc.; six or seven species of snakes, lizards, including the common gecko, and innumerable insects, amongst them a large black ant, which constructs in the bushes paper-like nests made of leaves, and about the size of a child's head. The spring near the top of the hill above alluded to contains a small fish which, according to J. C. Bowring, constitutes the type of a new genus, and others are met with in various fresh-water streams. Sponges and zoophytes are found on its shores, and the adjacent waters swarm with an infinite variety of fish, and a cephalopod resembling our cuttle-fish, which is eaten by the natives.

CHAPTER XV.

Departure from Hongkong—Pulo Aor—Singapore—Straits of Sunda—Sumatra—Death of Mr. Woodward—Keeling Islands—Arrival at the Cape of Good Hope.

ON the 22nd of December the Herald departed from Victoria, and calling on the 29th of the same month at Pulo Aor, a small island, she reached on the following day the roads of Singapore. The ship had hardly taken up her position, when she was surrounded by a number of shore-boats, offering crockery, clothing, eggs, parrots, monkeys, different articles made of gutta-taban, bananas, mangoes, pine-apples, limes, jacks, oranges, pomeloes, and even some ready-made curry.

Singapore makes a favourable impression upon the voyager. A mass of stately buildings, half-concealed by groves of bamboos, fig-trees, pucurus, catechu and cocoa-nut palms, encircle a bay over which the busy operations of shipping diffuse animation and life. On a hill, the slopes of which are clothed with numerous nutmeg-trees and a turf of brilliant green, stands the Government-house, while the background, as if to make up for the want of elevated mountains to complete the picture, is generally hidden from view by the dense vapour, fog, or rain, hanging over the thick jungle with which the greater part of the island is still covered. The aspect of the whole however is destitute of that grandeur by which Hongkong is so eminently distinguished; but Singapore, from its geographical position, its salubrious, though hot, climate, and its fertile soil, as well as from the incalculable advantages arising from its being a free port, is of far greater importance than Hongkong is, or ever will be. While the latter is merely a place carrying on a trade with a limited portion of the Chinese Empire, the former concentrates all the rich commerce of the Indian Archipelago.

I have said that the greatest portion of Singapore is still covered with jungle; but this does not seem destined to remain long. Every year fresh emigrants arrive from China, Siam, Cochin-China, Bengal,—in fine, from almost every part of Asia; the forests are fast disappearing, substantial roads intersect the colony in different directions, and extensive plantations are everywhere springing up. The cultivation of the nutmeg, especially, has lately been prosecuted with great zeal. When the settlement was established, much prejudice existed with regard to it. A general belief then prevailed that with so great an investment of capital which such plantations require, and without special protecting laws, much risk was incurred. Now however the fallacy of these views has been demonstrated; several far-sighted individuals, who early commenced the cultivation of the spice, are now reaping a golden harvest from their enterprise. This has induced others to follow their example, for it has been ascertained that the Singapore planters, with free labour and without any protecting laws whatever, are enabled to produce their nuts and mace at a cheaper rate than the Dutch, with all their antiquated institutions: another decisive proof—if indeed any was wanting—that industry only requires to be free, unfettered, in order to be productive of the best results.

The perseverance, care, and foresight which are required in order to cultivate the nutmeg successfully are truly astonishing. The preparation of the soil, manuring, shading of the young plants, etc., are very laborious operations, and often meet with disappointment. After years of attention, and the expenditure of considerable sums, the trees begin to blossom, when, alas! not unfrequently more than one-half turn out to be either male or monœcious plants, only to be felled by the axe. This circumstance is of great importance; in order to remedy the evil various experiments have been made to propagate the female plant by grafting, or by layers, and although these processes have been successful, it remains yet to be ascertained whether trees multiplied in this manner are as productive and durable as those raised from seed.

Besides the nutmeg, extensive plantations of the Cassava (*Manihot utilissima*, Pohl*) have been established,

---

* It seems to be little known that from this plant, and through the following mistake, Yucatan derives its name. "*Yuca*," in the language of that country, is the term applied to *Manihot utilissima;* "*tal*," to the field on which the shrub grows. When in 1517 the plant was shown to the prisoners brought to Cuba by Hernandez de Cordoba and his followers, they immediately recognized it, exclaiming, "Yuca-

and it is stated that they pay exceedingly well. The farinaceous substance prepared from the plant is exported partly raw, partly in the form of pearl sago; and so well has the latter preparation been imitated that it has actually been mistaken for real sago. The manihot is naturalized—not indigenous, as some contend—in different parts of the island. The white residents of Singapore call it Tapioca; the Malays, Ubi caju; while the Mexicans, it may be added, term it Quauhcamotl; the West Indians, Cassava, Cuzabi, and Mandioc; and the New Granadians, Eucadorians, and Peruvians, Yuca. It is a curious coincidence that both the Malayan and Aztec name signify exactly the same, viz. woody tuber, as the roots of this shrub, or, properly speaking, the tubers, when remaining too long in the ground, become as hard as wood, and unfit for use.

The *Areca Catechu* has not yet received the attention of capitalists, and consequently no plantations of any size are to be found. The Malays in Singapore chew its nut, together with gambir, tobacco, lime, and the leaves of the Siri (*Piper Siriboa*, Linn.), while the Chinese practise the same filthy habit, with the only difference that they use the foliage of the black pepper (*Piper nigrum*, Linn.) instead of that of the siri. This statement how-

tal!" which was supposed to signify their native land; and this expression, corrupted into Yucatan, has ever since been applied to that part of America which now bears the name. See Bernal Diaz del Castillo's History for further information. The edition of that work consulted by me contains several typographical errors. Yuca is written both "Yuca" and "Yucu;" "tale," as well as "tal:" which is the most correct I am unable to say. *Tal* is probably the same as the Aztec *tlan*, or *tlalli*, which signifies *country, territory, soil, earth,* and occurs in the composition of several Mexican names, as Mazatlan, Metzitlan.

ever has only reference to the colonists in the island; in the southern parts of China the people avail themselves of the leaves of *Piper Betel*, Linn. Though the quantity of tannin contained in the betel must exercise a baneful influence, yet it is a mistake to suppose that the mere chewing of it gives to the mouth an offensive appearance: unless the other ingredients are added the saliva hardly changes its natural colour.

Black pepper (*Piper nigrum*, Linn.) and Gambir (*Uncaria Gambir*, Roxb.) are grown in great quantities, and exclusively by the Chinese, for the profits made by both these articles are so small that Europeans have not deemed it worth their while to engage in the speculation. Pepper and gambir plantations are always coupled together, because the refuse of the gambir-leaves serves as an excellent manure for the pepper-shrubs, and moreover, what is of equal, if not of still greater importance, kills the Lalang (*Andropogon caricosum*, Linn.), a plant which, like the couch-grass (*Triticum repens*, Linn.), spreads with astonishing rapidity over the fields, growing so close together, and so high, that within a short space of time valuable plantations are rendered useless, and many have to be given up, from the impossibility of freeing the ground from this weed.

The process by which gambir is extracted and prepared is very simple. The leaves are boiled in water until all the astringent property is extracted; the decoction is then poured into another vessel, in which it becomes inspissated; and when nearly dry it is cut in small square pieces, and thus brought into the market. M'Culloch states that sago is used in thickening it; this however, at least in Singapore, is not the case, but instead of sago a piece of wood is dipped into the vessel, by which the desired effect is produced. It must indeed be an extraordinary substance the mere dipping of which into a fluid can cause it to become a thickened mass. I was very eager to obtain a piece of this wood; unluckily the Chinaman whose laboratory I visited could not be persuaded to part with his, and a friend of mine who was exerting himself to procure a sample had not succeeded at the time of the Herald's departure.

Genuine cutch is not a production of Singapore, but an adulteration of it is sometimes made. Specimens which I obtained were composed of alum, chromic acid, vitriol, and gambir. The compound was so well mixed and prepared that it resembled real cutch very closely, and similar preparations are, I dare-say, frequently mistaken for it. If such is the nature of some of the "raw products," need we wonder that chemical analyses of the same substance differ so widely from each other?

The arrow-root is different from that of the Sandwich Islands, being made from the tubers of the *Maranta arundinacea*, Linn. The cultivation of the plant has only lately commenced, and is at present not very extensive, but it is said to be annually increasing. Cloves, cinnamon, cacao, rice, and siri (*Piper Siriboa*, Linn.) are as yet grown only in small quantities; indeed it is stated that all the rice produced in Singapore is hardly sufficient to feed its population for a single week. Sago is not an indigenous production; it is brought from Cochin-China, Borneo, Java, Sumatra, Penang, and Celebes, and is only prepared in Singapore by the Chinese to be afterwards exported. The cultivation of the sugar-cane and the manufacturing of the different preparations of it have hitherto, in a pecuniary point of view, proved abortive, and several large estates have had to be given up in consequence. It is difficult to account for this failure; climate, soil, the low price of labour, and the facilities for shipping the produce, all argue in favour of success. Similar disappointments have been experienced in rearing cotton and coffee, though in this case several physical circumstances constituted insurmountable difficulties.

Indigenous productions of any great commercial value Singapore has none. Rattan is common; from an Acanthaceous plant the Chinese extract, merely for their own immediate use, a blue dye, which is perhaps the same as that called *Room* in Lindley's 'Vegetable Kingdom,' and said to be a *Ruellia*. The Taban, or, as it is erroneously called, Gutta-percha tree (*Isonandra Gutta*, Hook.), which was formerly tolerably abundant, is now almost extinct. A few isolated trees may here and there occur, but they are very scarce, and are considered, in the gardens of the white residents, as a curiosity. The geographical range of the tree however appears to be considerable; it being found all up the Malayan peninsula as far as Penang, principally in the alluvial tracts at the foot of hills, where it forms the principal portion of the jungle. The exportation of the indigenous Gutta-taban from Singapore commenced in 1844, but as early as the end of 1847, all, or at least most, of the trees producing it had been exterminated. That at present shipped from the place is brought in coasting vessels from the different parts of Borneo, Sumatra, the Malayan Peninsula, and the Jahore

Archipelago*. The difference existing in its appearance and property the merchants attribute to the intermixture of gutta-percha, jelotong, geggrek, litchu, and other inferior guttas, made by the natives in order to increase the weight. Though far from being extinct in the Indian Archipelago, gutta-taban will every year be more difficult to obtain, as the coast region is said to be pretty well cleared, and a long transport from the interior must, by augmenting the labour, increase the value of the article. The tree is from sixty to seventy feet high, from two to three feet in diameter, and in its general aspect it resembles the *Durian* (*Durio zibethinus*, Linn.), so much so as to strike the most superficial observer. The quantity of solid gutta obtained from each tree varies from five to twenty catties, so that, taking the average of ten catties, which is a tolerably liberal one, it will require the destruction of ten trees to produce one picul ($133\frac{1}{3}$ lbs.). Now the quantity exported from Singapore to Europe from the 1st of January, 1845, to the middle of 1847, amounted to 6918 piculs, to obtain which 69,180 trees must have been sacrificed! How much better would it be to adopt the method of tapping the tree practised by the Burmese

---

* " The total export of Gutta-taban was in 1844, 1 picul; in 1845, 169 piculs; in 1846, 5364 piculs; in 1847, 9296 piculs; in 1848, to the 1st of July, 6768 piculs; total, 21,598 piculs, valued at 274,190 Spanish dollars. About 270,000 trees have probably been felled during the four years and a half that the trade has existed, and the value of each tree has thus on an average been about a dollar."—J. R. Logan : ' On the range of the Gutta-taban Collectors, and present amount of import into Singapore.' Mr. Logan has promised an article on the various substances intermingled with the gutta-taban—a subject of the highest interest—but he has hitherto disappointed his readers.

in obtaining caoutchouc, than to continue the present process of extermination.

It must ever be an object of regret that on the first introduction of the taban gum its proper name was not promulgated. Now everybody in Europe and America speaks of gutta-percha, when in fact all the time he means gutta-taban. The substance termed by the Malays gutta-percha is not the produce of the *Isonandra Gutta*, Hook., but that of a botanically unknown tree. The confusion of these two names has become a popular error,— an error which science will have to rectify.

Of quadrupeds of the island, a deer, a tiger, and a pig (*Sus babyrussa*, Buff.) may be enumerated. The depredations of the tigers are so frequent that hardly a week passes without some person being carried off, and their daring is indeed great. In one of my excursions I came to a gambir plantation, which, being situated rather far in the jungle, is very often subject to their attacks. Only the night previous to my arrival a large tiger had come close to a hut in which ten of the Chinese labourers were lodged, and commenced there a most terrible howling. The people tried, by hissing, clapping their hands, and beating of metallic vessels, to frighten it away, but the animal continued its howling, when the ten, now almost driven to despair, gave such a yell that made the woods resound and the tiger abandon his prey.

Some contend that the tigers show a greater predilection for the coloured than the white man, as ever since the establishment of the colony no European has been killed; we may however, I think, safely ascribe this to the circumstance that the whites do not expose themselves so much as the coloured people, nor enter the forests without being well armed and in parties together. It is also stated that the tigers recruit their declining numbers by swimming across the narrow strait which separates Singapore from the mainland of Asia; but this is again disputed by others, who maintain that all the tigers are bred in the island; be this as it may, it is certain that they are very numerous, and that the Government, in order to lessen the accidents resulting from their attacks, has been compelled to offer a reward of fifty Spanish dollars for every tiger killed. The hunters are therefore well paid for their trouble. Besides the prize, they obtain eight or ten dollars for the skin, and realize about an equal sum from the flesh, which is eagerly bought by the Chinese, who eat it with the vain hope that it will make them strong.

Elephants are not now indigenous: only a few domesticated ones are kept in the plantations for working; on the adjacent mainland however both elephants and tapirs (*Tapirus Indicus*) abound. One of the latter—in comparison with which the American species, the Macho de monte, or Gran Bestia of the Panamians, is a mere dwarf —was during our visit offered for the sum of 150 Spanish dollars. It certainly would have been a most splendid specimen for any zoological collection.

The feathered tribe is numerous and brilliant, and fish seems to exist in almost as great a variety as in China. Of snakes, mosquitoes, centipedes, scorpions, and similar tormentors of the human species, Singapore has its due share. The scorpions are larger than I ever saw them elsewhere. One I caught in the jungle was nearly seven inches in length, and of a dark brown, almost black colour. I find that the Malays know as well as the Mexicans that the best remedy for scorpion-bites is the scorpion itself, though they differ somewhat in the application. The Mexicans plunge the animal in spirit, and then apply the infusion to the wound, while the Malays make a direct use of its pounded body.

"New Year's Day," says Captain Kellett, "was completely given up by the good people of Singapore of every nation to amusements. It was commenced with a regatta, in which both the native and men-of-war boats took part. It was really beautiful to see a crowd of the native proas and caics start with a fresh breeze under sail that it could not be supposed that they could carry. However, being good swimmers, they do not care much if they are occasionally capsized; they right the boat again, and off as if nothing had happened. They have outriggers, to which one, two, or three men can hang, according to the breeze. The result of the race between the men-of-war's boats was—first round, at which there was no tide, the Herald's barge and yawl were leading on passing the starting-point, and so far ahead that I supposed it was not possible they could be caught, unless through some accident. The barge would have had the race, but, for want of knowledge of the tides, made a short tack, besides running off the wind to close the ship to give her a cheer, and, being too confident, not only did not win, but came in third. The yawl was thrown out by her mizen-strap being carried away; a decked cutter taking first prize, a gig belonging to the Amazon the second.

"On the esplanade there were pony races with riders, and the same with Syces running at their heads; climbing a greasy pole; dancing girls and jugglers, besides numberless performances in the way of fighting between Chinese and Malays. The dancing would disappoint most people, being nothing more than a mere movement of the body and hands to most barbarous music at particular stages, the musicians repeating something in praise of the lady's beauty, etc. The girl is generally young, and dances with bare feet, but is dressed as gaily as she can afford. She is surrounded by a multitude of men, who leave her a space of not more than three feet to perform in. The jugglers and tumblers, who are all Madras men, were expert and active. Some curious tricks were performed; one passed down his throat a blade of iron fourteen inches long—a disgusting sight. The tumblers certainly beat any I had ever seen.

"A European visiting Singapore at this time would be particularly struck with the various costumes, as well as the great concourse of men, without a single woman, except some stray dancing girl, or a few of the same class driving about in gurries to see and be seen. The gurries, to which I have thus alluded, are not the least remarkable feature of this place; they are comfortable, airy, four-wheeled carriages, capable of holding four persons, and are drawn by little stout ponies, not much larger than an Irish pig, who go at a rapid pace, and never tire. They are never driven, but are led by a Syce. A European would pity the man, but a Syce will outrun any pony or horse, and the pony will die before he gives in. Wherever you go he follows you. You go out to dinner, he waits for you; you go on board, he watches for your landing again. A dollar is the hire of one of these vehicles for a day,—that is, from daylight in the morning until *you* go to bed."

On the 9th of January, 1851, we continued our voyage, and passing between the numerous islands of the Indian Archipelago, the Strait of Rhio, and Gaspar Strait, reached the Strait of Sunda, where a series of calms and light winds detained us a few days. The sight of this strait is indeed beautiful. On one side Java, on the other Sumatra, both teeming with vegetation, and presenting a variety of tints, a freshness, a luxuriance truly wonderful, rendered still more imposing by the elevated mountains, the light blue of which charmingly contrasts with the dark green of the primeval forest.

We approached Sumatra very closely, and cast anchor in the afternoon of the 15th of January. A party of us landed. The forests extended close to the water's edge, and the trees were very high and close together. Rattan, a spiny *Mimosea*, and numerous other creepers, were climbing from tree to tree, and often obstructed the passage. Of *Orchideæ* not one was to be seen. One of the most common trees was the *Cycas circinalis*, Linn., attaining a considerable size—about sixty feet high, three feet in circumference, and diverging towards the top into three, four, and even six branches.

That part at which we landed appeared to be but thinly peopled. We only found a single hut occupied by a few Malays, who were employed in cooking some fish, and eating a large jack just taken from a neighbouring tree. A few fowls were running about the place, but the whole looked wretched and uncomfortable, and a single glance at the scene would have cured many a European of his romantic notions of savage life. Mosquitoes were very numerous, and we were glad to find a path which led some distance in the forest, and took us, in a considerable measure, out of their range.

On the 26th of January we had to lament the death of one of our shipmates. Mr. Thomas Woodward, purser, having caught a severe cold while in the Arctic regions, was, after leaving the Sandwich Islands, taken so seriously ill, that, although both Mr. Goodridge and Mr. Billings were unceasing in their attention, it soon became evident that the disease would terminate fatally. Mr. Woodward, from his true-heartedness, good-nature, and cheerful disposition, his ready wit, and his great flow of conversation, made friends wherever he went, and was so well known in that service of which he was so bright an ornament, and so generally esteemed, that it would be looked upon as a grave omission were I not to accompany the notice of his death with some sketch of his life.

Thomas Woodward was born at Portsea on the 27th of August, 1811, and in 1821, at the age of ten years, he was sent to the Collége Royal, or Lycée, at Caen in Normandy, where, with twenty-six other English boys, many of them from his own town, he remained until the end of 1823, when a decree having been issued from the authority at Paris, that all teachers in public seminaries should be Roman Catholic priests, it became necessary for the Protestant boys to leave. The advantage Mr. Woodward obtained on being located in France at such an early age, may be gathered from a complaint that he made when at the next school at which he was placed in England, that " he led a dog's life," as from his complete French accent "the boys would not believe he was English, and dubbed him Monsieur." He was often taken for a French boy even by gentlemen who were acquainted with his friends. He was afterwards removed to a large proprietary school in the neighbourhood, St. Paul's, Southsea, where he made some progress in mathematics and drawing, as he was intended by his parents to try for the first vacancy in the School of Naval Architecture at Portsmouth Dockyard, which however did not occur until he was past the age required for admission.

In April, 1829, he entered the service as Naval Instructor on board the Southampton frigate, proceeding to the East Indies with the flag of Rear-Admiral Sir Edward Owen. After serving in this capacity for twelve months, a vacancy as clerk occurred, and he remained as Captain's Clerk until October, 1830, when, from ill health, he was compelled to invalid home. In March, 1831, he was attached to the office of Vice-Admiral Sir H. Hotham, under John Irvine, Esq., secretary, and remained in the St. Vincent in the Mediterranean until the death of that highly esteemed and gallant officer; and in April, 1834, on the St. Vincent quitting the station, he was transferred to the office of Vice-Admiral Sir Jonas Rowley, under Thomas Triphook, Esq., secretary. He remained in this office until June, 1835, when he was appointed acting purser to the Columbine brig; but the vacancy being only an invaliding one, the Admiralty sent out an officer to supersede him, and he returned to the office until the 18th of May, 1836, when a vacancy having occurred in the Vernon, by the death of her purser, Mr. Woodward was promoted into the Medea steam-vessel, Captain Horatio Austin, and continued serving in her until she was paid off at Woolwich, in October, 1837. In December following he was appointed to the Phœnix, on the north coast of Spain, under Captain W. H. Henderson, C.B., and was paid off in her in November, 1838. In February, 1839, he joined the Wasp, Captain the Hon. D. Pelham, and in her was present at the bombardment of Beyrout, and, during the remainder of the Syrian campaign, was employed on shore in the Commissariat Department, connected with the Royal Marine Artillery. Here he remained, after enduring much hardship from the want of stores, ignorance of the language, and having daily rations to provide for a hundred men, with fifty on the sick list from the fever of the country, among whom was the assistant-surgeon, until February, 1841, when they were fortunately released from their miserable position, and left, in H.M.S. Benbow, for Malta, when Admiral Sir R. Stopford, in acknowledgment of his services, appointed him to H.M.S. Daphne, then at Smyrna. From want of opportunity, he did not join her until she was ordered home, and was paid off in May, 1842, having been just three months on board. In February, 1844, he joined the Volage, then the flag-ship of Sir Hugh Pigot, at Cork, and remained in her until she was paid off at Plymouth, in February, 1845. As all his service had hitherto been in ships with "broken time," he applied and was appointed to H.M.S. Herald, then fitting at Plymouth, to survey the west coast of South America, and was employed in her for nearly six years, during which time he thrice visited the Arctic regions. On the last occasion he caught a severe cold while off Cape Lisburne, which terminated his life, on the 26th of January, 1851, and on the following day his body received a sailor's funeral.

The expedition was thus deprived of one of its most useful and zealous officers. Mr. Woodward had not only always been distinguished by a strict discharge of his official duties, but rendered besides the greatest service to the expedition by giving it the benefit of his various accomplishments. From his excellent knowledge of different languages, he often acted as interpreter, and translated sailing directions and other nautical remarks obtained at the various places visited. He was a superior draughtsman, and made many a sketch for our charts; and once he delineated nearly the whole coast of Eastern Kamtchatka, with its numerous volcanoes,—a sketch well deserving to be published. Whenever he went on shore he collected objects of natural history, and some of the best specimens of antediluvian animals in Eschscholtz Bay were discovered by him.

To his shipmates his death was a source of the deepest regret. From having sailed together so long, and shared both in the pleasures and privations of the voyage, a brotherly feeling had sprung up among us, that can only be understood by those who have been in a similar situation. When we found that so near home our little society was deprived of one who had done so much to enliven it and to make it agreeable, his death was almost looked upon, I may say, as a family misfortune; and much as his relations may regret their absence from the scenes of his last suffering, they have at least the satisfaction of knowing that he died surrounded by friends who, though unconnected with him by the ties of blood, were not strangers to his private worth, and not ignorant of his public merit.

On the 27th, in lat. 11° south, long. 98° 36' east, we got the trade-wind, south-south-east and south-east, and on the following day sighted the Keeling or Cocos Islands. We carried the trade-wind until the 15th of February, when we lost it in lat. 25° 30' north, long. 58° 30' east. On the 1st of March we made the land of South Africa about the mouth of the Great Fish River, and on the 6th of the same month anchored in Simon's Bay, Cape of Good Hope, where we learnt that our former tender, the Pandora, after leaving us when we started a second time for the Arctic regions, had reached England in safety, and that she had been recommissioned and was daily expected to arrive.

CHAPTER XVI.

Stay at the Cape of Good Hope—Departure—St. Helena—Ascension—Flores and Corvo—Arrival in England—Conclusion.

THE passage from India to the Cape of Good Hope had been so short, that the mind still retained a lively impression of the former. What a contrast was thus produced! Instead of the dense jungle there appeared a ridge of mountains but thinly covered with verdure; instead of the large foliage of the tropics, low hard-leaved bushes; instead of the noble timber, no trees, except those taken by man under his particular care; and instead of the elegant festoons of airy rattans, the leafless Vrouwenhaar (*Cassyta filiformis*, Linn.). Nevertheless, to a European the Cape flora presents a most pleasing aspect. He is no longer perplexed, as in the forests of equinoctial America or Asia, by the curious habits and strange foliage of the vegetation, but meets at every step forms which have for centuries, not only been cultivated in botanic gardens, but have become naturalized in every cottage of his native soil; the heaths, the ice-plants, the geraniums, the callas, and many others are welcome sights, recalling to mind many a happy scene; and even the botanist, if on one hand he must regret that he fails to discover additional genera and species, on the other cannot but rejoice that his favourite science has already made such progress as to render so remote a portion of the globe, in aspect at least, familiar.

The neighbourhood of Simon's Town consists of a ridge of rugged mountains, which are chiefly composed of sandstone, and present, especially during the dry season, the time of our visit, a barren and uninviting appearance. Like many similar localities however, it is very productive, and, on account of its climate, by far richer than the vicinity of Cape Town. *Proteaceæ* are particularly abundant. The *Protea cynaroides*, Linn., may be seen here in the greatest perfection, producing heads frequently more than eight inches in diameter. It is however less frequent than its congener, the *Protea grandiflora*, Thunb., which indeed is so common that it imparts a bluish hue to some places, and thus forms a peculiar feature in the landscape. The colonists call it Wagenboom, and employ its wood to make felloes—a purpose for which, on account of its toughness, it is admirably adapted. The wagenboom is from eight to fourteen feet high, and supplies, with several other *Proteaceæ*, the principal fuel of Simon's Town. We can hardly reconcile ourselves to the idea that any one should be so inconsiderate as to cut down plants which we esteem so highly, and on the structure and cultivation of which so many learned treatises have been written. I must confess that on witnessing the proceeding for the first time my feelings were almost akin to those of the soldier in a certain comedy, who, on entering France, discovers to his surprise that even the children speak French, a language which hitherto he had considered merely as an accomplishment for adults.

I was much struck with the *Myrica cordifolia*, Linn., which covers whole tracts of the downs, and appears at first sight to be about two or three feet high; on a closer inspection however it becomes evident that what seems to be little bushes are only the branches of subterranean trees! I succeeded in freeing several from the sand,— not a very difficult operation,—and found regular stems creeping a few inches below the surface, and attaining, in some instances, as much as sixty feet in length. The plant performs therefore the same office at the Cape as several *Carices* in Northern Europe—that of keeping down the loose shifting sand. Another plant, which both man and nature have applied to the same purpose, is the Paarde Vygen (*Mesembryanthemum edule*, Linn.). On the road between Simon's Town and Wynberg whole acres are planted with it.

On the 10th of March I took a place in the omnibus, and passing through a sandy, dusty country, and the villages of Kalkbay, Wynberg, and Drikoops, arrived after about three hours' ride at Cape Town. On inquiry I succeeded in finding the residence of my friend Mr. C. Zeyher, who has for more than twenty-five years been exploring the fauna and flora of Southern Africa. Mr. Zeyher's neighbour, also, Mr. Rheede van Outhoorn, was a gentleman of interest to me, he being a descendant of the celebrated author of the 'Hortus Malabaricus;'

and I may mention that on the following day I was introduced to Mr. Van Reenen, a nephew of Persoon. I became subsequently acquainted with Dr. C. F. Ecklon, Mr. Zeyher's former partner, and Dr. L. Pappe, the author of the 'Floræ Capensis Medicæ Prodromus.' Dr. Pappe intends, I understand, to follow up his late work by an enumeration of the economic plants of the South African flora. In executing this task he encounters however many difficulties,—the want of assistance on the part of those from whom he had reason to expect it, the retrograding movements of the Botanic Garden, and various other obstacles; but it is to be hoped that these impediments will not induce Dr. Pappe to abandon his design. At a time when the arts have arrived at such a state of perfection, and are ready to seize upon any new substance presented to them, works on economic botany cannot be valued too highly. The least hint on the part of a scientific explorer may lead to results which even the most sanguine could not have anticipated.

During my stay at Cape Town I paid several visits to the Botanic Garden. This institution occupies a space of ground formerly known as the " Government Garden." Considering that it was only established a few years ago, and possesses limited pecuniary means, it has already made some progress, containing a good many plants, two little hothouses, and a library. It is now however retrograding, chiefly through the mismanagement of the commissioners, a body of men who, with a few exceptions, seem to be quite incapable of exercising the supreme direction, and who, by a series of measures, have brought not only ridicule upon themselves, but the whole institution; and unless the chief direction is vested in a scientific person, this establishment, which, if conducted properly, might have been productive of much good both to the colony and botany in general, must soon fall to the ground, or at least fail to accomplish the object for which it was originally designed.

On Thursday, March 13th, Messrs. Zeyher, Baur, and Juritz and myself ascended Table Mountain. We started at dawn, and took the usual road, up the kloof. Seldom have I enjoyed an excursion so much. The day was beautifully clear, the company delightful. At an elevation of 1000 feet we found a grove of the *Leucadendron argenteum*, R. Br., which produces its branches with the regularity of a pine, and is the only indigenous tree I saw in the Cape Town district; for the *Virgilia Capensis*, Lam., which is frequent, has been brought from some distant part of the colony, and the others from Europe, Asia, America, Australia,—in fine, from every part of the globe. A strange mixture, indeed, is thus produced. Here stands a tall *Eucalyptus* near the *Populus alba*, there the *Nicotiana glauca* in company with the cypress of the Levant and the *Casuarina* of the Indian Archipelago; all apparently growing as vigorously as in their native soil.

It was nearly ten o'clock when we reached the summit. Most places generally fall short of the expectations formed of them, but never was I more disappointed than with Table Mountain. During my travels I have visited several mountains far more deserving of renown than this; the Montaña, or Galera de Chorcha, in Veraguas, is certainly more regular, larger, and bolder in outline.

The view of the town, the bay, and the island, however, and the surrounding flora, made up in some measure for the disappointment. Having taken our breakfast near a little fountain, we commenced ransacking the platform. On descending a few hundred feet we came to a valley. There the *Disa grandiflora*, Linn., probably the finest of all terrestrial *Orchideæ*, grew in great perfection on the sides of rivulets, places which during the wet season are entirely under water. Towards dusk our attention was attracted by a number of baboons, which were jumping with great dexterity from rock to rock and chattering so loudly that their voice could be heard at a great distance. We descended on the opposite side to that we had come, in order to make a semi-circuit, and arrived at nine o'clock in Cape Town, tired, but highly pleased with our excursion.

The Herald left Simon's Bay on the 27th of March, and anchored on the 8th of April off James Town, St. Helena. The Old Rock, as the inhabitants of St. Helena affectionately term their native isle, has been described so often by writers of all nations, that a detailed account of it would only be a useless repetition. The island has moreover been ably treated by Lockwood*, who thus alludes to its characteristic features :—

"St. Helena," he says, "is famous for an inexhausti-

---

* 'A Guide to St. Helena, Descriptive and Historical, with a Visit to Longwood and Napoleon's Tomb.' By Joseph Lockwood. St. Helena, 1851. The produce realized by the sale of this book the author has contributed to the fund for erecting a new church in James Town; not only on that account ought the work—the largest, I believe, ever published in St. Helena—be more extensively known, but because it contains a vast amount of useful information.

ble supply of fresh water, without a river; for an indigenous 'wire-bird,' with legs like a sandpiper; for a splendid display of prickly pears; an iron-bound coast; a ladder six hundred feet high—the high road to the upper regions; a time-ball like a Dutch cheese on a Maypole; for the possession of 'Lot and his wife;' a petrified Friar; for extinct volcanoes which cannot be found; the grave of Napoleon; and for not having had a wreck on its shores for time out of mind."

James Town, which is built in a narrow valley, has mean appearance; the houses are low, the windows small. The whole makes an unfavourable impression, especially to one coming from China, the East Indies, or the Cape of Good Hope, and retaining a recollection of the fine edifices of Hongkong, Singapore, and Cape Town. The state of society a casual visitor could of course not attempt to depict without committing some serious blunders, but being unwilling to pass over the subject in silence, I shall once more have recourse to the pages of Mr. Lockwood.

"The grand street—what may be called the 'Place de la Concorde' of St. Helena—contains somewhere about thirty houses; if we perform a grand arithmetical operation, and deduct from this number all the shops, stores, and similar places, we shall have a remainder of some ten or twelve houses, which are occupied by what I suppose must be called the fashionable residents of the place, or, in the language of the 'Court Journal,' the enlightened aristocracy of the island, who may be truly said to be alike distinguished for their wit and wealth, as far as they go.

"Now, as society here is so limited as to be amply sheltered in ten or a dozen houses, a reasonable man, unacquainted with the ways of the world, in the simplicity of his heart would delude himself into the belief, were he a stranger, that they are all as happy and social with each other as bees in a hive or ants in their hill—that they afford a beautiful picture of friendly feeling and sociability, mix with each other as readily as milk and water, and practise all the generous courtesies of gentlemanly bearing, friendly sincerity, and Christian kindness, freed from the pollutions of all assumed consequence, low egotism, and a vulgar affectation of what they call standing on their dignity; but, alas! it is not so.

"There are the Dumpys for example, who once had a relative a captain, cannot think of associating with the Stumpys, whose first cousin, the great man of the family, was only a lieutenant, for many years on half-pay, with a large family of small children to maintain; while the Lumpys, whose maternal grandfather had, at some remote time, married a daughter of the second cousin of no less a dignitary than a 'member of council,' cannot think of mixing in anything like a public place with either the Dumpys or Stumpys. The Lumpys however have no very great objection to visit in a private way both the Dumpys and Stumpys, eat their 'devils,' drink their wine, play at cards with them, or do anything of the kind *sub rosá*, on the sole condition that the Lumpys may cut the Stumpys and Dumpys whenever they meet them in public places or in the front street; they however, for decency sake, giving each other a careful nod in the back streets, if none of the Lumpys' aristocratic friends are sufficiently near to witness their friendly recognition.

"Then the Glumpys, who endeavour to make a great show, are rivals of the Mumpys, who are very musical, and twice a year get up a grand ball of half-a-dozen people, to which they invite two or three infantry officers, who go to ornament the room and dance in spurs, and are, in consequence, expected to escort the young ladies of the family to a fancy fair when one occurs, or at least once or twice to church, in full regimentals, which is a great triumph for the Mumpys. But as the Glumpys are determined not to be outdone by the Mumpys, they maintain their consequence by giving a dinner and a counter ball, to neutralize the effect of that given by the Mumpys, taking great care to have it when there is a man-of-war in the bay, so as to enable them to secure a few naval officers, to give it a consequence which it would not otherwise have had, and at the same time to secure, as a matter of course, a return invitation from the gallant captain, to see the ship and partake of his ready hospitality, which leaves them again on equal terms with the Mumpys, neutralizes their rivalry, and keeps them quiet for the next twelve months to come.

"The Lumpys are delighted to meet the Glumpys in the street, and chat with them about the weather and other interesting matters of the kind, which is courteously reciprocated by the Glumpys, till in an evil minute they catch sight of the Mumpys coming out of the garden, which immediately induces them to quit the Lumpys, and in spite of their rivalry to join company with the Mumpys, and agree with them in a laugh at the awkward pretensions of the odious Lumpys, who really have no sense of decency, and will persist in stopping them in public, although all the world knows they are not on visiting terms; for, say the Glumpys, the Lumpys have no right to presume on a mere private acquaintance, but what can be expected from such low people? to which the Mumpys assent, for somehow or other the Mumpys are under obligations to the Lumpys for sundry loans of money, which the Mumpys have spent without any prospect of repayment, in maintaining their dignity, and keeping themselves on an equality at least with the Glumpys.

"The eldest Miss Dumpy has set her cap at one of the young Humpys, which leads the Stumpys to wonder however the Dumpys can demean themselves by noticing young Humpy, who is only the son of one of the Company's 'uncovenanted' servants, while she belongs to a family that once had a captain in it. While the Stumpys are equally surprised that one of the Dumpys should ever think of presuming to catch one of the young Lumpys, which also becomes a tender point with the Glumpys, because if the Lumpys do form any such connection with the Dumpys, they can never think of associating, even in private, with the Lumpys, who are thus going to sink themselves on a level with the Dumpys, who may be very good people, but certainly cannot be recognized in society by Glumpys, because the Mumpys have a great objection to the Dumpys, and indeed to all such low people as the Stumpys and the Humpys; all of which coming to the ears of the Humpys, Dumpys, and Stumpys, as well as the Lumpys, they affect, every one of them, to despise the Glumpys and the Mumpys, because Glumpys' father was only a purser and Mumpys' a clerk in the Honourable Company's service; and therefore they have nothing to boast about, although they make such a fuss about their dignity. And so all the Lumpys, Dumpys, Humpys, Glumpys, Mumpys, and Stumpys, are at loggerheads with each other as far as they can be, to live in the same place without getting up a civil war, which they would do, were it not that the Lumpys, Glumpys, and Mumpys are under Government, and the Humpys, Dumpys, and Stumpys, in the merchant line, who would be as fierce and inveterate to each other as the factions of the Guelphs and Ghibellines, the Bianchi and the Neri, or even as the Kabblegauers and Hoeckens, to say nothing of the Montagues and Capulets, if they had it in their power."

We made several excursions to Longwood, which is now tumbling to ruins; Napoleon's tomb also, since the removal of the lid, no longer protected from the influence of the weather, is sharing the same fate, and in a few years the island will probably retain nothing save the recollection of having been the residence of one of the great heroes of the nineteenth century. The weeping willows which formerly shaded the grave have long since perished, and their last stumps were carried to France in 1840. The tree standing in the Royal Gardens at Kew has therefore as good a claim to be considered genuine as those now at St. Helena; for they are all only offshoots from the former ones. The little fountain, from which Napoleon used to drink, still pours forth its crystal water. It is overhung by a mass of brambles (*Rubus pinnatus*, Willd.) and birdlayer (*Buddleia Madagascariensis*, Lam.).

We also paid visits to Diana's Peak, the most elevated spot in St. Helena, and the only one where the indigenous vegetation still prevails; yet even there it is fast receding,—like the Indian race before the Caucasian,—and in almost every other part has been completely superseded by plants introduced from foreign countries. The Jackson willow, as the people call the *Acacia longifolia*, Willd., has overspread whole districts, and forms regular thickets. The *Buddleia Madagascariensis*, Lam., is abundant, and makes very good hedges, through which cattle cannot break, as its branches, being decumbent and one over the other, form regular layers like those of a bird's nest; hence its vernacular name, birdlayer. The furze (*Ulex Europæus*, Linn.), with its golden blossoms, is found almost everywhere, and appears to be more robust than in Europe, a change probably produced by climate. Its young sprouts are considered an excellent fodder, and are also, when bruised, given to the cattle as a vermifuge. The *Pelargonium inquinans*, Ait., *Mesembryanthemum edule*, Linn., *Leonotis Leonurus*, R. Br., and several Phylicas and other plants brought from the Cape, are now mingled with Mexican agaves and opuntias, and European oaks and firs. The date-palm is cultivated in the valleys; several avenues near the town consist of the *Ficus religiosa*, Linn., and other species of fig; in short, in the lower grounds the eye meets everywhere plants originally derived from other parts, and even on the highest summits

I noticed already a great mass of the fuchsia, and other intruders.

In ascending Diana's Peak the country assumes a different and peculiar aspect. Brambles (*Rubus pinnatus*, Willd.) become more plentiful, and gradually mingle with shrubby *Campanulaceæ* and *Scævoleæ*, with mosses, *Lycopodia*, tree-ferns, and the cabbage-tree (*Pterolobium arboreum*, R. Br.), with other arborescent *Compositæ*. The tree-ferns (*Dicksonia arborescens*, Herit.) are generally about eight feet high; here and there however specimens are seen attaining as much as fourteen feet. The top of the mountain is reached without difficulty by a footpath, and presents a charming view of the surrounding country. One can hardly imagine more lovely scenery, or that the foot rests upon an island which from the sea appears to be merely a barren rock. What could have induced the people to dedicate the peak to Diana is difficult to explain. That goddess has certainly little here to preside over; the wire-bird (*Charadius pecuarius*), some pheasants, formerly introduced from China, a few partridges and wild rabbits, field-mice, and perhaps now and then a herd of cattle that have strayed, are the only larger animals seen on the mountain.

On the 12th of April we departed from St. Helena, and in five days reached Ascension. Never have I set my foot in a more desolate place, and it is certainly no figure of speech when the people of St. Helena say, "We live upon a rock, the inhabitants of Ascension upon a cinder." The neighbourhood of the garrison, and indeed the greater portion of the island, is extremely barren; the only green spot is the highest peak, which has most appropriately been named "Green Mountain." On Good Friday several parties from our ship ascended it. The distance is seven miles, but appears considerably more, probably on account of the monotonous aspect of the district through which the road leads. It was interesting to notice how at every step the vegetation increased. In the immediate vicinity of the landing-place there were only a few isolated and crippled euphorbias and castor-oil plants. On advancing two miles they became more frequent, and were joined by the *Vinca rosea*, *Argemone Mexicana*, *Nicotiana Tabacum*, an herbaceous *Composita*, an *Amaranthus*, and the *Lycopersicum esculentum*. A little further on a *Crucifera*, a *Panicum*, and a *Sida* made their appearance; and thus by degrees the soil became more and more clothed with verdure, until at last, when approaching the actual summit, a total change took place, and we found ourselves in a comparatively fertile region.

Ascension was formerly uninhabited, and, excepting a few mosses, lichens, and ferns, destitute of any vegetation. About eighteen years ago however the British Government ordered trees to be planted, and the land of Green Mountain to be cultivated. Collectors were sent to St. Helena and the Cape of Good Hope, to gather the vegetable productions of those regions. The newly introduced plants grew up, and by their attraction the moisture has increased. Considering the progress already made, it is not unreasonable to expect that in time the whole of Ascension will be capable of supporting vegetation. This time could undoubtedly be hastened if the cultivation were extended to the lower parts. Hitherto the want of fresh water has been deemed the great obstacle, but this might be successfully surmounted if plants were selected which can be sustained by salt water as well as by fresh, so that, after these have attracted sufficient moisture for their own support, the irrigation with salt water might be discontinued without injury to them. I only know two trees of this nature, the Overal (*Varronia rotundifolia*, Alph. DC.) and the Algaroba (*Prosopis horrida*, Kunth); these are found in Ecuador and New Granada on the very verge of the ocean, and also in the most arid places of the Peruvian deserts, where sometimes for years nothing save dew is known to fall. They are moreover highly useful. The berries of the overal form excellent food for poultry, and the algaroba produces a bean which is almost the sole support of the numerous horses, mules, donkeys, and goats of the arid regions of Peru. It would be difficult to find in the whole vegetable kingdom two plants the constitution of which is better adapted for the island, or the introduction of which would be attended with more beneficial results, both directly and indirectly, than the two alluded to*.

In the Government Garden we met a corporal of marines, who had been one of the party that planted the first trees. He seemed to be an intelligent person, and, as the head-gardener was absent, conducted us over the whole establishment. We soon after fell in with two naval officers, and, guided by them, went through the various tunnels. They explained to us the way in which

* Seeds in large quantities may easily be obtained of any trader on the Peruvian coast, at little or no expense.

the water is collected and conducted to the coast; a contrivance so nicely regulated that hardly a drop of rain is lost. We were also shown what may be considered the Lion of Ascension, the great "Pride of India" (*Melia Azedarach*, Linn.), the largest tree in the island; it stands in a creek, is fifty feet high, and has a stem from nine to twelve inches in diameter. After having made the circuit of the mountain, we ascended to its summit—the "*Big Peak*." It is 2800 feet above the sea, and almost entirely overgrown with ferns and bramble (*Rubus pinnatus*, Willd.), the latter being one of the plants brought from St. Helena. Several seats and a table have been put up on the highest point. The view is quite pleasing: all around are fields cultivated with sweet potatoes, vegetable marrow, pumpkins, and bananas, while at a distance nothing save desolation prevails. How great must have been the labour, perseverance, and foresight that could produce such an effect, and change, as it were, a dreary desert into a fertile and inhabitable region!

On the 20th of April the Herald left Ascension, and, crossing the equator on the 26th of the same month, she passed in latitude 30° north through numerous floes of *Sargassum* weed, sighted on the 20th and 21st of May the islands of Flores and Corvo, two of the Azores, and arrived on the 6th of June, 1851, at Spithead, whence she proceeded to Chatham to be paid off.

Thus was completed a voyage which will ever remain remarkable. There are few ships that have gone in an equal space of time over so extensive a portion of the globe, furnished a greater amount of hydrographical data, or brought together more extensive collections of objects of natural history, than H.M.S. Herald, during the years 1845–1851, and I need only, as proofs of this assertion, refer to the foregoing pages, the series of charts which the Admiralty has made public, and the two works on the Zoology and Botany, which have already received the approbation of the press.

Captain Kellett, in his official communications to the Admiralty, more than once alludes to the excellent conduct of the officers and men under his command, and, had he undertaken the task of writing this Narrative, he would no doubt have pointed out, with that deep sense of justice which characterizes all his proceedings, those who had principally co-operated with him in bringing about results so favourable. Unfortunately, his sudden departure for the Polar regions has prevented him from paying this tribute to their merit; and, although I am not ignorant of the distinguished services rendered by most of my shipmates, yet it would ill become me to carry out on these points the intentions of the gallant Captain under whose command it is my pride to have been placed. The best proof that their services were duly acknowledged in those quarters in which every naval man is most desirous they should be known, is that the Admiralty marked their sense of approbation not only by remunerating all engaged in the arduous voyages to the Arctic regions with double pay for a portion of the time they were thus occupied, but promoted the greater number of the officers to a higher rank or employed them in important expeditions; while their estimation of Captain Kellett was marked in the most decisive manner by giving him the command of one of the vessels in search of Sir John Franklin, placing him in a position requiring qualifications of the highest order. Let us hope that Captain Kellett's talents, energy, and perseverance, which have hitherto been so successfully directed, whether to the promotion of science, or against the enemies of his country, may be equally successful when employed in the cause of humanity.

THE END.

APPENDIX.

NAUTICAL REMARKS, BY HENRY TROLLOPE, Com. R.N.

Bay of Panama; Trollope Rock, San Jose Bank.

THIS shoal is situated in the eastern entrance of the Bay of Panama; from the shoalest part a rocky patch of very small extent with only *three feet* water upon it. The tree on Galera Island, a very remarkable one, towering above all others on the island, bears N. 57° 40' W. (true), distant nine miles. The shoal has 4, 5, and 6 fathoms upon it, and is at the utmost about two miles from north to south and three from east to west; surrounded by much deeper water, 10, 11, 15, and 20 fathoms. The marks for clearing it, if coming from the southward, are as follows:—if intending to pass to the eastward of the shoal, keep well over on the main towards Garachine Point, observing that before the Island of St. Elmo is brought on, or is open of the east end of Galera, to be at least ten miles S.E. by E. of Galera: observing these directions will clear the shoal altogether. When Cocoa Island, a remarkable tree-capped rock on the south end of San Miguel Island, comes on with the small end of Galera Island bearing west, a ship will be to the northward of it; always bearing in mind that you should be, if passing east of the shoal, ten or twelve miles from Galera, if west of the shoal, not more than four or five miles from Galera. After passing Galera the course to Pelado will be N. ¼ W. (magnetic), distance twenty-five miles. The course is plain and clear throughout; the lead and a good look-out will amply suffice, as the shores on both sides are generally steep to, and free from dangers. Pelado is a flat level island of very small extent and moderate height, perhaps sixty or seventy feet high; it has no trees, but is covered with a coarse prickly shrub, making the machete (a sort of bill-hook and pruning-knife combined) a useful article in getting to the summit. From Pelado the course to Flaminco will be W. by N. (magnetic), forty-seven miles distant. This part is equally free from hidden dangers as the foregoing; the lead and a commonly decent look-out will amply suffice; the northern shore is shallow and must not be approached too closely, but the lead points this out far better than any description, as the shoaling is very gradual. Chepillo Island, and tree on the north shore, will be remarked, and if approaching the Pearl Islands the small isle of San Bartolomé between the bright silvery beaches of Taboga. Pacheque and Contadora Islands will be remarked as solely covered with palm-trees, the appearance of which, unmixed with any other, I do not remember in any other spot. Cabrera, with its three peaks; Taboga, for which it is sometimes mistaken, from its also having three peaks; lastly Flaminco, Ancon, and the towers of the cathedral, rise to view, and you may anchor as convenient off Perico and Flaminco Islands, in 6 or 7 fathoms, or go nearer the town in $3\frac{1}{2}$ and 4 fathoms, being however careful to avoid the Baja d'Afuera, the marks for avoiding which are as follows:—Centre of Portola Island on with San Jose (N. 38° E., magnetic) leads to the eastward of it three-quarters of a mile. Centre of Portola just touching the east tangent of Flaminco, leads about a cable's length to the eastward of it. The south end of Ancon Hill on with the south-east bastion of the city, clears it on the south about a cable's length. The north end of Ancon Hill on with the north-east bastion, leads a quarter of a mile of it. The south end of Ancon Hill on with the inner part of the north-west bastion, leads on the Baja d'Afuera, in its shoalest part $1\frac{3}{4}$ fathoms at low water. The northern and highest part of Changmel on with the east tangent of Perico Island, bearing S.W. (magnetic), leads just to the southward of the shoal. This rocky patch is of very small extent, and is said to have at lowest spring-tides only $1\frac{3}{4}$ fathoms. I sounded all round and had great difficulty in finding it; at low water, neap-tides, we had 2 and $2\frac{1}{4}$, surrounded by $3\frac{1}{2}$ and 4 fathoms on all sides.

Bearings of anchorage at Panama:—$3\frac{1}{2}$ to $3\frac{3}{4}$ fathoms (lowest springs); Uraba Peak on with San Jose, S. 5° W. (magnetic); Bruja Point on with the west tangent of Nao Island S. 47° W. (magnetic); Venado Isle on with Punta Bruja.

Bearings of anchorage off Flaminco Island:—6 fathoms (lowest springs); east tangent of Taboguilla on with or open of the west tangent of San Jose Rock, and the north end of Changmel midway between Flaminco and Perico; San Jose Rock S. 13° E.

High water at full and change at Taboga 3h. 16m.; greatest rise 20 feet.

San Jose del Cabo, California.

The Bay of San Jose is an indifferent roadstead at the extreme of the Californian Peninsula. It is entirely exposed from N.E. by the E. to S.S.W.; the water is deep even close to the shore, and a hole having 40 or 50 fathoms exists in the best part. It is however a convenient place for obtaining water, as well as for fresh beef and vegetables. Fruit, such as figs and oranges, milk, Mexican cheese, and one or two other articles may be procured from the village, which is about three-quarters of a mile from the stream. One of the marks for the bay will be the high range of hills running to the N.E.; the remarkable thumb peak of San Lazaro standing up like a pinnacle is the highest of the range, while the valley of the river is clearly defined between this range on the left and a much lower range of pinnacles, craters, and flat table-lands on the right. The coast for five or six leagues to the N.E. is free from danger. Running along the coast from the eastward, Punta Gorda (the northernmost point of the bay) is too remarkable to escape notice—a flat white hill of moderate height, perhaps 150 or 180 feet high, with several pyramidal hills to the left, particularly a group of three in one with a flat-topped crater-like hill or truncated cone near it, and a flat level plain with a single conical hill in it to the right; the long playa, or sandy beach, will then be seen, running along which you will soon distinguish the stream and a flagstaff on a slightly elevated mound. The coast may in any part be approached without danger, having 5 or 6 fathoms close to, but deepening very rapidly. To avoid letting go your anchor in the 50-fathom hole, keep the flagstaff open to the westward of the high peak of San Lazaro, or thumb, as we called it, the latter bearing N.W. by W., when a vessel may anchor in 13 to 15 fathoms (soft mud), three-quarters of a mile from the shore. The river is 50 yards to the left of the flagstaff, and at low water, when there is but little surf on the beach, affords an excellent supply. It is however liable to interruptions; strong north-west breezes raise a heavy surf on the beach, rendering landing somewhat difficult. However, with a party on shore filling and a hauling-line for the casks, we completed very expeditiously, getting forty tons on board in thirty hours. The sea at high water percolates through the sand, rendering the water brackish and unfit for use: this can be remedied by going higher up the stream, but the labour is of course more. Horses are good and easily obtained. There are no remains of the Franciscan Mission of San Jose, the origin of the place; and the village is but a poor straggling place, which, I believe, almost grew up during the war with America. The flagstaff is in 23° 3' 15" N., 109° 37' 53" W., variation 2° 28' 53" easterly. Off a rocky cliff between Capes Palma and Pafia there is a shoal about one mile off the shore, which we did not examine; the cliff is in 23° 26' 53" N., 109° 23' 30" W.

Angles for anchorage at San Jose del Cabo:—13¼ fathoms, mud. Punta Gorda and Peak of San Lazaro 113° 48'; Punta Gorda N. 41° E. (magnetic); Punta Gorda and Coast Peak 26°; Coast Peak and Flagstaff 97°; Flagstaff N. 82° W. (magnetic).

Guaymas, Gulf of California.

Guaymas once having been seen cannot, with ordinary attention, be mistaken; the whole coast is so remarkable that one is only at a loss to say which is the most prominent landmark; nevertheless, as Pajaros Island lies right before the entrance when ten or twelve miles to the eastward, it is a perfectly blind harbour; a stranger without a chart might well be in doubt as to the entrance. Cape Haro, a bold, bluff headland, jutting out due south to seaward, and rising with a wall-like cliff 200 feet from the water, is the best mark for the harbour; it has 14 or 15 fathoms touching the rocks, and the entrance between Trinidad (an island so called from the distinct manner in which it is formed in three divisions united at their base) and Pajaros is clear and free from danger, only taking care to give the points, particularly Punta Baja, a berth of half a cable's length; the lead is quite sufficient guide for going in. Secondly, the white smooth beach of Cochore, extending uninterruptedly from the Morro Inglese at the entrance of the harbour, twelve miles to the eastward, and terminated suddenly by a still more remarkable hill, called Cerro Tordillo, or, as we termed it, Morro Afulva, lies in such contradistinction to the extraordinary mass of hills forming the peninsula, out of which the harbour of Guaymas is hollowed like the crater of a volcano, that it is from the contrast almost equally remarkable. Further to the northward are the remarkable peaks called Tetas de Cabra (Goat's Teats). Some have recommended these to be made, as the prevalent wind is from N.W., and there is certainly no advantage to be gained by getting over on the Cochore shore, while by making the land to the windward of Cape Haro a ship will have the prevalent breeze and current in her favour. The Tetas de Cabra are about ten miles N.W. by W. of Cape Haro; they stand on the west shore of a large deep bay, which has several patches of rocks and islets in it. Pajaros Isle forms of itself an excellent harbour; in fact, the space between Trinidad, Pajaros, and Morro Inglese is equal as far as security, and superior as to depth of water, to the harbour itself; the advantage the latter has, is in there being a better access into the interior. The tides are very irregular except at full and change; there appears to be only one tide in the twelve hours, but then the usual interval occurs between high and low water. The greatest rise and fall we observed during our stay was 4 feet; high water 8h. A.M.

Latitude, Punta de Arena 27° 55' 15" N.; longitude, 110° 51' 10" W.; 17' 53" west of Mazatlan. Cape Haro, S.E. extreme, 27° 50' 30" N.; longitude, 110° 51' 40" W. Variation of the compass, 10° 29' 19" easterly. The average height of the barometer in January was 29·94 inches. Mean temperature 76° Fahrenheit.

Notes relating to the Currents in the North Pacific Ocean.

On the 9th of May, 1848, we weighed from the Isle of Taboga, and were taken in tow by H.M. Steam-ship Sampson. We made sail to a moderate breeze from N.W., standing to the southward, the Pandora astern of us. When in the latitude of Punta Mala we hauled up west, and, the wind heading, shortened and furled sails; the difference was at once perceptible; we were going 7 and 6½ before, now, with calm and moderate breezes ahead, only 6 and 5½; westerly and S.W. winds prevailed. On Friday, the 12th of May, we cast off the Pandora; she made sail N.W. for the Sandwich Islands, and we continued our course to the westward: having her in tow did not make so material a difference in our speed as we might have expected. Sunday, the 14th of May, in 7° 19' N. and 89° 20' W., the Sampson, having towed us 660 miles, cast us off on a drizzling rainy morning; she stood east on the starboard tack with a light breeze from S. and S.S.E., while we continued our course to the westward. We had now a succession of baffling winds, S.W., W., and N.W., so that she appeared to fall off on both tacks; heavy rains, occasional squalls, then a day or two of fine weather, but the wind never favouring us for a moment. On Tuesday, the 23rd of May, in 10° 54' N., 96° 42', we were one thousand miles W. by N. of Punta Mala. The table shows the set of the current on each day, but the mean of the whole amounted to 170' S., 69° E.

In 1846 we sailed from Taboga on the 16th of April, running out of the Bay of Panama with a fine north-west breeze, which, as at this time (May, 1848), failed us as we cleared Punta Mala. In three days we were off Quibo and Quicara, meeting light south-west and southerly breezes. A current in that time set us S. 56°, W. 75'. We were baffled with light airs, calms, etc., S.W. and N.W., making very slow progress. On the 11th of May in 10° N. and 96° W., or one thousand miles W. by N. of Punta Mala; the daily set is seen in the table, but the mean will be S. 10°, W. 88', forming a most striking difference to what we have this year experienced in the same part of the ocean. In 1848 the wind still continued to baffle us; sharp squalls, heavy rain, calms occasionally, but without bringing any change in the breeze; it was steady in unsteadiness, N.W., W., S.W., so that she fell off on both tacks most provokingly; our progress was thirty or forty miles a day, sometimes S.W., at others N.W.

On June the 12th we were in the meridian of Cape San Lucas, 11° 28' N., 109° 56' W., about nine hundred miles W. by N. of our position on the 23rd of May. The daily set is seen in the table, but the mean only amounts to nineteen miles N. 43° W., forming again a striking difference from what we experienced in 1846. We passed over nearly the same tract of ocean in that year between May 11th and 19th; the set then amounted to ninety-eight miles N. 83° W., but we then fell in with the trade-wind on May 17th in 9° 51' N. and 103° 57' W., which no doubt influenced the set. In fact, the sets of the currents during the early part of both passages were so different, yet the general direction of the wind so similar, that on this ground alone the difference cannot be accounted for. In 1846, between Panama and our falling in with the trade-wind, April 16th and May 17th, in 10° N., 104° W., the currents set with a great degree of regularity in three different directions:—

April 16th to 20th	7° 13' N.	84° 45' W.	S. 56° W. 75'
April 20th to May 1st	10° 23' N.	89° 00' W.	N. 47° E. 139'
May 18th to 17th	9° 51' N.	103° 37' W.	S. 52° W. 154'.

After falling in with the trade-wind in 1846 until we got into the latitude and longitude of our meeting with the trade-wind in 1848 (14° 24' N., 121° W.), the currents followed the direction of the wind with great regularity, averaging about 20' a day, or S. 57', W. 171' in eight days. In 1848, with different winds in the same part of the ocean (9° 51' N., 103° 37' W., to 14° 24' N. and 121° W.). June 4th to June 24th, the first ten days with variable winds from W.S.W. and

N.W., the set was S. 46° W. 96'. The last ten days the whole set was N. 45°, W. 91', the winds generally the same, with the exception of three days, June 20 to June 23, when we were carried four hundred miles N.W. by a steady breeze from S.W. This apparently gave a direction to the current in accordance to the wind, for during the second and third days the direction was found to be N.E. 29', both days included.

Thus we find in the last-named tract of ocean, in one year, with the regular trade-wind, during eight days, in a distance of one thousand miles, we were set S.W. by W. 171', or about 20' a day, *with the wind*. In the next year, with variable winds from N.W., W., and S.W., during twenty days we were set 133 miles nearly due west, or six miles and a half a day, directly *against the average wind*. Whether to attribute these apparently contradictory results to current or error in the reckoning is the question. On the one hand we may be led to place some confidence in the difference between dead reckoning and observations, by its uniform rate in two different years. When running through the trade-wind in 1846, steering a N.W. by W. course for 2700 miles, we were set 270 miles S. 53° W. in twenty-five days, or nearly eleven miles a day. In 1848, steering a W. by N. course for 4300 miles, we were set S. 56° W. 273 miles in twenty-nine days, or nine miles and a half a day. Again, on leaving the trade-wind and hauling in for the Straits of Juan de Fuca, the whole difference amounted only to thirteen miles N. 7° E., and this with westerly winds prevailing seven days out of the ten we were getting over the 1100 miles. In 1848, when going to Petropaulowski, the difference was still less; in 1360 miles the whole set only amounted to eight miles S. 35° W. But as if to destroy these results, Captain Beechey says, in the Blossom the whole set between Oneehow and Petropaulowski was N. 25° W. fifty-two miles: ours was S. 63° W. ninety-three miles. A current which Captain Beechey and Admiral Lütke mention in the thirty-fifth parallel, we did not experience, in an equal degree at all events. On May 26, in 35° 45' N. and 160° E., our difference was N. 73° E. 20'; on the day before N. 47° W. 6'; on the day after S. 19° W. six miles; whereas Captain Beechey's was S. 40° E. 50' in three days, but he had light winds and calms, and we a steady breeze from S.W.

In our passage from Chepoonskoi Noss to Cape Derby, Norton Sound, the winds varied between S.W. and N.W. generally; very moderate, occasionally a heavy swell, but not remarkably so. The whole set amounted to one hundred miles S. 27° E. in thirteen days, the distance about 1300 miles. Going up between Behring's Island and the main, we kept on the Asiatic shore, but did not make the land until the 26th of August, when Cape Navarin was in sight. Crossing the Gulf of Anadir the set was in one day S. 22° W. and the next S. 21° E., giving in forty-eight hours a set of 40' to the southward. On Wednesday, the 30th of August, off Cape Tchapline and Tchukotsky Noss, a boat was lowered and anchored in 30 fathoms water, five or six miles from the shore; but this trial gave a different result altogether, it being E.N.E. (true), one to two knots an hour. Captain King mentions having lowered a boat off Cape Tchapline, and gives the set N. by E. half a mile an hour; but he adds that it was not considered to be a current, but the effect of a long southerly swell.

On the 31st of August St. Lawrence Island was in sight. We passed it to the northward, and with a fresh north-westerly breeze ran for Norton Sound, and, to our surprise, made Sledge Island at 4h. in the afternoon, having been set thirty-seven miles S. 76° E. in forty-eight hours; it must be remembered however that we were baffled for twelve or fourteen hours with calm light winds and fogs, during which little could be observed as to how she was drifting, etc.

Between Cape Derby and Behring's Strait the whole amount of current or difference between the dead reckoning and observations amounted to 37', S. 58° W. Captains King and Beechey both mention a strong northerly current, particularly the former, who says in both years the Resolution and Discovery were set 20' in 24h. through the Strait. In our own case, both going and returning, we found it the reverse, particularly when leaving Kotzebue Sound for the southward. On each day the set was so regular that it could hardly have been the effect of accident or error; it would seem, from its direction, to have come from the American shore towards the coast of Asia, where, finding itself checked, it, with increased velocity, found vent between the Diomede Isles and East Cape; it was here we found it in its greatest strength. The daily set is seen in the table, the whole amounting to S. 60° W. 160 miles, or nine miles a day; the going and returning passage giving a somewhat similar result, particularly in that part where the passage was the same, namely, between Petropaulowski and St. Lawrence Island. When off St. Lawrence Island, returning from Kotzebue Sound in October, the current amounted to twenty-two miles S. 82° E., and, as mentioned before, in August S. 76° E. 37', a sufficient resemblance at different times and under different circumstances to make it remarkable. A discrepancy appears, according to general report, in the currents we met with in the entrance of Behring's Strait, and also in one respect in what we ourselves experienced. Captains Cook, King, and Beechey, all speak of a northerly current; Sir John Barrow mentions it as a well-known and undoubted fact, but does not state his authority; the one instance in our own case was in the boat off Tchukotsky, when its direction was E.N.E. (true), one to two knots an hour.

Between Petropaulowski and Guadelupe there is nothing to remark upon. We did not experience anything of the strong easterly set mentioned by Admiral Lütke and Beechey. Strong N.W. and westerly breezes carried us on two hundred miles a day, a rolling swell after us; on the 22nd one struck the ship heavily, and stove the galley on the starboard quarter. We made Guadalupe on the 15th of November twenty-five days from Petropaulowski; avoiding the trade-wind we fell into the N.W. winds off the coast of California in 37° N. and 132° W., having had a spurt of N.N.E., E., and S.E. winds for three days in 44° and 43° N., 160°, 153° W. The whole amount of current in the four thousand miles S. 30° W. 100', averaging four miles a day.

This was the second time we had made the voyage from San Blas to Panama, but the results are little satisfactory as to forming any conclusion of their general direction, except in one respect, that they always appear contrary, and that it is about the most tedious and provoking piece of navigation that could well be found.

From San Blas to Acapulco the land was in sight from three to five leagues distant; the winds were light and variable with frequent calms; they were very much the same in 1846, when we were nearer the land. In this year the mean direction in eight days was S. 36° E. twenty-five miles, while in 1846 in the same time it was N. 81° W. sixteen miles. In 1846-47 we kept the land in sight the whole way from Acapulco to Cape Blanco; the mean of all the currents in nineteen days amounted to S. 29° E. 74' in this year 1848-49. We were 180 miles off the shore and were sixteen days in getting sight of Cape Blanco de Nicoya; the mean of all the currents amounted to forty-two miles N. 77° W. During the 23rd and 27th of December, 1848, in 11° 35' N. and 93° W., and 9° 36' N. 90° 35' W., the currents were strong and more regular than usual; a heavy westerly swell accompanied light winds from N.E. and N.N.E.; a Tehuantepec gale had probably been blowing, and the waters were now returning northwards, the direction modified by the N.E. winds, which were steady for two or three days. But it was on making Cape Blanco that we experienced the full strength of adverse currents. For six days we kept the Cape and Island in sight; even after clearing it the currents increased rather than diminished, as will be best seen by the table.

We were sixteen days getting over a distance of 450 miles, during which time we were set S. 84° W. 260'. In 1847, at the same time of year, the weather generally speaking very similar, we were only eight days doing the same distance, and the mean of all the currents only amounted to thirty-nine miles west. On the 17th of January, 1849, we made Port Pinas; on the 18th of January Galera Island was in sight, and at 1h. 30m. P.M. on the 19th anchored off Flaminco, Panama. Captain Hall's abstract of the currents on the south-west coast of Mexico, only prove the strength and even violence with which they occasionally run; his strongest set was experienced in 91° and 93° W. three or four leagues from the land; in six days it amounted to 210 miles S.S.E. When only 180 miles from Acapulco, a distance he took nine days to accomplish, he was, in that time, set 153' E. by S.

On the 19th of March, 1849, we sailed from Point Burica for the Sandwich Isles, leaving the coast one month earlier than in 1846, and nearly two months than in 1848. Although detained by frequent calms, the passage was certainly more favourable than in former years. The currents were strong and generally adverse, in the first part of the passage particularly; in fact, they divide themselves into different sets; the first between Point Burica and lat. 8° 45' N., long. 87° 10' W., secondly, from this to lat. 9° 35' N., long. 109° 55' W. In the first period of nineteen days the whole distance was only 264 miles, and the mean of all the currents amounted to 262' N. 85° E., but the calms were so long and frequent, and the winds so light and baffling, that much of this must be attributed to error or the impossibility of keeping a correct reckoning. In the second period, eleven days, the whole distance was 1360 miles; the mean of all the currents amounted to S. 77° W. 222 miles.

On the 8th of April a breeze from N.E. set in so steadily that we considered it the trade-wind, but, after carrying us seven or eight hundred miles, it died away, and we had a period of calms, light airs, variable winds, rain, thunder and lightning, and it was not until the 12th of April, in 8° 39' N. and 102° 31' W., that we fairly may be said to have had the trade-wind; it certainly was not so strong as in previous years, when we were later in the season. This was the third time we had made this passage; it is interesting to compare the results of the mean of all the currents in different years.

APPENDIX.

Year.	Currents.	Dates.	Route, Distance, etc.
1846	S. 72° W. 112°	April 16 / May 18	Panama to 10° N. and 104° W.: 1450 miles in 31 days.
1848	S. 72° E. 152°	May 10 / June 12	Panama to 8° 39' N. 100° W.: 1500 miles in 33 days.
,,	N. 45° W. 91°	June 13 / June 14	8° 39' N. 110° W. to 14° 51' N. and 119° 34' W.: 700 miles in 10 days.
1849	S. 59° E. 50°	March 19 / April 19	Point Burica, Costa Rica to 9° 35' N. and 109° 55' W.: 1580 miles in 31 days.
1850	S. 60° E. 57°	April 4 / April 12	Mazatlan to Clarion Island: 550 miles in 8 days.

RUNNINGS THROUGH THE TRADE-WINDS.

Year.	Currents.	Dates.	Distance.		
1846	S. 54° W. 274'	May 19 / June 13	2460 miles in 24 days		
1848	S. 52° W. 189'	June 25 to July 12	2450	,,	17 ,,
,,	S. 65° W. 86'	July 12 to July 23	1700	,,	11 ,,
1849	S. 69° W. 234'	April 20 to May 8	2500	,,	16 ,,
,,	N. 83° W. 165'	May 20 to June 7	1700	,,	19 ,,
1850	S. 67° W. 168'	April 12 to May 5	2400	,,	23 ,,
,,	S. 85° W. 101'	May 25 to June 7	1800*	,,	14 ,,

In 1846 fell in with the N.E. trade-wind on the 19th of May in 10° N. 103° W.; after carrying us 2450 miles it failed in 34° N. 141° W. In 1848 (June 25) fell in with the trade-wind in 14° 24' N. and 121° W.; after carrying us 2300 miles to the Sandwich Isles (July 12) and 1700 miles further, it failed on the 23rd of July, in 31° N. and 169° E. In 1849 fell in with the trade-wind in 9° 35' N. and 100° 55' W.; it carried us to the Sandwich Isles, a distance 2900 miles, on the 8th of May. Leaving Tahoora on the 20th of May it carried us 1680 miles further, when we lost it, the 7th of June, in 31° 44' N. and 170° 41' E. In 1850 we did not meet the regular trade-wind (leaving

* Averaging nine miles and a half a day, following generally the direction of the wind.

Mazatlan on April 4) until off Clarion Island in 18° 22' N. and 114° 38' W.; it carried us to the Sandwich Islands on the 5th of May, a distance of 2200 miles. Leaving Tahoora on the 25th of May, after carrying us 1800 miles, it failed in 34° N. and 172° E. on June 7.

The regular action of the currents within the influence of the trade-winds is seen at once, but in other parts of the ocean they apparently follow no law. Our results must necessarily be imperfect, and to a certain degree unsatisfactory. Wind appears to have but little effect, even with the prevalent westerly gales between Kamtchatka and the north-west coast of Asia. In one year the mean of the currents amounted to 100 miles S. 30° W., and in the following to 162 miles S. 54° E. Such differences, occurring again and again, diminish very much one's faith in the accuracy of the means employed, and in fact, were it not for the regularity of the set in four successive voyages within the influence of the trade-winds, we should be inclined to put the whole on one side as worse than useless, and only calculated to mislead. It must however be remembered that the voyages of one ship, however extended, form little more than a single link in the chain; and further knowledge may clear up contradictions and prove that Nature, here as elsewhere, has nothing contrary.

Heights ascertained with the Barometer and by Trigonometrical Measurement, by Captain Henry Kellett, C.B., H.M.S. Herald.

		Feet.
Santiago, Chile	(Bar.)	1868
Curacaria, on the road to Santiago from Valparaiso	(Bar.)	667
Cuesta Prado	(Bar.)	2585
Cuesta Zapato	(Bar.)	2008
Casa Blanca	(Bar.)	846
Mountain of Aconcagua (Tr. Mt. from Valparaiso and Pichidanque)		23004
Right Peak of San Martin's Isle, coast of California	(Bar.)	548
Back Peak Station, one of the lower peaks in the south-east part of Cerros Island, coast of California	(Bar.)	954
Cross Hills, City of Guayaquil, Eastern	(Bar.)	247
,, ,, Middle	(Bar.)	326
Western	(Bar.)	284

APPENDIX. 295

		Feet.
Table Hill, Punta St. Elena, Guayaquil . . .	(Bar.)	424
Taboga, Bay of Panama, south-east summit . .	(Bar.)	935
Taboguilla	(Bar.)	710
Cerro Congo, Isle San Miguel	(Bar.)	481
Valparaiso Lighthouse, centre of lantern (base of tower 136 feet)	(Tr. Mt.)	188
Lima, Callao Gate (by levelling)	(Tr. Mt.)	453
Santa Clara Island, River Guayaquil . . .	(Tr. Mt.)	220
Lighthouse on Santa Clara (30 feet) . . .	(Tr. Mt.)	250
Charles Isle, Galapagos; the Puebla	(Bar.)	461
The Chacre	(Bar.)	1049
Southern Coronados Isle, coast of California .	(Bar.)	585

GULF OF CALIFORNIA.

		Feet.
Highest hill over Guaymas Harbour . . .	(Tr. Mt.)	1584
,, ,, . . .	(Bar.)	1556
Black Mountain, Guaymas	(Tr. Mt.)	1364
Round Mountain	(Tr. Mt.)	1574
Haro Peak	(Tr. Mt.)	900
Peak right of Haro Peak	(Tr. Mt.)	1316
Soldado Peak	(Tr. Mt.)	428
Pajaros Island	(Tr. Mt.)	190
Morro Inglese	(Tr. Mt.)	83
Almagro Island	(Tr. Mt.)	256
Peak over the south-west end of San Marco Island	(Bar.)	526
Peak of Coronados Island	(Bar.)	935

INDEX.

Acapulco, i. 139.
Achira, an eatable root, i. 180.
Adobes, derivation of the name, i. 48.
Agnew, Mr. J., i. 263, ii. 78.
Agricultural Society of the Hawaiian Islands, ii. 217.
Alanje, canton of, i. 278.
Albemarle Island, i. 58.
Alce, Señor, i. 56.
Alfalfa, i. 200.
Almendral, i. 37.
Amaro, Don Vicente, i. 126.
Amortajado, i. 53.
Ancon, Hill of, i. 87, 293.
Aconcagua, height of, i. 42.
Anderson, Mr. J., ii. 227.
Andes, i. 164.
Anta, i. 223.
Aracacha, i. 200.
Araucanians, i. 29.
Ascension, Island of, ii. 276.
Atahualpa, i. 174.
Austin, Captain H., his expedition, ii. 202.
Awatcha Bay, ii. 6, 92.

Bayanos, i. 321.
Beechey, Captain, ii. 4.
Behring's Strait expedition, ii. 191.
Behring, Vitus, ii. 3.
Belcher, Captain Sir E., his expedition, ii. 212.
Billings, Mr. W., ii. 156, 182.
Bocas del Toro, territory of, i. 277.
Bosky, ii. 8, 70.
Botafogo, i. 17.
Bowring, Mr. J. C., ii. 245.

Brandt, F., death of, i. 91.
Buckland river, ii. 120.
Buenaventura, town of, i. 79, 80.
Bueso, Don Alejandro, ii. 161.
Byer's Island, ii. 91.

Calête, i. 17.
California, Gulf of, ii. 153.
Callao, i. 44.
Canton, ii. 228.
Cape Classet, i. 95.
,, Collnett, i. 119.
,, Corrientes, i. 82, 227.
,, Finisterre, i. 2.
,, Flattery rocks, i. 95.
,, Gavarea, ii. 91.
,, Horn, i. 27.
,, Mendocino, i. 113.
,, of Good Hope, arrival at, ii. 263
,, San Francisco, i. 63.
,, San Lucas, ii. 155.
,, Velas, i. 136.
Cariamango, i. 167.
Cayos, i. 235.
Cedron-tree, ii. 74.
Cedros Island, i. 120.
Cerros Island, i. 120.
Chacayaque, river and cave of, i. 205.
Chagres, town of, i. 287.
,, river of, i. 238.
Challenger, wreck of, i. 30.
Chamisso, Adalbert von, ii. 4.
Charles Island, i. 54.
Chepillo, Island of, i. 83.
Chihuahua, ii. 171.
Chilian coaches, i. 40.

Chimborazo, i. 210.
Chimmo, Mr. W., ii. 9.
Chinese herbal, ii. 230.
Chiru, beach of, ii. 76.
Choco, Bay of, i. 2, 18.
,, province of, i. 73.
Cholera, ii. 149.
Cholo Indians, i. 321.
Chorera, canton of, i. 284.
Cochopato, i. 183.
Coffee, i. 18.
Collinson, Captain, his expedition, ii. 197.
Colosacapi, i. 165.
Concepcion Boy, i. 31.
Cook, death of, i. 91.
,, Captain, ii. 3.
Cook's visit to Rio, i. 13.
Cooper, Mr. E., ii. 99, 110.
Cope, Mr. W., i. 193.
Copper mines of Chile, i. 42.
Cormorant, H.M.S., i. 51.
Coronados, i. 118.
Corvo, island of, ii. 279.
Cotton, i. 19.
Coyba, i. 90.
Crossing the line, i. 6.
Cuenca, i. 194.
Cueva, Don Juan, i. 169.
Cujibamba, valley of, i. 171.
Cumbi, i. 192.
Cupica, i. 220.

Dalrymple rock, i. 59.
Darien, territory of, i. 294.
David, i. 279.
Deep soundings, i. 7.
De Haven, Lieutenant, his expedition, ii. 206.
Desert, Great South American, i. 52.
Desertas, i. 3.
Diana's Peak, ii. 275.
Diego Ramirez, i. 27.
Dorachos, i. 313.
D'Ozery, Viscount, i. 142.
Duncan rock, i. 95.
Durango, ii. 166, 168.

Earthquake, i. 32.
Edmonston, Mr. T., i. 55, 66.
Ekins, Dr. R., i. 172, 173.
El Parco, i. 157.
Enterprise, H.M.S., ii. 175, 185.
Erebus and Terror, H.M.S., ii. 190.
Eskimos, their customs and manne described, ii. 49.
Esmeraldas, river and town of, i. 70.
Espino, i. 39.
Esquimalt, i. 101.

Falkland Islands, i. 21.
Fernando de Noronha, i. 8.
Finger-point, i. 61.
Finlayson, Mr., i. 105, 112.
Flaminco, Island of, i. 88.
Flattery Jack, i. 112.
Flores, Island of, ii. 279.
Forsyth, Captain, his expedition, ii. 207
Fort William, i. 21.
Fossil animals, ii. 35.
Franklin, his probable position, an plan for his relief, ii. 213–216.
Freshwater Bay, i. 60.
Fuchsia spectabilis, discovery of, i. 204

Gallo Island, i. 71.
Gambir, ii. 250.
Gardiner's Island, i. 54.
Gonzanama, i. 167.
Goodridge, Mr. J., i. 120, 129; ii. 110.
Gorgona, island of, i. 73.
Guacos, in Veraguas, i. 313.
Guadelupe, Island of, ii. 72.
Guaymas, ii. 156.
Guayaquil, Gulf of, i. 153.
,, river of, i. 211.
,, town of, i. 208.
Gutta percha, ii. 252.
,, taban, ii. 252.

Half-castes, i. 302.
Hance, Dr. H. F., ii. 233.
Harris, Colonel, i. 194, 202.
Harris, W., death of, i. 135.

Hawaiian Islands, ii. 79.
Herald Island described, ii. 116.
,, discovered, ii. 114.
Herald's first voyage to the Arctic regions, ii. 1; second voyage, ii. 91; third voyage, ii. 175.
Herz, Mr. H., ii. 173.
Hill, Mr. J., i. 127.
Hongkong, botany of, ii. 239.
,, climate of, ii. 236.
,, geology of, ii. 235.
,, zoology of, ii. 244.
Honolulu, ii. 217.
Hot springs, i. 244.
Hull, Mr. T., ii. 158.
Hutchinson, Mr. J., ii. 156.
Hydrographical surveys, i. 139.

Ice-cliffs in Kotzebue Sound described, ii. 33.
Ilha Raza, i. 11.
Indians, i. 198.
Indiarubber-tree, i. 70.
Inglefield, Captain, his Arctic voyage, ii. 210.
Investigator, H.M.S., ii. 175, ii. 179.
Isthmus of Panama, i. 231.
,, climate of, i. 245.
fauna of, i. 261.
flora of, i. 249.
,, inhabitants of, i. 296.

Jago, Mr. E., i. 224, ii. 121.
Jangadas, i. 9.
Jervis, Dr., i. 194.
Jiggers, i. 177.
John Bigge's reef, i. 118.

Kamehameha, his levee, ii. 218.
Keeling Island, ii. 263.
Kegel, Dr., ii. 170.
Kellett, Captain H., his expedition, ii. 197.
Kellett, Captain H., taken prisoner, i. 126.
Kelp, i. 93.

Kennedy, Charles, death of, ii. 188.
,, Mr., his voyage, ii. 209.
Kerr, Mr. W., ii. 167.
Keys, i. 235.
Kicker Rock, i. 59, 60.
King George, i. 106.
Koa, table of, ii. 225.
Koolan, district of, ii. 80.
Kotzebue, Otho von, ii. 4.

Ladrones, i. 235.
La Ligua Bay, i. 41.
Language, English, ii. 89.
,, Eskimo, ii. 68.
,, Hawaiian, ii. 88.
,, Quichua, i. 184, 191.
La Peñete, i. 157.
Las Juntas, i. 181.
Lee, Mr. W., ii. 98.
Lehmann, Mr., ii. 167.
Lima, i. 48.
Lobos de la Mar, i. 51.
,, Tierra, i. 51.
Lockwood, Mr. J., ii. 270.
Loja, i. 176.
Longwood, ii. 274.
Los Santos, canton of, i. 283.
Loxa, i. 176.

Maguire, Mr. R., i. 224, ii. 177.
Manta, i. 215.
Manzanilla-trees, i. 141.
Mariviña, i. 191.
Mazatlan, ii. 149.
,, port of, i. 122.
Mesquital, ii. 172.
M'Gowan's reef, i. 59.
Michaelowski, ii. 8, 184.
Miguel, Don Jose, i. 174.
M'Clure, Commander, ii. 175, 179.
,, his expedition, ii. 197.
Monte Christi, i. 215.
Monterey, California, i. 117.
Montezuma, King Lora, i. 317.
Moody, Lieutenant R. C., i. 22.
Moore, Commander, ii. 98.

Moore, Commander, his expedition, ii. 197.
Mormons, i. 116.
Morrell's Island, ii. 91.
Mosquita Point, i. 30.
Mowett, Captain, i. 23.
Murphy, W., death of, i. 91.

Naranjal, town of, i. 206.
Nata, canton of, i. 284.
„ town of, i. 284.
Navon, i. 190.
Neagh Bay, i. 111.
Nelson, i. 4.
„ Mr., consul, i. 229.
New Dungeness, i. 109.
New Year's Day in Singapore, ii. 256.
Nueva Granada, boundary of, i. 72.
Nutmeg, account of, ii. 247.
Nunanu, valley of, ii. 79.

Oahu, flora of, ii. 81.
„ island of, described, ii. 80.
„ shells of, ii. 87.
Ocotes, ii. 164.
O'Higgins, Don Ambrosio, i. 47.
Old Concepcion, i. 35.
Old Mazatlan, ii. 160.
Oña, i. 183.
Orchil, i. 3.

Paavil Oglayuk, the interpreter, ii. 8.
Pacific Ocean, i. 43.
Pakenham, Mr. R., ii. 73, 161.
Pali, ii. 80.
Palm cactus, i. 58.
Panama, city of, i. 84, 289.
„ hats, i. 213.
„ province of, i. 283.
„ Viejo, i. 87.
Pandora, ii. 263.
Papudo Bay, i. 41.
Paredes, i. 235.
Parita, canton of, i. 283.
Payta, i. 52, 144.
Pearls, i. 268.
Pearl Islands, i. 137, 234, 235.

Penny, Captain W., his expedition, ii. 199.
Petermann, Mr. A., ii. 93, 189.
Petropaulowski, ii. 71.
Peru, coast of, i. 48.
Piedra de la Tierra, i. 124.
„ del Mar, i. 123.
Pim, Mr. B., i. 147, 173, ii. 130.
Piscobamba, i. 173.
Piura, i. 152.
Plover, H.M. Brig, ii. 1.
„ Island, ii. 116.
Point Curaomilla, i. 36.
„ Gordo, i. 69.
Poisonous plants, i. 254.
Port Clarence, ii. 185.
„ Discovery, i. 107.
„ Luis, i. 22.
„ Townshend, i. 108.
„ Victoria, i. 99.
Portobelo, canton of, i. 285.
„ port of, i. 232.
„ town of, i. 286.
Porto Santo, i. 2.
Post-office Bay, i. 55.
Proteaceæ, ii. 265.
Pullen, Lieut., his expedition, ii. 193.
„ Mr. W., ii. 101, 104.
Pulo Aor, ii. 246.
Punta de Cocos, i. 137.
„ Piñas, i. 220.
Pustau, Mr. W., ii. 227.

Quadra's and Vancouver's Island, i. 98.
Quibo, i. 90.
Quichua language, i. 184.
Quina fina de Loja, i. 180.
Quiros, rivers of, i. 159.

Rae, Dr., his journey, ii. 208.
Ramirez, Don F., ii. 167.
Raza lighthouse, i. 20.
Remedios, ii. 74.
„ village of, i. 280.
Reptiles, i. 264.
Richardson, Sir J., his expedition, ii. 19

INDEX.

River Buenaventura, i. 79.
,, Catamayo, i. 171.
,, Iscuande, i. 77.
,, Macara, i. 160.
,, San Jose, ii. 154.
,, Sua, i. 63.
Rivers of the Isthmus of Panama, i. 237.
Riofrio, Don Mariano, i. 172.
Rio Janeiro, i. 11.
Rock goose, i. 25.
Ross, Sir J., his expedition, ii. 204.
Roys, Captain, ii. 93.

Salango Island, i. 213.
Sampson, H.M.St., ii. 8.
San Antonio, i. 5.
,, Blas, i. 123.
,, Diego, California, i. 119.
,, Carlos, Castle of, i. 134.
,, Francisco, Bay of, i. 113.
,, ,, mission of, i. 114.
,, Guayange, i. 74.
,, Lucas, i. 181.
,, Martin, Island of, i. 119.
,, Miguel, Gulf of, i. 234.
,, Quintin, Isle of, i. 120.
,, Sebastian, ii. 161.
Santa Clara, i. 53.
,, Cruz, Fort of, i. 20.
,, Lucia, ii. 163.
,, Teresa, ii. 172.
Santiago, canton of, i. 281.
,, de Chile, i. 38.
,, de Veraguas, i. 282.
Sandwich Islands, ii. 79.
Saragura, i. 182.
Sasaranga, i. 164.
Saunders, Mr. J., his expedition, ii. 195.
Savanerics, i. 317.
Search for Franklin, ii. 189.
Secos, i. 235.
Seymour, Sir G., ii. 72.
,, Rear-Admiral Sir G., i. 140.
Shedden, Mr. R., ii. 118, 129.
,, his search for Franklin, ii. 96.
Shells, i. 267.
Sierra Madre, 163.

Siguantenejo, i. 126.
Silla de Payta, i. 81.
Simon's Town, neighbourhood of, ii.
Singapore, described, ii. 247.
Solano, Bay of, i. 224.
Solis, i. 12.
Soundings, i. 43, 63, 92, 94, ii. 107.
Soviango, i. 162,
Spanish schooner in distress, i. 5.
,, vessels, i. 2.
Spithead, arrival at, ii. 279.
Stanley harbour, i. 21.
Staunton, Mr., i. 127.
Straits of Juan de Fuca, i. 97.
Sua Head, i. 64.
Sua, village of, i. 217.
St. Helena, ii. 269.
St. Michael, Fort of, ii. 8.
St. Stephen's Bay, i. 60.
Stephens, Mr., i. 229.
Sunda, Strait of, ii. 258.
Survey, commencement of, i. 78.
Swift, wreck of, i. 23.

Taboga, i. 88.
Table-mountain, ascent of, ii. 268.
Talbot, Colonel, i. 194, 202.
Talcahuano, i. 33.
Tapir, Asiatic, ii. 255.
Tartar soldiers, ii. 229.
Tatooche Island, i. 95.
Taylor, Dr. J., i. 193, 194.
Tambo, name and origin of, i. 164.
Tea, cultivation of, i. 19.
,, preparation and adulteration of, ii. 231.
Teneriffe, Peak of, i. 3.
Tepic, town of, i. 124.
Theatre, Limenian, i. 143.
Theatre Royal, Kotzebue, ii. 10.
Tides, ii. 236.
Timber, i. 257.
Tobacco, i. 19.
Trollope, Mr. H., i. 121, 127.
,, ii. 106, 154.
,, his mission to Behring's Strait, ii. 212.

INDEX.

Moore, Co*ght, i. 9.
197. *, i. 217.
Mor*
Mo*land goose, i. 24.
M*
M*aldivia, i. 28.
M*lparaiso, i. 37.
*egetable ivory, i. 222.
Venado Island, i. 122.
Veraguas, i. 278.
Victoria, Straits of Juan de Fuca, i. 101.
Vinda of St. Peter and St. Paul, i. 81.

Western Eskimo-land, description of, ii. 11.
,, ,, animals of, ii. 23.
,, ,, climate of, ii. 13.
Western Eskimo-land, islands of, ii. 12
,, ,, plants of, ii. 14.
Whalers, American, ii. 94.
Whiffin, Mr. J. G., i. 216, 224, ii. 9, 218
Winds, i. 10.
Wood, Mr. J., i. 127, 213.
Woodward, Mr. T., i. 130, ii. 9.
,, death of, ii. 259.
Wreck Bay, i. 59.

Yierba Buena, California, i. 114.
,, Ecuador, i. 204.
Yucatan, derivation of the name, ii. 248

Zamora, i. 169.
Zapote blanco, ii. 170.
Zeyher, Mr. C., ii. 266, 267, 268.

I.
THE NARRATIVE OF THE VOYAGE OF H.M.S. HERALD,

Under the Command of Captain Henry Kellett, R.N., C.B., during the Years 1845–1851; being a Circumnavigation of the Globe, and Three Cruizes to the Arctic Regions in Search of Sir John Franklin. By BERTHOLD SEEMANN, F.L.S., Member of the Imperial L.C. Academy Naturæ Curiosorum, Naturalist of the Expedition. In two volumes, octavo, with a Map and tinted Lithographs. Price 21s.

II.
THE ZOOLOGY OF THE VOYAGE OF H.M.S. HERALD,

Under the Command of Captain Henry Kellett, R.N., C.B., during the Years 1845–51. Edited by Professor EDWARD FORBES, F.R.S. In one volume, quarto, 400 pages and 100 lithographic plates (issued in Parts). Price 21s.

Opinions of the Press.

"An abstract of the reports [on the ice-cliffs in Kotzebue Sound] of Dr. Goodridge and Mr. Berthold Seemann, who accompanied Captain Kellett, is given in this [the first] part. . . . . No pains have been spared by Sir John Richardson himself to make his descriptions of these [fossil] remains as perfect as he could; . . . . and the accuracy of the descriptions is much increased by the employment of the nomenclature suggested by Professor Owen in his work on the Archetype of the Vertebrate Skeleton. . . . . We have seldom seen better specimens of natural history lithography. They are highly creditable to artist and publishers,—and worthy of the work which they accompany."—*Athenæum*.

III.
THE BOTANY OF THE VOYAGE OF H.M.S. HERALD,

Under the Command of Captain Henry Kellett, R.N., C.B., during the Years 1845–51. By BERTHOLD SEEMANN, F.L.S., Member of the Imperial L.C. Academy Naturæ Curiosorum. In one volume, quarto, 400 pages and 100 lithographic plates (issued in parts). Price 31s. 6d. coloured; 21s. plain.

Opinions of the Press.

"The parts now published possess an interest independent of scientific botany, inasmuch as any new information respecting the natural features both of the Arctic Regions and of the Isthmus of Panama must at the present time be particularly acceptable. In this respect we like the plan followed by Mr. Seemann's work; which is, not to give merely a synopsis of the flora, but to preface each of his divisions with an 'Historical notice,' detailing the events and scientific labours which led to our present knowledge of the districts treated of,—and an 'Introduction' conveying a general notice of the country and an account of the conditions under which the animal and vegetable kingdoms flourish. The general reader will indeed find under these two heads a comprehensive picture of the country, drawn by a hand whose study of nature and scientific attainments are evidently of a high order. . . . . The Flora of Eskimo-land (Part I.) is a valuable addition to Arctic literature. . . . The Flora of the Isthmus of Panama (Part II. *et seq.*) contains altogether a larger amount of information respecting the natural features and resources of that at present important country than we had previously possessed. . . . . The way in which Mr. Seemann has performed his task is, as we have said, deserving of great praise. The general descriptions are in a graphic and lucid style, and call to mind the writings of a Humboldt or a Darwin; while the accuracy and value of the scientific parts are guaranteed by the names of Harvey, Wilson, Nees von Esenbeck, Bentham, J. D. Hooker, J. Smith, Churchill Babington, and others, who have lent the author a helping hand. Sir William Hooker has, with his accustomed liberality, allowed Mr. Seemann the use of his extensive library and herbarium."—*Athenæum*.

"No traveller was ever better fitted for his task than Mr. Seemann. He looks at his favourite science of phytology with all the ardour of a devoted lover. Nothing can exceed the assiduity of his attentions, or the careful manner in which he has bestowed them. He has considered the subject in all its bearings. His summaries of the botanical products of the country, whether statistical, economical, or ornamental, are replete with instruction, and bespeak the possession of one of those comprehensive minds which can appreciate at once, and correctly, all the features of the scene before him. Instead of those dry, and shall we say unprofitable, details which have too often filled the pages of works designed as records of the discoveries made under Government patronage and at Government expense, we have here a series of written pictures, presenting vividly to the mind's eye the very scenes which the author himself beheld, and grouping, with exact method, yet with agreeable ease, the characters which communicate to the landscape and the land their greatest interest, alike to the enthusiastic explorer, and the sober, plodding student in the science-halls of distant Europe."—*Phytologist.*

"It happened fortunately that there was attached to Captain Kellett's expedition Mr. Berthold Seemann, a German naturalist, of much intelligence and industry, and great power of observation, who neglected no opportunity of making himself thoroughly acquainted with everything relating to botany which came within his reach. . . . . The first part contains a graphic and cleverly-written description of Western Eskimo-land and its vegetation. . . . . In the second part of this important work an account will be found of Panama, which gives a graphic and ample description of what it is most desirable for the cultivator to know, and draws a striking picture of the beauty of the vegetation."—*Prof. Lindley, in Gardeners' Chronicle.*

REEVE AND CO., HENRIETTA STREET, COVENT GARDEN.

Published on the 1st and 15th of every Month, price 10s. per Annum,

BONPLANDIA,

A BOTANICAL PERIODICAL, THE OFFICIAL ORGAN OF THE IMPERIAL L.C. ACADEMY NATURÆ CURIOSORUM.

EDITED BY BERTHOLD SEEMANN, F.L.S.,
Member of the Imperial L.C. Academy Naturæ Curiosorum.

This Journal will be devoted principally to Economic Botany, but contain, besides, Leading Articles on all subjects of general interest to Phytologists, Treatises on the Geography of Plants, Biographical Sketches of eminent Men, Reports of Learned Societies, Reviews of Books, Official Communications by the Imperial L.C. Academy Naturæ Curiosorum, and Scientific News from all parts of the world. Communications may be written in all European languages, but appear only in German; and they must be addressed either to the Editor (B. Seemann, Kew, near London), or to the Publisher (C. Rümpler, Hanover). The Paper may be ordered in London by

WILLIAMS and NORGATE, Henrietta Street, Covent Garden.

LIST OF WORKS

PRINCIPALLY ON

NATURAL AND PHYSICAL SCIENCE,

PUBLISHED BY

REEVE AND CO.,

5, HENRIETTA STREET, COVENT GARDEN.

BOTANY.

PARKS AND PLEASURE-GROUNDS; or, Practical Notes on Country Residences, Villas, Public Parks, and Gardens. By CHARLES H. J. SMITH, Landscape Gardener and Garden Architect, Fellow of the Royal Scottish Society of Arts, Caledonian Horticultural Society, etc. Crown 8vo. Price 6s.

CONTENTS:—The House and Offices—The Approach—Pleasure Grounds and Flower Gardens—The Park—Ornamental Character of Trees detached and in combination—Planting—Fences of the Park and Pleasure Grounds—Water—The Kitchen, Fruit, and Forcing Gardens—Public Parks and Gardens—The Villa—The Laying-out and Improvement of Grounds.—The Arboretum—The Pinetum.

"Mr. Smith expresses himself with frankness as well as precision, and with such an evident reliance on the sympathy of his readers, as to make him a favourite with those who are familiar with his pages. In short, his book is what was really wanted in these busy times to bring the elegant in country residences abreast of the useful."—*North British Agriculturist.*

"In describing the characters and requirements of the various descriptions of ornamental grounds, Mr. Smith has happily chosen language so plain, and rules so simple, that he leaves nothing to be wished for."—*Liverpool Standard.*

"The author gives the result of some twenty years' study and observation in a methodical form and practical style."—*Aberdeen Journal.*

"Mr. Smith, who is a landscape-gardener and garden-architect of great experience, has worked out his design with ability and judgment."—*Globe.*

"The character of this publication is altogether practical, from the opening hints upon the house and offices, to the closing directions about the arboretum and the pinetum."—*Spectator.*

"Mr. Smith is an experienced landscape-gardener, and a man of much good sense. His opinions are therefore entitled to attention."—*Gardeners' Chronicle.*

THE VICTORIA REGIA. By Sir W. J. HOOKER, F.R.S. In elephant folio. Illustrated on a large scale by W. Fitch. Reduced to 21s.

The work on the Royal Water Lily contains four plates of very large size, expensively coloured, illustrative of the different stages of flowering and fruiting, with analyses of structure, as follows:—

1. A view of the entire plant, flower, fruit, and leaves, on the water.
2. A flower *of the natural size* in progress of expanding, together with as much of the enormous foliage as the broad dimensions of the paper will admit.
3. A fully expanded flower *of the natural size*, with foliage, &c.
4. A vertical section of the fully developed flower, with various dissections and analyses.

"Although many works have been devoted to the illustration and description of the *Victoria regia*, it seemed still to want one which, whilst it gave an accurate botanical description of the plant, should at the same time show the natural size of its gigantic flowers. This object has been aimed at by the combined labours of Sir W. Hooker and Mr. Fitch, and with distinguished success. The illustrations are everything that could be desired in the shape of botanical drawings. They are accurate, and they are beautiful."—*Athenæum*.

THE RHODODENDRONS OF SIKKIM-HIMALAYA. With drawings and descriptions made on the spot. By J. D. HOOKER, M.D., F.R.S. Edited by Sir W. J. HOOKER, D.C.L., F.R.S. In handsome imperial folio, with thirty coloured plates. Price 3*l*. 16*s*.

"In this work we have the first results of Dr. Hooker's botanical mission to India. The announcement is calculated to startle some of our readers when they know that it was only last January twelvemonths that the Doctor arrived in Calcutta. That he should have ascended the Himalaya, discovered a number of plants, and that they should be published in England in an almost UNEQUALLED STYLE OF MAGNIFICENT ILLUSTRATION, in less than eighteen months—is one of the marvels of our time."—*Athenæum*.

"A most beautiful example of fine drawing and skilful colouring, while the letter-press furnished by the talented author possesses very high interest. Of the species of *Rhododendron* which he has found in his adventurous journey, some are quite unrivalled in magnificence of appearance."—*Gardeners' Chronicle*.

SANDERS'S PRACTICAL TREATISE ON THE CULTURE OF THE VINE, as well under Glass as in the Open Air. With plates. 8vo. 5*s*.

"Mr. Assheton Smith's place at Tedworth has long possessed a great English reputation for the excellence of its fruit and vegetables: one is continually hearing in society of the extraordinary abundance and perfection of its produce at seasons when common gardens are empty, and the great world seems to have arrived at the conclusion that the kitchen gardening and forcing there are nowhere excelled. We have, therefore, examined with no common interest the work before us, for it will be strange indeed, if a man who can act so skilfully as Mr. Sanders should be unable to offer advice of corresponding value. We have not been disappointed. Mr. Sanders's directions are as plain as words can make them; and, we will add, as judicious as his long experience had led us to expect. After a careful perusal of his little treatise, we find nothing to object to, and much to praise."—*Gardeners' Chronicle.*

"A clever, well-written, and nicely illustrated horticultural pamphlet, telling us all we want to know on the subject."—*Guardian.*

PHYCOLOGIA BRITANNICA; or, History of the British Sea-weeds; containing coloured figures, and descriptions, of all the species of Algæ inhabiting the shores of the British Islands. By WILLIAM HENRY HARVEY, M.D., M.R.I.A., Keeper of the Herbarium of the University of Dublin, and Professor of Botany to the Dublin Society. The price of the work, complete, strongly bound in cloth, is as follows:—

In three vols. royal 8vo, arranged in the order of publication................ } £7 12 6

In four vols. royal 8vo, arranged systematically according to the Synopsis ...... } £7 17 6

A few Copies have been printed on large paper.

"The 'History of British Sea-weeds' we can most faithfully recommend for its scientific, its pictorial, and its popular value; the professed botanist will find it a work of the highest character, whilst those who desire merely to know the names and history of the lovely plants which they gather on the sea-shore, will find in it the faithful portraiture of every one of them."—*Annals and Magazine of Natural History.*

"The drawings are beautifully executed by the author himself on stone, the dissections carefully prepared, and the whole account of the species drawn up in such a way as cannot fail to be instructive, even to those who are well acquainted with the subject. The greater part of our more common Algæ have never been illustrated in a manner agreeable to the present state of Algology."—*Gardeners' Chronicle.*

POPULAR HISTORY OF BRITISH SEA-WEEDS, comprising all the Marine Plants. By the Rev. DAVID LANDSBOROUGH, A.L.S., Member of the Wernerian Society of Edinburgh. *Second Edition.* With twenty-two plates by Fitch. Royal 16mo. 10*s.* 6*d.* coloured.

"The book is as well executed as it is well timed. The descriptions are scientific as well as popular, and the plates are clear and explicit. Not only the forms, but the uses of Algæ, are minutely described. It is a worthy SEA-SIDE COMPANION—a handbook for every occasional or permanent resident on the sea-shore."—*Economist.*

"Those who wish to make themselves acquainted with British Sea-weeds, cannot do better than begin with this elegantly illustrated manual."—*Globe.*

"This elegant work, though intended for beginners, is well worthy the perusal of those advanced in the science."—*Morning Herald.*

A CENTURY OF ORCHIDACEOUS PLANTS, selected from those most worthy of cultivation figured in Curtis's Botanical Magazine, with coloured figures and dissections, chiefly executed by Mr. FITCH; the descriptions (entirely re-written) by Sir WILLIAM J. HOOKER, F.R.S. With an introduction on the culture of Orchidaceæ generally, and on the treatment of each genus; by JOHN C. LYONS, Esq. Royal 4to, containing one hundred plates. Price *Five Guineas*, coloured.

"In the exquisite illustrations to this splendid volume full justice has been rendered to the oddly formed and often brilliantly coloured flowers of this curious and interesting tribe of plants."—*Westminster and Foreign Quarterly Review.*

"A very acceptable addition to our knowledge of the Orchis tribe. The plates are beautifully executed, and have been selected with great care. Each species has a brief character attached, and to each genus botanical and practical observations, from the pen of Sir William Hooker, are prefixed. The work is enriched with a prefatory memoir by Mr. Lyons, full of sound judgment and experience, on the most approved method of growing Orchids."—*Literary Gazette.*

POPULAR HISTORY OF BRITISH FERNS, comprising all the Species. By THOMAS MOORE, F.L.S. With twenty plates by Fitch. Royal 16mo. 10*s*. 6*d*. coloured.

"Mr. Moore's 'Popular History of British Ferns' forms one of the numerous elegant and instructive books by which Messrs. Reeve and Co. have endeavoured to popularize the study of Natural History. In the volume before us, Mr. Moore gives a clear account of the British Ferns, with directions for their cultivation; accompanied by numerous coloured plates neatly illustrated, and preceded by a general introduction on the natural character of this graceful class of plants."—*Spectator.*

"We have rarely, if ever, seen a publication relating to plants where the object aimed at is more fully accomplished than in this elegant volume."—*Hooker's Journal.*

"A prettily got-up book, and fit for a drawing-room table."—*The Friend.*

THE BRITISH DESMIDIEÆ; or, Fresh-Water Algæ. By JOHN RALFS, M.R.C.S., Honorary Member of the Penzance Nat. Hist. Society. The Drawings by EDWARD JENNER, A.L.S. Royal 8vo, thirty-five plates. Price 36*s*. coloured.

NEREIS AUSTRALIS; or, Illustrations of the Algæ of the Southern Ocean. By Professor HARVEY, M.D., M.R.I.A. To be completed in Four Parts, each containing twenty-five coloured plates, imp. 8vo. Price 1*l*. 1*s*. Parts I. and II. recently published.

"Of this most important contribution to our knowledge of exotic Algæ, we know not if we can pay it a higher compliment than by saying it is worthy of the author. It should be observed that the work is not a selection of certain species, but an arranged system of all that is known of Australian Algæ, accompanied by figures of the new and rare ones, especially of those most remarkable for beauty of form and colour."—*London Journal of Botany.*

CURTIS'S BOTANICAL MAGAZINE (commenced in 1786); Continued by Sir WILLIAM JACKSON HOOKER, K.H., D.C.L., &c., Director of the Royal Gardens of Kew.

⁎ Published in monthly numbers, each containing six plates, price 3s. 6d. coloured; and in annual volumes, price 42s.

HOOKER'S JOURNAL OF BOTANY and KEW GARDENS MISCELLANY. Edited by Sir WILLIAM JACKSON HOOKER.

This Botanical Journal, in addition to original papers by Eminent Botanists, contains the Botanical News of the month, Communications from Botanical Travellers, Notices of New Books, &c.

⁎ In monthly numbers, with a plate, price 2s.

THE LONDON JOURNAL OF BOTANY. Edited by Sir W. J. HOOKER, K.H., D.C.L., F.R.S., etc. Vol. VII., completing the series. 8vo, with plates. 30s. plain.

ICONES PLANTARUM; or, Figures, with brief descriptive characters and remarks, of new and rare Plants. 8vo. New Series. Vol. V. 31s. 6d. plain.

(*Under the Authority of the Lords Commissioners of the Admiralty.*)

FLORA OF NEW ZEALAND. By Dr. J. D. HOOKER, F.R.S. To be completed in Five Parts, each containing Twenty Plates. Price 31s. 6d. coloured; 21s. plain.

"The work is written in good plain English, with a view to the conveniency of colonists, but without, on that account, being rendered in the smallest degree unscientific. Quite the contrary. .... Let us add, that the beautiful execution of the work renders it a 'library-book,' even to those who are not interested about natural history."—*Gardeners' Chronicle.*

(*Under the Authority of the Lords Commissioners of the Admiralty.*)

BOTANY OF THE VOYAGE OF H.M.S. HERALD. By BERTHOLD SEEMANN, Member of the Imperial Academy Nat. Curiosorum. To be completed in Ten Parts. Plates. 4to. 10s. plain.

(*Under the Authority of the Lords Commissioners of the Admiralty.*)

FLORA ANTARCTICA; or, Botany of the Antarctic Voyage of H.M. Discovery Ships *Erebus* and *Terror*, during the years 1839–1843, under the command of Capt. Sir James Clark Ross, R.N., F.R.S. By JOSEPH DALTON HOOKER, M.D., R.N., F.R.S., &c., Botanist to the Expedition. In two vols. royal 4to, cloth, containing 200 plates. Price 10*l*. 15*s*. coloured; 7*l*. 10*s*. plain.

"The descriptions of the plants in this work are carefully drawn up, and much interesting matter, critical, explanatory, and historical, is added in the form of notes. The drawings of the plants are admirably executed by Mr. Fitch; and we know of no productions from his pencil, or, in fact, any botanical illustrations at all, that are superior in faithful representation and botanical correctness."—*Athenæum*.

CRYPTOGAMIA ANTARCTICA; or, Cryptogamic Botany of the Antarctic Voyage of H. M. Ships *Erebus* and *Terror*. By JOSEPH DALTON HOOKER, M.D., F.R.S., &c. Royal 4to, cloth, containing 74 plates. Price 4*l*. 4*s*. coloured; 2*l*. 17*s*. plain.

THE ESCULENT FUNGUSES OF ENGLAND; a treatise on their History, Uses, Structure, Nutritious Properties, Mode of Cooking, Preserving, &c. By the Rev. Dr. BADHAM. Super-royal 8vo, plates. 21*s*. coloured.

"The English are not a fungus-eating nation; and though we do not eat frogs like our neighbours, we are rather celebrated for our love of another of the reptilian family—turtle. There is no reason why we should eschew frogs and relish turtle; still less is there for our eating one or two of the numerous edible funguses which our island produces, and condemning all the rest. To draw attention to this fact, and to supply an accurate account, with a correct delineation, of the esculent species of this family in Great Britain, are the objects of the book before us. Such a work was a desideratum in this country, and it has been well supplied by Dr. Badham; with his beautiful drawings of the various edible fungi in his hand the collector can scarcely make a mistake. The majority of those which grow in our meadows, and in the decaying wood of our orchards and forests, are unfit for food; and the value of Dr. Badham's book consists in the fact, that it enables us to distinguish from these such as may be eaten with impunity."—*Athenæum*.

ILLUSTRATIONS OF BRITISH MYCOLOGY; containing Figures and Descriptions of the Funguses of interest and novelty indigenous to Britain. *First Series*. By Mrs. HUSSEY. 4to, cloth gilt, with ninety beautifully drawings. Price 7*l*. 12*s*. 6*d*. coloured.

"This talented lady and her sister were in the first instance induced to draw some of the more striking Fungi, merely as picturesque objects. Their collection of drawings at length became important from their number and accuracy, and a long continued study of the nutritive properties of Fungi has induced the former to lay the results of her investigations before the public, under the form of illustrations of the more useful and interesting species. The figures are so faithful that there can be no difficulty in at once determining with certainty the objects they are intended to represent; and the observations will be found of much interest to the general reader."—*Gardeners' Chronicle.*

"This is an elegant and interesting book: it would be an ornament to the drawing-room table; but it must not, therefore, be supposed that the value of the work is not intrinsic, for a great deal of new and valuable matter accompanies the plates, which are not fancy sketches, but so individualized and life-like, that to mistake any species seems impossible. The accessories of each are significant of site, soil, and season of growth, so that the botanist may study with advantage what the artist may inspect with admiration."—*Morning Post.*

ILLUSTRATIONS OF BRITISH MYCOLOGY; containing Figures and Descriptions of the Funguses of interest and novelty indigenous to Britain. *Second Series.* By Mrs. HUSSEY. Publishing in Monthly Parts, coloured drawings, price 5s.

VOICES FROM THE WOODLANDS; or, History of Forest Trees, Lichens, Mosses, and Ferns. By MARY ROBERTS. Elegantly bound. With twenty Plates of Forest Scenery, by FITCH. Royal 16mo. 10s. 6d. coloured.

"This work includes a wide range of genera, from the lichen to the oak, and by way of giving variety to a subject so commonplace, the several plants are supposed to tell their own stories, and describe their own family peculiarities."—*Atlas.*

"The fair authoress of this pretty volume has shown more than the usual good taste of her sex in the selection of her mode of conveying to the young interesting instruction upon pleasing topics. She bids them join in a ramble through the sylvan wilds, and at her command the fragile lichen, the gnarled oak, the towering beech, the graceful chestnut, and the waving poplar discourse eloquently, and tell their respective histories and uses."—*Britannia.*

POPULAR FIELD BOTANY; containing a familiar and technical description of the plants most common to the British Isles, adapted to the study of either the Artificial or Natural Systems. By AGNES CATLOW. *Third Edition.* Arranged in twelve chapters, each being the Botanical lesson for the month. Containing twenty plates of figures. Royal 16mo. 10s. 6d. coloured.

"The design of this work is to furnish young persons with a Self-instructor in Botany, enabling them with little difficulty to discover the scientific names of the common plants they may find in their country rambles, to which are appended a few facts respecting their uses, habits, &c. The plants are classed in months, the illustrations are nicely coloured, and the book is altogether an elegant, as well as useful present."—*Illustrated London News.*

THE TOURIST'S FLORA. A Descriptive Catalogue of the Flowering Plants and Ferns of the British Islands, France, Germany, Switzerland, and Italy. By JOSEPH WOODS, F.A.S., F.L.S., F.G.S. 8vo. 18s.

"The appearance of this book has been long expected by us; and we can justly state that it has quite fulfilled all our expectations, and will support the high reputation of its author. Mr. Woods is known to have spent many years in collecting and arranging the materials for the present work, with a view to which he has, we believe, visited all the most interesting localities mentioned in it. This amount of labour, combined with extensive botanical knowledge, has enabled him to produce a volume such as few, if any other, botanists were capable of writing."
—*Annals of Natural History.*

ZOOLOGY.

(*Under the Authority of the Lords Commissioners of the Admiralty.*)

ZOOLOGY OF THE VOYAGE OF H.M.S. SAMARANG. Edited by ARTHUR ADAMS, F.L.S., Assistant-Surgeon, R.N., attached to the Expedition.

VERTEBRATA. By JOHN EDWARD GRAY, F.R.S., Keeper of the Zoological Department of the British Museum.

FISHES. By Sir JOHN RICHARDSON, M.D., F.R.S.

MOLLUSCA. By the EDITOR and LOVELL REEVE, F.L.S. Including the anatomy of the *Spirula*, by Prof. OWEN, F.R.S.

CRUSTACEA. By the EDITOR and ADAM WHITE, F.L.S.

*** Complete in one handsome royal 4to volume, containing 55 plates. Price, strongly bound in cloth, 3*l.* 10s.

CONTRIBUTIONS TO ORNITHOLOGY. By SIR WILLIAM JARDINE, Bart., F.R.S.E., F.L.S., &c.

The "CONTRIBUTIONS" are devoted to the various departments of Ornithology. They are published at intervals in Parts, and form an annual Volume, illustrated by numerous coloured and uncoloured Plates, Woodcuts, &c.

The Series for 1848, containing ten Plates, price 9s.

The Series for 1849, containing twenty-four Plates, price 21s.

The Series for 1850, containing twenty-one Plates, Vignettes, and Woodcuts, price 21s.

The Series for 1851, containing fourteen Plates, price 18s.

CONCHOLOGIA ICONICA; or, Figures and Description and their Shells of Molluscous Animals, with critical remarks, eighteen synonyms, affinities, and circumstances of habitation. LOVELL REEVE, F.L.S.

⁎ Demy 4to. Published monthly, in Parts, each containing eight plates. Price 10s.

SOLD ALSO IN MONOGRAPHS:

	£	s.	d.		£	s.	d.		£	s.	d.
Achatina	1	9	0	Dolium	0	10	6	Oliva	1	18	0
Achatinella	0	8	0	Eburna	0	1	6	Oniscia	0	1	6
Arca	1	1	6	Fasciolaria	0	9	0	Paludomus	0	4	0
Artemis	0	13	0	Ficula	0	1	6	Partula	0	5	6
Buccinum	0	18	0	Fissurella	1	0	6	Pectunculus	0	11	6
Bulimus	5	12	0	Fusus	1	6	6	Phorus	0	4	0
Bullia	0	5	6	Glauconome	0	1	6	Pleurotoma	2	10	6
Cardita	0	11	6	Haliotis	1	1	0	Pterocera	0	8	0
Cardium	1	8	0	Harpa	0	5	6	Purpura	0	17	0
Cassidaria	0	1	6	Hemipecten	0	1	6	Pyrula	0	11	6
Cassis	0	15	6	Ianthina	0	3	0	Ranella	0	10	6
Chama	0	11	6	Isocardia	0	1	6	Ricinula	0	8	0
Chiton	2	2	0	Lucina	0	14	0	Rostellaria	0	4	6
Chitonellus	0	1	6	Mangelia	0	10	6	Strombus	1	4	6
Conus	3	0	0	Mesalia } Eglisia	0	1	6	Struthiolaria	0	1	6
Corbula	0	6	6					Turbinella	0	17	0
Crassatella	0	4	0	Mitra	2	10	0	Triton	1	5	6
Cypræa	1	14	0	Monoceros	0	5	6	Turbo	0	17	0
Cypricardia	0	3	0	Murex	2	5	6	Turritella	0	14	6
Delphinula	0	6	6	Myadora	0	1	6	Voluta	1	8	0

The genus HELIX *is in course of publication.*

SOLD ALSO IN VOLUMES:

VOL. I. CONUS   PHORUS   DELPHINULA
PLEUROTOMA   PECTUNCULUS   CYPRICARDIA
CRASSATELLA   CARDITA   HARPA

[122 *Plates, price* 7l. 16s. 6d. *half-bound.*]

VOL. II. CORBULA   GLAUCONOME   MITRA
ARCA   MYADORA   CARDIUM
TRITON   RANELLA   ISOCARDIA

[114 *Plates, price* 7l. 6s. 6d. *half-bound.*]

VOL. III. MUREX   MANGELIA   MONOCEROS
CYPRÆA   PURPURA   BULLIA
HALIOTIS   RICINULA   BUCCINUM

[129 *Plates, price* 8l. 5s. 6d. *half-bound.*]

VOL. IV. CHAMA   FICULA   FUSUS
CHITON   PYRULA   PALUDOMUS
CHITONELLUS   TURBINELLA   TURBO
FASCIOLARIA

[110 *Plates, price* 7l. 1s. 6d. *half-bound.*]

Vol. V.	Bulimus	Cassis	Oniscia
	Achatina	Turritella	Cassidaria
	Dolium	Mesalia	Eburna
		Eglisia	

[147 *Plates*, price 9*l*. 7*s*. 6*d*. *half-bound*.]

Vol. VI.	Voluta	Artemis	Strombus
	Fissurella	Lucina	Pterocera
	Partula	Hemipecten	Rostellaria
	Achatinella	Oliva	Struthiolaria

[129 *Plates*, price 8*l*. 5*s*. 6*d*. *half-bound*.]

The figures are drawn and lithographed by Mr. G. B. Sowerby, Junr., of the *natural size*, from specimens chiefly in the collection of Mr. Cuming.

"This great work is intended to embrace a complete description and illustration of the shells of molluscous animals, and, so far as we have seen, it is not such as to disappoint the large expectations that have been formed respecting it. The figures of the shells are all of full size; in the descriptions a careful analysis is given of the labours of others; and the author has apparently spared no pains to make the work a standard authority on the subject of which it treats."—*Athenæum*.

CONCHOLOGIA SYSTEMATICA; or, Complete System of Conchology, illustrated with 300 plates of upwards of 1500 figures of Shells. By Lovell Reeve, F.L.S.

"The text is both interesting and instructive; many of the plates have appeared before in Mr. Sowerby's works, but from the great expense of collecting them, and the miscellaneous manner of their publication, many persons will no doubt gladly avail themselves of this select and classified portion, which also contains many original figures."—*Athenæum*.

*** In two quarto volumes, cloth. Price 10*l*. coloured; 6*l*. plain.

ELEMENTS OF CONCHOLOGY; or, Introduction to the Natural History of Shells and their animals. By Lovell Reeve, F.L.S. Parts I. to X., price 3*s*. 6*d*. each.

"The work before us is designed to promote a more philosophical spirit of inquiry into the nature and origin of Shells."—*Ecclesiastical Review*.

CONCHYLIA DITHYRA INSULARUM BRITANNICARUM. The Bivalve Shells of the British Isles, systematically arranged. By William Turton, M.D. Reprinted verbatim from the original edition. The illustrations, printed from the original copper-plates, are distinguished for their accurate detail. Twenty coloured plates. Price 2*l*. 10*s*.

POPULAR HISTORY OF MOLLUSCA; or, Shells and their Animal Inhabitants. By MARY ROBERTS. With eighteen plates by Wing. Royal 16mo. 10s. 6d. coloured.

"This volume forms another of the excellent series of illustrated works on various departments of Natural History, for which the public is indebted to Messrs. Reeve & Co. . . . When we add, that the plates contain no fewer than ninety figures of shells, with their animal inhabitants, all of them well, and several admirably, executed, and that the text is written throughout in a readable and even elegant style, with such digressions in poetry and prose as serve to relieve its scientific details, we think that we have said enough to justify the favourable opinion we have expressed."—*British and Foreign Medico-Chirurgical Review*.

THE DODO AND ITS KINDRED; or, the History, Affinities, and Osteology of the DODO, SOLITAIRE, and other extinct birds of the islands Mauritius, Rodriguez, and Bourbon. By H. E. STRICKLAND, Esq., M.A., F.R.G.S., F.G.S., President of the Ashmolean Society, and A. G. MELVILLE, M.D., M.R.C.S. Royal quarto, with eighteen plates and numerous wood-illustrations. Price 21s.

"The labour expended on this book, and the beautiful manner in which it is got up, render it a work of great interest to the naturalist. . . . It is a model of how such subjects should be treated. We know of few more elaborate and careful pieces of comparative anatomy than is given of the head and foot by Dr. Melville. The dissection is accompanied by lithographic plates, creditable alike to the Artist and the Printer."—*Athenæum*.

POPULAR BRITISH ORNITHOLOGY; comprising a familiar and technical description of the Birds of the British Isles. By P. H. GOSSE, Author of 'The Ocean,' 'The Birds of Jamaica,' &c. In twelve chapters, each being the Ornithological lesson for the month. With twenty plates of figures. Royal 16mo. 10s. 6d. coloured.

"To render the subject of ornithology clear, and its study attractive, has been the great aim of the author of this beautiful little volume. . . . It is embellished by upwards of 70 figures of British birds beautifully coloured."—*Morning Herald*.
"This was a book much wanted, and will prove a boon of no common value, containing, as it does, the names, descriptions, and habits of all the British birds, handsomely got up."—*Mirror*.

CURTIS'S BRITISH ENTOMOLOGY, being Illustrations and Descriptions of the Genera of Insects found in Great Britain and Ireland, comprising coloured figures, from nature, of the most rare and beautiful species, and, in many instances, of the plants upon which they are found. By JOHN CURTIS, F.L.S.

The 'British Entomology' was originally brought out in Monthly Numbers, size royal 8vo, at 4s. 6d., each containing four coloured plates with text. It was commenced in 1824, and completed in 1840, in 193 Numbers, forming 16 volumes, price £43 16s.

The work is now offered new, and in the best condition:—
Price to Subscribers for complete copies in sixteen volumes, £21.
Price of the new issue, and of odd Numbers . „ 3s. 6d. per No.
*** Vols. I. II. & III. of the New Issue are now ready for delivery.

INSECTA BRITANNICA. DIPTERA. By F. WALKER, Esq., F.L.S. Vol. I. Illustrated with plates. Price 25s.

POPULAR BRITISH ENTOMOLOGY, comprising a familiar and technical description of the Insects most common to the British Isles. By MARIA E. CATLOW. *Second Edition.* In twelve chapters, each being the Entomological lesson for the month. In one vol., with sixteen plates of figures. Royal 16mo. 10s. 6d. coloured.

"Judiciously executed, with excellent figures of the commoner species, for the use of young beginners."—*Annual Address of the President of the Entomological Society.*

"Miss Catlow's 'Popular British Entomology' contains an introductory chapter or two on classification, which are followed by brief generic and specific descriptions in English of above 200 of the commoner British species, together with accurate figures of about 70 of those described; and will be quite a treasure to any one just commencing the study of this fascinating science."—*Westminster and Foreign Quarterly Review.*

POPULAR HISTORY OF MAMMALIA. By ADAM WHITE, F.L.S., Assistant in the Zoological Department of the British Museum. With sixteen Plates of Quadrupeds, &c. By B. WATERHOUSE HAWKINS, F.L.S. Rl. 16mo. 10s. 6d. coloured.

"The present increase of our stores of anecdotal matter respecting every kind of animal has been used with much tact by Mr. White, who has a terse chatty way of putting down his reflections, mingled with that easy familiarity which every one accustomed daily to zoological pursuits is sure to attain. The book is profusely illustrated."—*Atlas.*

POPULAR SCRIPTURE ZOOLOGY; or, History of the Animals mentioned in the Bible. By MARIA E. CATLOW. With Sixteen Plates. Royal 16mo. 10s. 6d. coloured.

"It contains a short and clear account of the animals mentioned in the Bible, classed according to their genera, and illustrated by a number of well-executed and characteristic coloured plates. It is a seasonable addition to a very nice set of books."—*Guardian.*

"Miss Catlow's abilities as a naturalist, and her tact in popularizing any subject she undertakes, are too well known to need reiteration on this occasion."—*Notes and Queries.*

"It is a pleasant mixture of popular and scientific matter. . . . The book is illustrated by characteristic coloured plates."—*Spectator.*

(*Under the Authority of the Lords Commissioners of the Admiralty.*)

THE FOSSIL MAMMALS COLLECTED IN NORTH-WESTERN AMERICA DURING THE VOYAGE OF H.M.S. HERALD, under the command of Captain Henry Kellett, R.N., C.B., while in search of Sir John Franklin. By Sir JOHN RICHARDSON, C.B., F.R.S. In royal 4to, with Fifteen double Plates. Price 21s.

THE ARTIFICIAL PRODUCTION OF FISH. By PISCARIUS. Price 1s.

"The object of this little book is to make known the means by which fish of all descriptions may be multiplied in rivers to an almost incalculable extent. . . . . This principle of increase Piscarius has carried out by argument and experiment in his little treatise, which, we think, is worthy the attention of the legislator, the country gentleman, and the clergyman; for it shows how an immense addition may be made to the people's food with scarcely any expense."—*Era.*

POPULAR HISTORY OF BRITISH ZOOPHYTES. By the Rev. Dr. LANDSBOROUGH. With Twenty Plates. Royal 16mo. 10s. 6d. coloured.

"This work constitutes one of the popular series of scientific treatises which, from the simplicity of their style, and the artistic excellence and correctness of their numerous illustrations, has acquired a celebrity beyond that of any other series of modern cheap works. With this manual of Zoophytes, and that upon Seaweeds by the same author, the student can ramble along the sea-shores and glean knowledge from every heap of tangled weed that lies in his pathway."—*Liverpool Standard.*

"Parents who sojourn for a few months at the sea-side will find him a safe and profitable companion for their children. He will tell them not only to *see*, but to think, in the best acceptation of the term; and he is moreover a cheerful, and at times a merry teller of incidents belonging to his subject."—*Belfast Mercury.*

"We can cordially recommend this beautiful little book to our readers as one which will greatly add to the interest of a temporary or permanent residence by the sea-side, and which will give to those who have no opportunity of studying the creatures themselves, an excellent insight into the extent and beauty of this section of the deep."—*Weekly News.*

"It is unnecessary to observe that the coloured engravings and the various minutiæ of the publication, are all excellent—such being the characteristic of the whole of the above series."—*Sun.*

MISCELLANEOUS.

TALPA; or, THE CHRONICLES OF A CLAY FARM: an Agricultural Fragment. By C. W. H. With Twenty-four Illustrations by GEORGE CRUIKSHANK. 12mo. Price 8s.

"If there still remains a real living unsatisfied Protectionist, we in all heartiness and goodwill recommend to him the amusing and instructive 'Chronicles' before us. . . . To complete its attractions, every chapter of the work has been illustrated by the inimitable George Cruikshank."—*Sherborne Journal.*

"The writer handles this subject in such a masterly manner—his style is so piquant, as well as forcible, so scholarly, yet so racy—his wit and his wisdom are so skilfully blended—he has so cleverly worked out his motto, *Ridentem dicere verum*, by telling the truth laughingly—that the reader finds himself irresistibly carried along, and he and the book part not company until he has made himself master of the tale that he has to unfold."—*Leicestershire Mercury.*

"This is a rare little volume. We don't know which to admire most, the author's humour or his wisdom. He has set himself the task of illustrating, in an agreeable manner, the evils of Custom, Prejudice, and Feudalism, as they exist among agriculturists. It will create much laughter among the merry, and convey many a lesson to the tiller of the soil. There are some very capital illustrations too embellishing the volume."—*Era.*

"Cleverly written in a vein of pleasantry, the work perseveringly uproots the prejudice of the past, and demonstrates that scientific knowledge is an important element in successful tillage."—*Lincoln Mercury.*

"Serious truths in a garb of simple language laced with rich humour."—*Morning Advertiser.*

"The vignettes of Mr. Cruikshank are the happiest proofs we have lately seen that the genius of this fine artist's earlier day is still fresh and unimpaired. The farmers should be very grateful to have such a nice little book provided for their especial use, entertainment, and profit."—*Examiner.*

"It is a capital volume for a Christmas hour in the country."—*Daily News.*

POPULAR MINERALOGY; a Familiar account of Minerals and their Uses. By HENRY SOWERBY. With Twenty plates of figures. Royal 16mo. 10s. 6d. coloured.

"Mr. Sowerby has endeavoured to throw around his subject every attraction. His work is fully and carefully illustrated with coloured plates."—*Spectator.*

ILLUSTRATIONS of the WISDOM and BENEVOLENCE of the DEITY, as manifested in Nature. By H. EDWARDS, LL.D. Cloth, 2s. 6d.

"A little excursion in the track of Paley and the broad road of the Bridgewater Treatises. Animals, Atmosphere, Organic Matter, Light, and Electricity are the natural elements out of which the author deduces his pious lessons, leading to a First Cause in wonder, admiration, and worship."—*Literary Gazette.*

DROPS OF WATER; their marvellous and beautiful Inhabitants displayed by the Microscope. By AGNES CATLOW. Square 12mo, with plates. 7s. 6d. coloured.

"In this little book, illustrated with plates scarcely inferior to those of the well-known Ehrenberg, we have the wonders of the microscope revealed in the history of a drop of water. Miss Catlow's pleasing works on botany, &c., are all well known, and we can assure our readers that in this little history of infusorial animals and plants of a drop of water she has added much to her well-deserved reputation. The style in which it is got up renders it worthy of companionship with the choicest ornaments of the library table."—*Liverpool Standard.*

"A pleasant introduction to microscopic studies, having reference in particular to the animalcules, or infusoria, as they are now more commonly called, which inhabit water and other liquids. The little volume before us contains a goodly body of information touching the infusorial world, with some clearly and sensibly written information as to the species of water, and the seasons, in which certain varieties are to be found."—*Atlas*.

"'Drops of Water' is an introduction to one of Nature's inexhaustible sources of wonder and delight, performed in a very efficient and satisfactory manner. . . . As a specimen of typography, it is of a superior character; and the plates are indicative of no small degree of artistic skill as well as science."—*Observer*.

"An elegant little book, both in the getting up and its literature. . . . The text is accompanied by coloured plates, that exhibit the most remarkable creatures of the watery world."—*Spectator*.

"Of the manner in which this work is executed, we can say that, like Miss Catlow's previous productions on Natural History, it displays an accurate acquaintance with the subject, and a keen delight in the contemplation of the objects to which it is devoted. As far as the living beings which inhabit 'Drops of Water' are concerned, we know of no better introduction to the use of the microscope than the present volume."—*Athenæum*.

WESTERN HIMALAYA AND TIBET; the Narrative of a Journey through the Mountains of Northern India, during the Years 1847-8. By THOMAS THOMSON, M.D. With Maps and Tinted Lithographs. 8vo, 15*s*.

"Few more valuable volumes of travels than this by Dr. Thomson have been for a long time past published. Long after the interest which its novelty will create shall have passed away, it will be a standard book of reference on account of the valuable facts which it contains, and of the spirit of sound observation in which it is written."—*Athenæum*.

"The work is one of durable importance. The most general reader will not find Dr. Thomson's journey tedious. . . . . We have in this volume matter which will inform every man who reads it steadily, and follows the author's route with attention to the Map."—*Examiner*.

"To all those who desire to judge scientifically of what is possible in the cultivation of the Indo-Alpine Flora, which is now so rapidly enriching our gardens, works of this description have great interest."—*Gardeners' Chronicle*.

"We can most cordially recommend Dr. Thomson's work to all those who wish to obtain a clear idea of this magnificent and interesting region, to which our late conquest in the Punjaub has brought us into such close contiguity."—*Guardian*.

"This is a valuable contribution to our knowledge of a remote and lately explored tract of the earth's surface."—*Advertiser*.

TRAVELS IN THE INTERIOR OF BRAZIL; principally through the Northern Provinces and the Gold and Diamond Districts, during the years 1836–41. By the late GEORGE GARDNER, M.D., F.L.S., Superintendent of the Royal Botanic Gardens of Ceylon. *Second and cheaper Edition*. With a Map of the Author's Route and View of the Organ Mountains. Price 12*s*. cloth; 18*s*. bound.

"When camping out on the mountain-top or in the wilderness; roughing it in